Space, Place, and Sex

Why of Where
Series Editor: George J. Demko

The goal of this series is to provide new perspectives on important ideas and issues of our time in a relevant and lively style. Topics such as peace, migration, health, death, genius, music, homosexuality, and other global themes are explored across space and through time, highlighting relationships, patterns, and concepts. Intended to educate *and* entertain, these volumes will appeal to students and general readers alike as they demonstrate the significance of the geographical perspective in the world today.

Space, Place, and Sex

Geographies of Sexualities

Lynda Johnston
and Robyn Longhurst

ROWMAN & LITTLEFIELD PUBLISHERS, INC.
Lanham • Boulder • New York • Toronto • Plymouth, UK

Published by Rowman & Littlefield Publishers, Inc.
A wholly owned subsidiary of The Rowman & Littlefield Publishing Group, Inc.
4501 Forbes Boulevard, Suite 200, Lanham, Maryland 20706
http://www.rowmanlittlefield.com

Estover Road, Plymouth PL6 7PY, United Kingdom

British Library Cataloguing in Publication Information Available

Library of Congress Cataloging-in-Publication Data
Johnston, Lynda, 1964–
  Space, place, and sex : geographies of sexualities / Lynda Johnston and Robyn Longhurst.
     p. cm. — (Why of where)
  Includes bibliographical references and index.
  ISBN 978-0-7425-5511-2 (cloth : alk. paper) — ISBN 978-0-7425-5512-9 (pbk. : alk. paper) — ISBN 978-0-7425-6748-1 (electronic)
  1. Sex. 2. Gender identity. 3. Sex customs. 4. Space—Social aspects. 5. Human geography. 6. Queer theory. I. Longhurst, Robyn, 1962– II. Title.
  HQ23.J636 2010
  306.701—dc22   2009031098

Printed in the United States of America

Contents

Preface

Since the early 1990s "the body" has come to be in vogue in the social sciences. Geographers, sociologists, psychologists, and scholars in gender, cultural, and health studies have all shown a growing interest in the body, including the sexed and sexual body, as an important coordinate of subjectivity. The relationship between the body, space, place, and sex has been explored at numerous geography conferences over the past decade. The Association of American Geographers (AAG) has the Sexuality and Space Specialty Group that organizes conference paper and panel sessions. This group is one of approximately fifty established specialty groups of the AAG. It was formally established in 1996 with the aim of encouraging geographic research and scholarship on topics related to sexuality.

Work on sexuality and space has also appeared widely in articles in scholarly journals such as *Gender, Place and Culture* and *Body & Society*. It has also appeared in academic books such as David Bell and Gill Valentine's *Mapping Desire* (1995a) and Lynda Johnston's *Queering Tourism: Paradoxical Performances at Gay Pride Parades* (2005a). Over the past few years there have also been numerous documentaries on "space, place, and sex" created for general consumption. Some of the titles we use for teaching are *Boys with Breasts*, *Fa'afafine: Queens of Samoa*, *Why Men Wear Frocks*, *Gender Unknown*, *Make Me a Man*, and *Out in the Garden*. In short, there has been a burgeoning of scholarly and popular work on space, place, and sex.

We aim to introduce readers to some of the important ideas contained in this scholarly and popular work. A lot of new ground has been broken in geography over the past decade. The sexed and sexual body has been placed at the center of many theoretical and empirical enquiries. The body's differential construction, its regulation, and the way it is represented have become crucial to understanding sexual relations at every spatial scale.

Before we begin this book, however, we want to say something briefly about each of us individually, and jointly, as authors; that is, we want to position ourselves in the research. We were both born in Aotearoa New Zealand. *Aotearoa* is the Māori term for *New Zealand*. Since the late 1980s when Māori became an official language it has been used by a range of individuals and groups in both formal and informal contexts. Sometimes it is used alone, sometimes it is used in conjunction with the term *New Zealand*. Throughout this book we mainly use *New Zealand* but we want to alert readers to the idea that the naming of places is political. We both live and work in Hamilton, New Zealand. Hamilton is a small city by international standards with a population of 130,000. Living and working in Hamilton we often feel as though we occupy a position that in some ways is aligned with "the center" but in other ways is relegated to the margins of Anglo-American scholarship on sexuality and space.

Elsewhere we have argued that queer geographies "down under" are both similar to, and different from, Anglo-American work on sexuality and space (Longhurst 2008). Our Anglophone down under geographies of sexualities are intimately connected to wider (predominantly) Western ideas, yet it is clear that our research and teaching is embedded in, and responds to, down under issues. These local knowledges are both informed by and contribute to international debates. As Pākehā (white, non-Māori, European New Zealanders), English is our first language and we are easily able to access and contribute to debates in the Anglo-American geographical literature, but in Aotearoa New Zealand we often feel a long way from the metropolitan centers (read the United States and United Kingdom). The number of New Zealand geographers is quite small and there are no institutional arrangements in place that facilitate formal networking. There is a geographical society but it does not have study groups (like the Association of American Geographers, which has the Sexuality and Space group that holds meetings prior to its annual conference—as well as offering themed sessions within the conference— and the British Royal Geographical Society, which has a group called Sexualities, Space and Queer Geographies). In short, we see ourselves as being positioned paradoxically in the world of academic geography, including in work on sexuality and space.

In relation to our sexed identities one of us self-identifies as lesbian and/or queer and the other as "straight" and a mother of two teenage sons. Despite this difference in our sexual identities we share many things in common such as we are both in long-term relationships; we each have a large dog; and we share similar political views. Both of us have been highly influenced for more than two decades by feminist theory and practice and are actively engaged in researching various issues around sex, gender, bodies, spaces, and power.

We mention these things because who we are has undoubtedly manifested itself on the pages of this book. We don't pretend to be disembodied commentators on the subject of sex and sexuality. We are shaped by our past experiences, our present circumstances, and where we live, even if these things aren't always necessarily discussed up front in our work. For example, living in New Zealand has led us to choose examples in this book that are derived both from the metropolitan centers such as the United States and the United Kingdom but also from places that are often considered peripheral to these centers.

It is our hope that this book will help readers develop a deeper understanding of the ways in which individuals, communities, and nations simultaneously engage in various mutually constituted sexual power relations in different places and at different times. The sexed and sexual body is a contested site. Control over what we ourselves can do with and to our bodies, what we can do with and to other people's bodies, how we move, what spaces we have access to, what spaces we are excluded from are all issues that are explored in this book. Geographies of sexualities is an eclectic field (if one can even call it a field) of research and writing. We think it is an exciting field. We hope readers will too. Chapters in this book can be read as individual essays or the book can be read from cover to cover. Whichever is your preference, we hope you'll be prompted to question further some of the places and spaces that you occupy in relation to sex and sexed bodies.

Acknowledgments

This book has been written in the midst of other research projects. We've each been working on several individual projects and we've been working together, with Elsie Ho, on a project about migrant women and food. During the gestation and writing of this book we've also both served individually a term as chair of our department. Needless to say we have relied upon people's generosity of spirit to assist us. Our departmental administrator Brenda Hall deserves special mention because over the past few years she has generously supported each of us in our capacity as heads of department. At every turn Brenda has willingly gone beyond the call of duty to ensure that the department runs smoothly. We are both very grateful to her.

Cherie Todd, a graduate student and research assistant in the Department of Geography, Tourism and Environmental Planning, located excellent resource material for the project. She also took us to new technological heights teaching us how to use EndNote. Without her efforts the book would have taken much longer to write and the researching and writing would not have been as pleasurable. Max Oulton, a cartographer in the department, assisted with preparing figures. We are most appreciative.

Thanks also to Susan McEachern, editorial director of History, International Studies, and Geography at Rowman & Littlefield, who offered support throughout this project. In particular we appreciated her astute comments on our initial proposal and flexibility with the deadline! We also appreciate Mona Domosh suggesting to George J. Demko that we might be appropriate authors for this book. George made contact with us initially and was helpful in sending us another title in the series to view.

Last but certainly not least, a huge thank you must go to our supportive partners. We know that living with an academic poses a number of challenges one of which is that the work never ends. This is not always easy for partners. Thank you.

The authors and publishers also wish to thank a number of people for allowing us to reproduce their material. Thanks are due to the Hamilton City Council who offers an excellent online Photo Library of high quality downloadable images that are freely available for private and professional use. We are also indebted to the editor of *Sunday Star-Times*, Emily Simpson, and photographer Becky Nunes, for allowing us to reproduce the cover of their publication. Simon Woolf, from Photography by Woolf, and Georgina Beyer kindly permitted the use of a photograph of Georgina Beyer and Jim Bolger. Hamilton Pride Inc. allowed us to use its flier advertising Pride Week. Jordon Harris (Kaiarahi), senior health promoter at Hau Ora Takatāpui New Zealand AIDS Foundation, kindly gave us permission to reproduce the cover of the foundation's publication. Lisa Ebbing, director of HOTmilk lingerie, allowed us to include her advertisement. Matt Akersten provided us with one of his photos and permission to reproduce it in the book. Air New Zealand Limited also kindly permitted us to include one of its photos. We are enormously grateful.

Every effort has been made to trace copyright holders but if any have been inadvertently overlooked the publisher will be pleased to make the necessary arrangements at the first opportunity.

1

❦

Introduction

Geography, Bodies, Sex, and Gender

In May 2007 a story titled "Australian Pub Bars Heterosexuals" was published in a number of news forums around the world including the *Washington Post*, the *Independent*, BBC News, and Australia's *Herald Sun* and Channel 4 News. It was reported that the state and civil administrative tribunal in Victoria, Australia, ruled the Peel Hotel could ban patrons based on their sexual orientation. "Managers complained raucous hen nights and stag parties created a poisonous atmosphere for its gay clientele" (BBC News 2007). The hotel's management said the move would help stop groups of heterosexual men and women abusing gay men. Some came to stare in a "dehumanizing" manner at the gay men. They were being "gawked at" as if they were "exhibits in a zoo" (Marks 2007). Tom McFeely, the hotel's manager, said that Melbourne has two thousand venues catering to heterosexuals, but only one or two aimed exclusively at gay men.

As a result of the tribunal's decision, for the first time in Australian history, a pub will be able to legally ask people their sexual orientation at the door and turn patrons away based on their response. While some civil liberties and human rights groups have supported the ban arguing that homosexuals should be allowed to relax in places without fear of bullying or intimidation, others have questioned whether it furthers freedoms or creates barriers to understanding (Steiner 2007).

A couple of months later another story in the media caught our attention. A thirty-three-year-old English tourist, Helen Simpson, was asked

1

by a female staff member at the Christchurch Casino in New Zealand to either cover up her ample breasts or leave. Simpson said, "I was highly embarrassed—humiliated, absolutely humiliated." She continued, "I was wearing too low a top, which people found offensive." The casino claimed that they are reviewing their dress code. Simpson told the *Press* (Christchurch) newspaper, "I feel like I've been discriminated against for having big breasts." She said she didn't choose to be "well endowed in the upper region" and described herself as a "size 14 woman with the top half demanding a size 20" (*New Zealand Herald* 2007). Human Rights Commission spokesperson Gilbert Wong said Ms. Simpson was welcome to make a complaint although physical appearance—including breast size—was not a criterion for discrimination under the Human Rights Act. Mr. Wong said Christchurch Casino appeared to be enforcing its dress code, which it had a right to do (*Dominion Post* 2007). Wellington civil liberties lawyer Tony Ellis said he did not believe Ms. Simpson had adequate grounds upon which to argue she was discriminated against. Although rules that prohibit excessive displays of cleavage might adversely affect one section of one gender group, they are a result of prevailing moral standards. Mr. Ellis said the casino was entitled to control the behavior of its patrons—including ensuring that what they wore did not offend others. "Some punters don't want to be distracted while they gamble" (*Dominion Post* 2007).

These two stories from the daily press illustrate that sexuality (what we do and what we can talk about) is constantly being mapped and remapped across various cultural and social landscapes. The examples illustrate that space, place, and sex are inextricably linked. It matters that bodies occupy particular positions marked in time and space. It matters whether it is 1997 or 2007; it matters whether we are gay, have large breasts, are an English tourist, live in Australia, New Zealand, or somewhere else, are in a gay bar or a casino. Heidi Nast and Steve Pile (1998, 2) claim that "the ways in which we live out body/place relationships are political." They continue: "The body is both mobile and channeled, both fluid and fixed, into places. It is not only the 'geopolitics of the body' but also the politics of connection and disconnection, of rights over the body, of the body as a site of struggle" (Nast and Pile 1998, 3).

The cover illustration we chose for our book *Space, Place, and Sex* is a statue of Riff Raff, a cross-dressing character from the cult film and musical *The Rocky Horror Picture Show* (www.riffraffstatue.org), which is located in downtown Hamilton, New Zealand. The film was written by Richard O'Brien, who grew up in Hamilton and plays Riff Raff, the butler. We chose this image specifically because it epitomizes many of the issues we discuss. *The Rocky Horror Picture Show* is about Frank'n'Furter, "a sweet transvestite from transsexual Transylvania." The film parodies science fiction and horror genres by adopting a queer perspective to space, place, and sex. It illustrates the ways in which bodies become sexualized, included, or excluded depending upon place and time. The decision for Hamilton to support a statue of Riff Raff was bold and contested, yet support prevailed, and the statue was erected in 2004. The Riff Raff statue is provocative and unusual in that not only does it queer the streets of Hamilton but also it upsets the idea that city statues have to be heteronormative, commemorate, and celebrate conservative family values. The significance of the statue goes beyond the city of Hamilton. It has become a site of pilgrimage for tourists, as well as for those of us who gather there on International Transgender Day of Remembrance (November 20). Both of us attended the ceremony at the Riff Raff statue in 2008. Flowers were laid, candles lit, and we remembered and honored transgender people who are subject to gender bashing, have been killed, or have taken their own lives.

It appears, then, that sexed bodies are mapped, connected, and threaded not just through bars, casinos, and sites where statues are erected but through all spaces. Take, for example, the space of the home (see Blunt and Dowling 2006). Homes are sites of a range of differently configured sexual relations. Nuclear families, gay and lesbian homes, and young people living together are just a couple of examples of sexual relations that are constituted within the intimate space of the home. Whether it is a bar, casino, or home sexual politics permeate the space. There are no spaces that sit outside of sexual politics. Sex and space cannot be "decoupled."

In contemporary Western societies sexed bodies are constituted not just within real or material spaces but also within virtual spaces. Over the past decade millions of pornography, romance, "find a bride," gay, lesbian, bisexual, and transgendered websites have been created. The virtual world has provided new opportunities for sexual connections, interactions, and communities to emerge. It enables people to try out new sexual identities unrestricted by the limitations of their real bodies.

"Eroticised topographies" (Bell 1994a), or sexualized imagery in landscapes, can be found everywhere: hotels, homes, the Internet, suburbs, gay neighborhoods, red light districts, shop window displays, billboards, magazine covers, dating columns in newspapers are just a few examples. Sexual politics permeate all space—private and public, urban and rural, at the macro and micro level. In short, sex is everywhere and social, cultural, feminist geographers and others have begun to recognize this. Place and sexuality are mutually constituted. Sexuality has a profound effect on the way people live in, and interact with, space and place. In turn, space and place affect people's sexuality. Gill Valentine

(2001, 5) offers an example of the way place and sexuality are mutually constituted, explaining:

> Spatial visibility (e.g., in terms of the establishment of so-called gay ghettos or various forms of street protest or Mardi Gras) has been important to the development of lesbian and gay rights. In turn, these performances of sexual dissidents' identities (re)produce these spaces as lesbian and gay spaces in which sexual identities can be, and are forged.

What Valentine's example makes clear is that space and sexuality do not just interact with, or reflect, each other but rather are mutually constituted.

More than a decade ago most of the existing literature on space and sexuality was contained within one volume—David Bell and Gill Valentine's *Mapping Desire* (1995a). Bell and Valentine (1995a, 4) introduce the collection noting:

> The women's, gay and civil rights movements emerged in North America and Europe in the 1960s and 1970s on a wave of social and political upheaval. But despite a growing awareness amongst geographers in the following decade of the need to study the role of class, gender and ethnicity in shaping social, cultural and economic geographies, sexualities were largely left off the geographical map.

Bell and Valentine's edited collection was important in helping put sexuality on the geographical map. These days there are many articles on sexuality sprinkled throughout a variety of social, cultural, and feminist geography literature. There are also a number of edited (e.g., Browne, Lim, and Brown 2007) and authored books (e.g., Binnie 2004a; Johnston 2005a; Hemmings 2002) on the topic. Topics explored in this literature include the "pink economy," gay tourism, gay pride parades, bisexuality, sexuality in rural areas, sexuality and citizenship, the globalization of sexuality, HIV and AIDS, and sexuality and ethnicity.

More recently—2007—Kath Browne, Jason Lim, and Gavin Brown produced an edited collection *Geographies of Sexualities: Theories, Practices and Politics*. They say "geographies of sexualities" is a relatively young field that has "blossomed" over the past ten years. It is an area that is now taught in a number of undergraduate courses, at least in countries such as the United Kingdom, United States, Canada, Australia, and New Zealand, and has succeeded in striking up conversations with a range of other subdisciplinary areas such as gender studies, migration studies, cultural and social geography, and tourism.

Given that "geographies of sexualities" is not really a discrete intellectual field but more one that has emerged in conversation with other disciplinary areas it follows that our book is an expression of the many connections and links that exist across different areas of inquiry. We draw on the work of geographers who are positioned in a range of subdisciplinary fields but also on the work of people in cognate disciplines.

THE PRODUCTION OF SCALE

In this book, like Browne, Lim, and Brown (2007), we address themes of theories, practices, and politics but these themes run throughout. They are not grouped in particular sections. Instead we use the notion of geographical scale as a platform for thinking about specific kinds of sexual-social activities while acknowledging that the production of scale is itself a political process and that different scales overlap and are fluid and contingent (see Marston 2000 on the social construction of scale; Moore 2008 on "rethinking scale as a geographical category"; and Valentine 2001 for an example of a book which uses the notion of scale to structure ideas). It is the production of scale rather than scale *per se* that is important. There is nothing innate or inevitable about particular geographical scales. They are a product of different times and spaces. For example, in Europe nation-states rarely existed prior to the seventeenth century. Today, the existence of nation-states can also be called into question. Due to globalization it can be argued that governments have less sway than global corporate giants in the creation of relevant groupings of people.

Sallie Marston (2000, 219; italics in original) notes: "Over the last ten years, scholars in human geography have been paying increasing theoretical and empirical attention to understanding the ways in which the production of *scale* is implicated in the projection of *space*." Marston continues that it is not only capitalist production that is implicated in this production of scale but also social reproduction and consumption. David Delaney and Helga Leitner (1997) introduce a special issue of *Political Geography* that develops a social constructionist perspective on scale. A social constructionist approach takes as its starting point "the idea that the social context of inquiry, rather than the world which is investigated, determines—constructs—knowledge. Knowledge, therefore, is always relative to its social setting (there are no absolutes), and the outcome of an active process of fabrication rather than the discovery of a reality pre-existent and fully formed" (Johnston et al. 2000, 748). They focus on empirical work that showcases exactly how the construction of scale engages actors in various political projects. Delaney and Leitner (1997, 94) explain: "The politics of scale are a fundamental ingredient of the ways in which we go about creating, revising and living within a complex set of power relations." The essays in the collection make it evident that different geographical scales are likely to be appropriate for analyzing different kinds of social spaces and activities. Each scale represents an intersection between a range of different people and places.

Scale is not meant to be read as absolute, as in cartographic scales that are used to draw maps, but rather as overlapping and "nestled" (see Smith 1992). This perspective on scale can be traced to changes in social theory more generally (Delaney and Leitner 1997). Scale has not been immune to the social constructionist turn. Earlier conceptions of geographical and cartographic scales were inadequate for understanding some of the quite profound transformations that have taken place in the contemporary world, such as globalization.

Adam Moore (2008, 203) extends these arguments saying that a clear distinction needs to be made between scale as a category of *practice* and a category of *analysis*. Moore claims that using scale as a category of analysis tends to "reify it as a fundamental ontological entity" (much like "identity" has become reified as a conceptual category in the social sciences in recent years). This, argues Moore, is not helpful. Instead scale needs to be understood as a category of practice which "opens up new and fruitful avenues for investigating . . . the politics of scale—avenues that highlight epistemology, categorization and cognition." Taking on board Moore's comments, we think it is useful to examine representations and practices of sexuality using a variety of contingent and fluid geographical scales. Sexual relations cut across scales. This is evident in Michael Brown's book *Closet Space* (2000) in which he examines the metaphor of the closet at the scale of the body, urban space, the nation, and the world.

In the past geographers have privileged some scales over others. For example, there has been a great deal of research conducted using the scale of community and the nation. Other scales such as the home have not been paid as much attention. Home as a scale, however, can mean many things. In October 2008 Lynn Staeheli and David Ralph put out a call for papers to be presented in a session titled "Home and Migration: Mobilities, Belonging(s) and Identities" at the Association of American Geographers conference in Las Vegas. In an e-mail they explain that conceptions of home are not bound simply to the materiality of houses "but can take imaginative flight over multiple and overlapping scales." They point to the example of migrants who often have attachments to multiple "homes" at a variety of spatial scales.

We do not see any one scale (such as national or global) as inherently superior to any other scale (such as the body or home) and draw on a full range in this book to illustrate the complex ways in which sex, place, and space are interrelated. It also needs to be noted that we do not simply place events/actions/bodies at particular scales but rather throughout the book we point to the various ways in which sexual processes stretch across a variety of scales. Scales can exist simultaneously. They can also intersect. They are fluid and flexible. As Browne, Lim, and Brown (2007, 3) note: "The spaces that we can understand as structured by sexuality . . . are not just . . . everyday spaces. Rather these everyday spaces intersect with various other scales of spatiality, including national, international and transnational." Scales are both conceptual and material. Delaney and Leitner (1997, 97) write: "scale emerges . . . in the fusion of ideology and practice."

Neil Smith (1993, 99) argues that each scale is a platform not just for thinking about places *per se* but for the specific kinds of sociospatial relations that are constituted within places. He says: "Scale is produced in and through social activity which, in turn, produces and is produced by geographical structures of social interaction" (Smith 1993, 97). Another useful contribution Smith (1993) makes to thinking about the production of scale is his introduction of the concept of "jumping scales." This refers to the way power at one geographical scale can be extended to another. Paul Beere (2007) uses Smith's concept of jumping scales to think about "boy racers" (as young car enthusiasts are often dubbed by the media) in the context of New Zealand. Beere argues that geographical scale is one of a number of strategies used by social groups to dominate, control, and even define others and that young people are able to resist being confined to just one or two scales such as the home or neighborhood through having access to cars.

> Certain social settings become available through the car. The mobility a car provides facilitates greater access to more spaces and places. . . . In general, the teen years are a pivotal period in which much of our identities are formed. This occurs as a result of an increased self-awareness. At the same time, we begin to gain increased (and often contested) access to the public domain. The car allows us to break free from the tyranny of scale, particularly the scale of the home. (Beere 2007, 27)

Scale, then, can act as both a form of containment and empowerment. This is one of the reasons why it is such a useful device for the ordering of chapters in this book. The scales used—the body, home, community, city, rural, nation, and globe—are not discrete but formed out of many and varied sexed and gendered performances. So, as is suggested by Valentine (2001, 9) in *Social Geographies*, which also uses the notion of scale to group ideas, each of the spatial scales used "represents the intersection of a whole range of connections, interrelations and movements, and of different people who have very different ways of participating in, understanding or belonging to them." Unlike Valentine's book, however, we focus not on society and space broadly but more specifically on sex and sexuality.

METHODOLOGY

This book has been researched using a range of qualitative methods. The first three chapters are based mainly on our reading of a range of academic literature in the area of sexuality and space. Both of us have been engaged in reading this literature for more than a decade. We use alerts for new material on our e-mail systems, browse book catalogs, and check new issues of journals as they arrive in the library. We also employed the services of a research assistant who was directed to search for material on sex and sexuality thinking in particular about bodies, home, and communities (including virtual communities), and city, rural, national, and global spaces. In analyzing the material we have paid particular attention to places both inside and outside of the metropolitan centers of the United States and United Kingdom although it needs to be noted that the material is overwhelmingly Anglo-American in its focus.

Throughout the period of conceptualizing and writing the book we also have kept a watchful eye on various media accounts of events that we considered relevant to this project. As stories on sex and sexuality in relation to specific places and spaces emerged in local newspapers, magazines, film, and on television, we collected hard copies and took notes, all of which were placed in a large folder.

During the years it has taken to plan and write the book we have been keen observers in a wide variety of places often when traveling to conferences. For example, when attending the International Geographical Union (IGU) Commission on Gender and Geography in Taipei, Taiwan, in November 2007 we both visited the Women's Centre and were able to ask about women's experiences of being lesbian in Taipei. On yet another IGU Commission on Gender and Geography fieldtrip in Tunis, Tunisia, in August 2008 one of us—Robyn—was able to ask a similar question. While many of these observations are not discussed explicitly in the book we mention them because they have helped us to build up a larger picture of some of the spatial dimensions of sexuality.

For many of the chapters throughout the book, especially the second half of chapter 4, we collected data from Internet websites. There are a plethora of sites and routes to finding information about gendered and sexed identities, sexual practices, and sexual communities on the Internet. We were helped in thinking through how to approach this part of the chapter by an edited collection of essays on *Doing Internet Research: Critical Issues and Methods for Examining the Net* (S. Jones, 1999). We acknowledge that not everyone has access to information and communications technology (ICT). Many people in the world construct sexual identities without ever turning on a computer.

In chapter 5, which focuses on sex and the city, we present a variety of material collected from a range of sources. In 2007 Lynda was integral in setting up Hamilton Pride—a group that celebrates and supports the diversity of Hamilton's rainbow community. These experiences have been important in formulating ideas for this chapter on urban sexualities.

Chapters 6 and 7 are based mainly on the literature. We have woven together a variety of texts including academic literature, film, and media such as newspaper articles on agricultural field days, and gay marriages. We have also drawn on a variety of texts in chapter 8 coupled with material collected using semistructured interviews on wedding tourism.

As can be seen the material upon which this book rests has been collected using a mix of qualitative research methods (see Hay 2005 for a useful discussion of a variety of qualitative methods used in human geography) including critical reading of texts, online searches, interviews, and observational research. We also want to point out, as noted by Juliana Mansvelt and Lawrence Berg (2005, 248), that we have not simply "written up" the results of our qualitative research findings. Writing is not just a mechanical process that reflects some kind of reality or truth that we have discovered about sex, space and place, but rather "writing constitutes in part how and what we know about our research."

THINKING ABOUT LANGUAGE

The reason why writing constitutes what we know about our research is because language matters. It matters in that it is important and also in that it creates reality and gives meaning to the world. It does not simply reflect or label the world. Meaning is constituted within language, not by the subject that speaks it. Meaning does not exist prior to its articulation in language. This is the way in which poststructuralist theorists understand language. It is a view we share. Poststructuralism builds on linguist Ferdinand de Saussure's (1974) principle that meaning is produced within language rather than reflected by language. Language is viewed as a system existing within historically and geographically specific discourses. Poststructuralist ways of thinking allow for plurality of meaning and changes in meaning. This means that language is a site of political struggle. For example, if we take the word *queer*, the meaning of queer is not fixed by a natural world but is socially produced within language; it is plural and subject to change over time and space. This means that it is always important to think about language but especially when introducing a new field because the authors and readers may not share much by way of a common understanding of terms and concepts.

Social theorists, geographers included, employ different understandings of spaces, places, and bodies. Studies of sexualities are heavily influenced by poststructuralism and postmodernism. Postmodernism refers to a set of philosophical ideas, developed in the 1980s, which question the grand claims and single truths of the modernist era. The rejection of grand theories or metanarratives is at the core of postmodernism. Instead a postmodern approach recognizes that all knowledge is partial, fluid, and often contradictory. There is recognition of difference and multiple truths, realities and voices (Johnston et al. 2000).

In the remainder of this introductory chapter therefore we discuss some terms and concepts used frequently in geographies of sexualities, in queer studies, and throughout this book—terms such as the body, sex, gender, sexuality, gay, straight, heterosexual, bisexual, transsexual, transgender, queer, Other, space, and place. There are of course many other terms also associated with sex and sexuality such as love, sexual harassment, sadomasochism, butch-femme, transmen, bio-women, drag kings, trans lives, sexual citizenship, and voyeurism, but we cannot possibly address all of these. Therefore in the first instance we attempt to unravel only those that we consider to be vital to the arguments being made. Other terms are discussed later either explicitly or through the context in which they are used.

We begin by discussing the term *the body*. The meaning of the body seems so obvious it is tempting to overlook defining it. However, in thinking about sex and sexuality we are ultimately thinking about the body. We all *have* bodies, or at least, we all *are* bodies—they are more than just possessions (Nast and Pile 1998, 1) and surely, therefore, we all know what the body is. And yet there is a multiplicity that surrounds and inhabits the body, or bod*ies*, that makes it impossible to settle on any one definition. When we use the term *the body*—whether it be infant, child, or adult—we are referring to something that houses subjectivity, is a surface of social and cultural inscription, is a site of pleasure and pain, is public and private, has a permeable boundary, and is material, discursive, and psychical. Philosophers from the ancient Greeks to the postmodernists have been preoccupied over the centuries with attempting to understand the body but there has been little agreement. For example, does the body include the shadow (see Synott 1993), nail clippings, shaven hair, and feces? Its boundaries are not always as clearly demarcated as might be assumed.

In the seventeenth century, philosopher René Descartes formulated a dualistic conception of the body as separate from the mind. The body, according to Descartes, was simply a machine, much like a car. It was driven intellectually and spiritually by the mind, hence Descartes's well-known dictum *"Cogito ergo sum"* meaning "I think therefore I am." Valentine (2001, 16–17) notes: "Although his [Descartes's] view was contested by other philosophers both at the time and since, the Cartesian division and subordination of the body to the mind and the emphasis placed on dualistic thinking and scientific rationalization had a profound impact on Western thought."

This division between mind and body is gendered. The mind has been associated with positive terms such as *reason, rationality*, and *masculinity* whereas the body has been associated with negative terms such as *irrationality, nature*, and *femininity*. Men are thought to be able to transcend their bodies, or at least have their bodily needs met by others, whereas women are thought to be tied to their bodies because of their emotions, menstruation, pregnancy, and childbirth (Longhurst 1997). When we use the term *the body* or *bodies* in this book we are not implying that bodies are separate from minds but assuming the two cannot be separated. We could use the term *mind-body* but this seems cumbersome and for this reason we decided against it.

As can be seen already from the debate about minds and bodies outlined above, bodies have long been a focal point for feminist theorizing and politics. The ways in which they have been conceptualized, however, have varied greatly. Feminists have traversed many different intellectual and political routes in their attempt to understand bodies. In the 1960s feminists began to establish a firm distinction between sex as a biological given (nature, biology, the body) and gender as a social creation (nurture, socialization). This distinction between sex and gender did not originate from feminist work; rather, it was derived from the work of psychologist Robert Stoller (1968). It was, however, adopted by a number of influential feminist writers who used the distinction between sex and gender in order to argue that there are biological differences between the sexes at birth, but that it is primarily socialization that results in women and men having different gender characteristics. The advantages of this conceptualization were that it offered a way of distinguishing between the predetermined, inherent characteristics of men and women and the other social differences. Further, it carried an evaluation of the social as the determinant of women's unequal position.

In the late 1980s and early 1990s this distinction between sex and gender began to be questioned by feminist theorists such as Diana Fuss (1989), Moira Gatens (1991a, 1991b), and Elizabeth Grosz (1994). They persuasively argued that the distinction between sex and gender (between biology and social inscription) does not hold. It is not possible to say where sex stops and gender starts or vice versa. The body can never be extracted from the social. Sex and gender are always inextricably linked. Gender writes itself not *on* but *through* bodies. In this book, therefore, in talking about sex and the sexed body we are inevitably also talking about gender.

The term *sexuality* (as opposed to *sex*) refers to the expression of one's sexual desires and behaviors, or more generally to one's sexual identity or subjectivity. Heterosexuals (straights) are sexually attracted to those of the opposite sex whereas homosexuals (gays and lesbians) are sexually attracted to those of the same sex. Bisexuals are attracted to both the opposite and same sex. In reality, however, identities are never this clearcut. For example, is the married man who seeks sex with another man in a public toilet a couple of times each year heterosexual, homosexual, or bisexual? There is an array of difference surrounding categorizations such as man, woman, masculine, feminine, heterosexual, homosexual, and bisexual.

This is what, at least in part, has prompted use of the term *queer*. *Queer* in the 1970s and 1980s was a term of abuse used to refer to lesbians and gay men, but in the early 1990s it began to take on other meanings (see McDowell and Sharp 1999, 225). David Bell and Gill Valentine (1995a, 20; italics in original) explain: "Queer has become a notoriously indefinable watchword for certain so-called radical theoretical and activist stances in 1990s sexual politics, the first of which was arguably the act of reclaiming the very word 'queer' from its use as homophobic slang to be a label used *by* a variety of sexual dissidents." Bell and Valentine (1995a, 20), in an attempt to begin to define *queer*, quote a pamphlet circulating in New York, circa 1990, entitled *I Hate Straights*:

> Being queer means leading a different sort of life. It's not about the mainstream, profit margins, patriotism, patriarchy or being assimilated. It's not

about being executive directors, privilege and elitism. It's about being on the margins, defining ourselves; it's about genderfuck and secrets, what's beneath the belt and deep inside the heart; it's about the night.

Queer politics emerged at a particular historical juncture when numerous governments failed to respond adequately to the AIDS crisis, and a great deal of antigay legislature was put forward by a homophobic Thatcher government in the United Kingdom. Existing political strategies were proving impotent for lesbians and gays, "a new adversarial politics was needed; it was time for queers to bash back" (Bell and Valentine 1995a, 21). Queer politics are closely linked to queer theory, which is a diverse literature that is often seen as having emerged out of gay and lesbian literary criticism—particularly the works of Eve Kosofsky Sedgwick (1990). It is most commonly situated within postmodernist and/or poststructuralist frameworks which decenter normative notions of sexuality.

A key concern of queer theorists is the deconstruction and disruption of binary oppositions such as heterosexual/homosexual, gender/sex, and man/woman. How, for example, are we to understand the pregnant man? From time to time stories appear in the media about pregnant men. In 2008 the global media reported the story of a thirty-four-year-old transgender man in Oregon, United States—who kept his female reproductive organs—who was pregnant with a baby girl. Thomas Beatie, on the *Oprah Winfrey Show*, "stripped off for the cameras and bared his baby bump and also revealed pictures from his beauty queen days as a young woman" (*Daily Mail Online* 2008). Beatie and his wife, Nancy, had wanted to have a child but Nancy could not conceive. When asked by the media how it felt to be a pregnant man, Beatie responded, "Incredible." But lots of people did not think it was incredible; they thought it was unacceptable. But Beatie was not the first pregnant man. In 1999 trans man Matt Rice gave birth to a baby boy. Rice's trans man partner, Patrick Califia, told *Village Voice* magazine:

> Straight neighbours were "pretty sweet" about it. . . . The only people who have gotten upset are a handful of straight-identified homophobic FTMs [female to male transgender people] online who started calling Matt by his girl name, because real men don't get pregnant. (*Sunday Star-Times*, March 30, 2008, A17)

One of us has argued previously that "pregnant men do not (yet) make sense to most people. . . . Maternal bodies only make sense within specific geographical and temporal contexts" (Longhurst 2008, 146). Male embodiment and maternity are not easily linked. Clearly, in most cases it is *not* men who conceive, carry in utero, give birth, and breastfeed babies, but sometimes it is. It is important, therefore, not to simply ascribe these biological processes to women as though women are the only ones capable of being maternal bodies. Sex, gender, and identities such as "mother" can be configured in many different ways that queer the body. It is useful to note that the word *queer* tends to be used as a noun and a verb—someone/thing can be queer; it is also possible to queer someone/thing. Pregnancy queers men, and vice versa.

Scholars in many disciplines, including geography, have made effective use of queer theory and politics to understand further the performance of sexual identities in space. Bell et al. (1994), for example, use the work of Judith Butler (1990) to examine the construction of public space as heteronormative (also see Bell and Valentine 1995a). More recently, geographical knowledge has also been subjected to "queer readings" (see Binnie 1997; and Binnie and Valentine 1999, 181–82).

Like the terms *sex* and *gender*, the terms *transsexual* and *transgendered* are contested and subject to change over time and space. Petra Doan (2007, 59) argues that transsexuals are people "whose identification as a member of the other sex is so strong s/he MUST at minimum live full time in a gender appropriate role, and often will attempt to alter his/her anatomical sex through hormonal or surgical means" (capitals in original). Transsexuals believe their bodies do not correspond with their gender identities. They make reference to feeling like a man trapped in a woman's body or vice versa. Medical technology (hormones and surgery) has enabled some transsexuals to change their sexed body to fit their gender identity. Transgendered people live in the opposite gender role and may take gender appropriate hormones but do not desire surgical transformation.

Probably the most well-known openly transsexual where we live in New Zealand is Georgina Beyer. Beyer was the first transsexual in the world to be elected as mayor and the first transsexual to be elected as a Member of Parliament. She has now retired from Parliament after serving seven years (Georgina Beyer.com 2008). Beyer's story is in many ways incredible. She has done a great deal to help pave the way for transsexual and transgendered communities in New Zealand and beyond (for more information on Beyer see chapter 7).

Unlike transsexuals, drag queens are female impersonators who are often attracted to men. They do not feel the desire to necessarily live as full-time women. By way of another example, again in New Zealand, one of, if not the, most iconic queens is Carmen Rupe. Carmen is Māori and has been at the forefront of seeking recognition for those in queer communities in New Zealand and Australia for more than fifty years. Drag kings are male impersonators who are often lesbians. Cross-dressers are people who enjoy wearing clothing of the opposite sex. They are sometimes referred to as transvestites. Some cross-dressers frequently dress as the other sex; others engage in this activity more sporadically. They do not wish to live as that gender (Doan 2007). Intersexed people have genitals which are neither clearly male nor female. Often physicians attempt to "correct" an infant's ambiguous genitalia soon after birth. Babies that do not fit neatly into the binary notion of the sex model are labeled as "problems" or even worse as "anomalies" or "monsters" (Cream 1995). Androgynous people appear and identify neither as female or male and present a persona that tends to be either neutral or mixed.

A term that appears reasonably frequently in this book and one that can be used to describe all the various subjectivities discussed above is *Other*. The Other is someone who is different from the Self. The Other is understood to be lesser than and/or to lack in some way. Othering is a process by which some individuals, groups, and categories become constructed (psychically, discursively, and materially) as "different." The process of Othering is associated with unequal power relations that exclude and marginalize some individuals, groups, and categories.

Another term that appears throughout this text is *discourse*. The notion of discourse is complex, mainly because there are many conflicting and overlapping interpretations from a range of disciplinary and theoretical standpoints. In short, however, two general understandings of discourse can be identified. First, in linguistics, discourse tends to refer to examples of either written or spoken language. Second, and the meaning adopted in this book, in social theory, discourse tends to be understood in broader terms. Although social theorists recognize the centrality of language to understanding discourse, they use the term to refer to ways of structuring knowledge and social practice.

We want to move now to examine more geographical or spatial terms that are used throughout the book, in particular the terms *space* and *place*. These two terms occupy an important position in the discipline of human geography and enough books have been written on these concepts to fill a library (see Johnston et al. 2000, 767–73, for a definition of *space*, *place*, and *human geography* and for a comprehensive list of references on the terms *space* and *place*). Each "turn" in the production of geographical knowledge has been reflected upon and added into the large corpus of work. The terms *space* and *place* have long been, and are still, integral to the geographical imagination. Phil Hubbard (2005, 41) explains they provide "the basis for a discipline that insists on grounding analyses of social and cultural life in appropriate geographic contexts."

For our purposes we do not want to rehearse all these existing arguments here. Nor do we necessarily want to pin down *space* and *place*,
offering neat and tidy definitions. It is more that we want to continue to
work with them. When we use the term *space* we refer *not* to something
that is abstract, absolute, static, empty, "just there," ultimately measur-
able, and able to be mapped, but to something that is complex, change-
able, discursively produced, and imbued with power relations. Spaces
and bodies are intimately tied together, a point that is elucidated in the
next chapter.

We tend to use the term *place* to refer to specific places. In this way the
term highlights the materiality of spaces. It reminds us that real people
live in real places. More than four decades ago, in 1974, Yi-Fu Tuan developed the idea that place is created and maintained through "fields of
care" that result from people's emotional attachments to places. Tuan
used the dual concept of topophillia and topophobia to refer to desires
and fears that people associate with particular places. In thinking about
sexual identity and practices in relation to place these ideas are still relevant today. Our reference to the work of humanistic geographer Tuan is
not meant to deny the importance of the discursiveness of space, place,
and bodies (something that humanistic geographers did not discuss much
at the time) but rather to remind readers that places are bounded settings
and that the bodies that occupy them are flesh and blood and experience
a range of emotions in relation to these places. Places and bodies are not
just "linguistic territories" (Longhurst 2001). They have an undeniable
materiality that cannot be bracketed out when considering the relationship between people and place.

These are some of the key terms and concepts that are used throughout this book. We have provided brief definitions but it needs to be
remembered that the meanings of these terms are not fixed. They shift
depending on the time and context in which they are used. For example, we attempted to define the term *queer*, but how does *queer* with
its complex intellectual and political history translate into non-English
languages such as Māori? "In Māori the word takatāpui tends to be used
currently to embrace all non-heterosexual forms of sexuality but this
term has a colonial history that is different from the history of the term
queer" (Longhurst 2008, 383). The phrase "ko ia" is also used in Māori.
Ko is a word that is simply used before a definite article, *ia* means he
or she. Jordon Harris (2005, 3) explains: "In the language of our ancestors there was no pronoun distinguishing gender such as he or she,
there was ia." Consequently *Ko Ia: He or She* was the title chosen for an
information booklet on sexuality circulated by the New Zealand AIDS
Foundation (see figure 1.1).

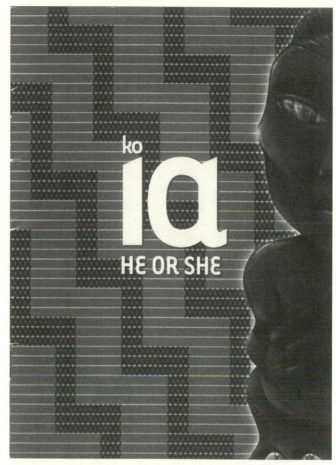

Figure 1.1. *Ko Ia: He or She*, 2005. Booklet compiled by Jordon Harris, produced and distributed in New Zealand by Hau Ora Takatāpui New Zealand AIDS Foundation. Reproduced courtesy of Hau Ora Takatāpui New Zealand AIDS Foundation.

In Samoa identities are constructed differently yet again. The word *fa'afafine* is used to describe men who are like women. Johanna Schmidt (2001, 1) explains: "The Samoan word fa'afafine literally translates as 'in the manner of a woman.' Fa'afafine are biological males who express feminine gender identities in a range of ways . . . fa'afafine are both viewed through the lens of and influenced by Western understandings of sexuality." Fa'afafine are biologically men who have been raised since childhood to take on stereotypical women's roles such as cooking and cleaning (although many fa'afafine also carry out stereo-typical men's roles such as heavy lifting and digging). Most fa'afafine seek sexual relationships with heterosexual men. In Samoan, as well as in Māori, culture there is an emphasis on the collective, that is, the family and community rather than on the individual. Therefore, there is a line of thought that suggests whatever is best for the group is best for the individual. A family may require an extra woman in the family and so may choose to raise a boy as fa'afafine (although some boys do resist). Words such as *homosexual, drag queen, queer,* or *transvestite* do not adequately describe or explain the identities of, or social contexts in which takatāpui or fa'afafine live. These contexts are undoubtedly complex and varied: for example, fa'afafine living in Apia, Samoa, and Auckland, New Zealand, are likely to have quite different experiences (see Schmidt 2001).

The material in this introduction, therefore, is just that, an introduction. It represents a start at unraveling some of the complex power relations that congeal around sexuality and spatiality. Clearly it is not possible to separate sex and sexuality from other markers of identity such as culture, age, skin color, ethnicity, social class, health, and so on. People do not just have one dimension to their subjectivities. Therefore, although in this book we highlight sex and sexuality, we are always cognizant that people cannot be *reduced* to their sexual desires, acts, or subjectivities. These simply interact with a variety of other factors at different times and in different contexts.

CHAPTER OUTLINE

As indicated at the beginning of this introduction, the rest of this book is concerned with exploring the diversity and complexity of embodied experiences of sex and sexuality, which are constructed through different social, cultural, and economic networks and through different spaces and places. It is argued that space, place, and sex are inextricably linked and embedded with complex power relations at a variety of different spatial scales.

Chapter 2 introduces readers to debates about nature/nurture, sex/gender, mind/body, and essentialism/social constructionism. We explain that the book is informed by a version of feminist poststructuralism that holds on firmly to the notion of materiality (in other words, we are not just interested in representations or social constructions of bodies but also in "real" fleshy bodies).

Chapter 3 explains that in recent years geographers have begun to examine the relationship between sex, sexuality, and home focusing on housing design and the meanings and experiences of home. It is noted that home has often been valorized as the site of heterosexual family relationships. Still today many houses are designed and built for nuclear families. Often, however, homes are occupied by Others such as gay couples, single mothers, roommates, polygamists, or polyamorists, all of who imbue homes with different social relations. Homes, therefore, can be spaces of relaxation, havens, and sites of oppression, danger, subversion, and resistance. In this chapter we also think about what it means to want to have sex but to not have a roof over one's head—to be homeless.

Chapter 4 focuses on the notion of community as a group of people sharing something in common, in this instance, a sexual identity. We look to the examples of the gay games, faith-based queer spaces or gay churches, gay men creating domestic gardens and online sexual communities. During the past decade most of us have heard about, or been engaged in, the phenomena of people using the Internet to look for love and romance. Other individuals and groups go online to seek out pornography and/or casual sexual encounters. Still others seek companionship with those who share a similar sexual orientation.

In chapter 5 it is argued that millions of people across the globe live in cities. This makes them extremely significant places. This chapter addresses the social relations surrounding sex and sexuality that are constituted within cities. Public rituals surrounding heterosexual sex are usually acceptable in cities, for example, a man and woman marrying in a public park or a straight couple kissing on a bus. Other sex, such as homo-, trans-, and bisexuality, is usually less acceptable. This chapter explores the idea that cities can be understood as sexually contested urban spaces where streets may be queered (Johnston 2005a).

Chapter 6 changes tack to focus on rural space. Rural space is often epitomized as natural, pure, and tranquil and has long been associated with those who wish to be "closer to nature." We explore the relationship between the rural and sexuality by examining farming men's attempts to find "appropriate" wives, a rural bachelor of the year competition, people who are considered to be Other in rural spaces, and animal-human sexual relations.

Chapter 7 begins by exploring sexual citizenship as a form of social identification, which some writers claim is replacing more traditional forms of national identity. Nations often assume their citizens are heterosexual men or women who engage in "natural" or "normal" sex. We examine the role of the state, churches, and pressure groups in relation to both straight and queer marriage, the ways in which transsexuals are excluded from the nation, and the story of Georgina Beyer, the world's first transsexual mayor and Member of Parliament.

In chapter 9 we examine the ways in which desire and romance transcend national boundaries to travel across the globe. One example of this is wedding tourism (also known as destination weddings). Another is the so-called mail-order bride business. Following this we look at how some women are now traveling to destinations within the Caribbean for sex and romance with "beach boys" and how queers are traveling to gay friendly destinations and events such as Mardi Gras in Sydney.

The book concludes in chapter 9 with an argument that exploring sex and sexuality points not only to the importance of place and space in the production of sexual identities, but also to the centrality of sexualities in constituting specific social spaces. In order to understand the production and expression of sexual identities whether they be lesbian, gay, bisexual, transsexual, intersex, queer, heterosexual, or something else it is useful to consider space and place at a variety of spatial scales. Sex and sexuality are important issues of our time and adopting a geographical perspective has the potential to deepen our understanding of these issues.

2

❦

"The Geography Closest In"
The Body

This chapter explores the body *as a* space and the body *in* space. Feminist writer and poet Adrienne Rich (1986, 212) describes the body as "the geography closest in." Our bodies make a difference to our experience of spaces and places. Our size, shape, health, appearance, dress, comportment, sexuality, and sexual practices affect how we respond to others and how people respond to us. Kirsten Simonsen (2000, 7) notes that we appear to live in the "era of the body" and that we are obsessed with bodies and bodily appearance. This body fixation can be seen in a number of examples such as eating disorders, plastic surgery, and an obsession with exercise. Geographers' interest in the body is clearly part of a much wider societal interest. Valentine (2001, 15; italics in original) says:

> It [the body] marks a *boundary* between the self and other, both in a literal physiological sense but also in a social sense. It is a personal *space*. A sensuous organ, the site of pleasure and pain around which social definitions of wellbeing, illness, happiness and health are constructed, it is our means for connecting with, and experiencing other spaces.

Geographers since the mid-1990s have been examining the body as a space, carrying out research that seeks to explore questions around sexual specificity, the differences between bodies, women's social subordination to men, and the mutually constitutive relationships that exist between bodies and places (see Duncan 1996; Nast and Pile 1998; Rose 1993).

Geographers have begun to conceptualize the discipline of geography as being one that is founded on an understanding of subjects as *embodied* and more specifically, as *sexually* embodied. We use this term *embodied* in the way that philosopher Benedictus Spinoza used it in the seventeenth century—the mind as an idea of the body rather than separate from it (see Lloyd 1993). We use the term *sexually embodied* in order to stress the point that there exist not just *human* bodies, but rather bodies that are usually either men's bodies or women's bodies (Gatens 1991a). We want to think about bodies and places and the complex relationship that exists between bodies and places. Recent critical theory on the body has much to offer geographers. In turn, geographers are making an important contribution to this literature by examining the complexities in the relationships between bodies and places (and between materialities and discourses, and nature and culture).

"FLESHY FEMINISM"

In this book we examine sexed bodies using a version of feminist poststructuralist theory that holds on firmly to the notion of materiality and discourse—a kind of "fleshy feminism" or more specifically a "fleshy version of feminist poststructuralism." Sexed bodies are not "natural" but rather tend to adhere to expected regulatory behaviors that are established over time. There is no preconstituted sexed body; instead, a variety of sexed and gendered behaviors can be attached to numerous different bodies, in different times and spaces. Julia Cream (1995, 31) asks: "What is the sexed body?" and answers by saying whatever it is, it is contingent upon time and place. Furthermore, the sexed body can be read as a historical outcome of a range of cultural meanings centering on biological sex, social gender, gender identity, and sexuality. This chapter draws on place-based theorizations, histories, and narratives of (trans)sexed bodies (see Meyerowitz 2002) to examine why and how some sexed bodies enjoy many privileges while others are marginalized. Despite arguing that bodies are constructed by history, space, text, representation, and discourse we do not want to deny the real fleshy materiality of bodies (think, for example, of transvestites who argue they have been born into the wrong body—there is no denying the fleshy materiality of bodies). We are interested in identity, representation, and discourse as well as in the undeniable fleshiness of bodies and the spaces in which they love, fight, sleep, eat, go to work, dress up, dance, have sex, and so on.

This theoretical framework shares something in common with that developed by Pamela Moss and Isabel Dyck (2002) to examine the lives of women with chronic illness. Moss and Dyck (2002, 9) refer to this as "a framework for a radical body politics—one that is feminist, one that draws out discursive formation, one that has a material base, and one that is spatialized." This is the lens through which we tend to read most of our data. It is not the only lens though.

Throughout the book we also draw on gay, lesbian, and queer perspectives not just in a way that constructs gendered and sexual subjectivities as completely performative and ethereal but one that recognizes the lived experiences of people who identify as queer and/or transsexual or transgendered. Over the past decade some geographers have alluded to tensions between those working from feminist, and queer, perspectives in the discipline. As one of us has noted elsewhere "in 1999 Jon Binnie and Gill Valentine argued that feminist geography has been both supportive but also restrictive in regard to homophobia remaining deeply seated in the discipline" (Longhurst 2008, 384). David Bell (2007, 85) reiterates these sentiments saying, "Feminist geography has sometimes been home to work on queer politics and theory, though I think it is fair to say there are on-going tensions between queer and feminism that are also being played out in geography" (also see Nast 2002 and Sothern 2004). This theme of the relationship between feminist and queer geographies was explored at the interdisciplinary conference Intersections: Feminist and Queer Geographies hosted by the School of Geography, University of Leeds, July 7–8, 2008. In New Zealand tensions have not been evident among feminist and queer geographies, possibly because there are far fewer and smaller groups of scholars and activists involved. Also, in New Zealand it is mainly women geographers working on queer spatial issues. In this book, therefore, it is likely that readers will note a melding of feminist and queer work rather than a careful carving of the theoretical terrain.

BODIES THAT DON'T FIT THE TWO-SEX MODEL

There are many bodies that don't fit the two-sex model and who do not fit neatly into the binary categories of man/woman or masculine/feminine. For example, there are people who have both male and female genitalia, usually known as intersexed, transsexuals, and people with XXY chromosomes. There are also people who exhibit gendered characteristics that do not align with the expected performances of their sexed body. Kath Browne (2006a, 121) explains, "Queer theorizations of sexed embodiments have rendered the dichotomies of man/woman problematic and unstable." Or to put it like one of Browne's research participants, it is possible to be "a right geezer-bird"—*geezer* being English slang for men and *bird* for women. In other words, it is possible to be a man-woman.

The *spatial* implications for such people are now beginning to be explored. Embodied difference can be a basis of discrimination and prejudice. Browne teases out some of the implications of having an ambiguous gendered and sexed body by focusing on public toilets or bathrooms. When there is a discontinuity or what some might term a mismatch between the gender and sex with which one identifies, and how others read their gender and sex, difficulties can occur. Browne, based on a study of nine women who participated in a wider research project about nonheterosexual women's lives, explores "how women negotiate the policing of sexed spaces such as that bodies, sexed sites (toilets) and the location of these sites (nightclubs, service stations) are mutually constituted within sexed regimes of power" (Browne 2004, 331). The boundaries of gender difference are often overtly enforced in such spaces.

Judith Butler's well-known book *Gender Trouble* (1990; also see Butler 1993) has prompted many to think carefully about what it means to trouble or disturb the presumed naturalness of the man-masculinity and woman-femininity binary. Individuals who prompt "gender trouble" are likely to find themselves subject to insulting comments, exclusions, aggression, and violence (Namaste 1996; Munt 2001). Butler (1990, 33) argues that gender is "the repeated stylization of the body, a set of repeated acts within a highly rigid frame that congeal over time to produce the appearance of substance, of a natural sort of being." In other words, gender is something that we "do," and do recurrently. Butler argues that the gendered body is a performative body. She suggests that "acts, gestures, enactments, generally construed, are *performative* in the sense that the essence or identity that they otherwise purport to express are *fabrications* manufactured and sustained through corporeal signs and other discursive means" (Butler 1990, 136; italics in original). In arguing that gender is performative, Butler displaces the alignment of gender and sex. She illustrates that it is not natural for women to be feminine and men to be masculine but rather repeated gendered acts that constitute the body's reality make it *appear* this way. Gender and sex are constructed social relations. Gendered and sexed bodies are acculturated and inscribed by discourse. This does not mean that they can be reduced to discourse or to being nothing more than cultural, social, or linguistic constructions. Bodies have a weighty materiality and biology that is undeniable but fleshy bodies always exist within the realms of political, economic, cultural, and social realms (see Nelson 1999 on "the limits of performativity"). Bodies require examination and explanation: they are "not a starting point" (Cream 1995, 31). Sexed bodies are an interface between culture and nature. They are both real and socially constructed.

What we are alluding to here is a debate that has been going on among feminists, queers, and others for a number of decades—a debate often referred to as the nature/nurture debate, or more recently in academic circles, the essentialist/social constructionist debate. Is there something inherent and unchangeable in people's being that makes them who they are and how they are? Clearly there are numerous political imperatives embedded in this question. Claiming that people have some kind of unalterable essence can work both for and against different individuals and groups. For many years (and still today) it has been argued by some—those who do not support equal rights—that women are naturally or essentially weaker than men and more suited to occupying domestic realms rather than public space. Such people argue that nothing can change this. It is universal and timeless.

This argument for essentialism, however, is not just used in the pursuit of conservative political agendas. Many lesbians and gay men have claimed an essence in relation to their sexual orientation arguing that it is simply the way we/they were born, or "the way God made us/them" and no one can or should attempt to change this. This is sometimes referred to as strategic essentialism, that is, claiming essentialism in order to further a particular social and political project. Judith Butler charts a path through this complex theoretical and political territory by arguing that repeated performances of gendered and sexed expected behaviors establish regulatory practices for bodies. One such regulatory practice is heterosexuality. Heterosexuality constitutes an unmarked category in contemporary Western culture and as such has been subject to rigorous critique over the last decade (Puar 2006). A great deal of this critique has been produced under the label "queer." It is useful to look at an example of what has come to be a well-known and cited "queer geography" that probes these issues.

Geographers David Bell, John Binnie, Gill Valentine, and Julia Cream (1994) drawing on queer theory, particularly the work of Judith Butler, examine the performance of two different sexual identities in space—the hypermasculine gay skinhead and the hyperfeminine lipstick lesbian. They argue that in the early 1990s the skinhead look became trendy in gay London, including a number of bars and clubs such as Club 4 Skins. A No. 1 cut or completely shaven head, tight-fitting Levi 501 jeans, Fred Perry and Ben Sherman label clothing, and Doc Marten boots complete the look. Also in the late 1980s–early 1990s some lesbians began adopting a hyperfeminine image that enabled them to "pass" as heterosexual and derive the privileges of being heterosexual in a variety of everyday spaces. High heels, dresses, and makeup were donned by some who previously preferred boots, denim, and leather. In the final instance Bell et al. (1994) could not reach a unanimous conclusion about sexed and gendered performances in spaces which are assumed to be heterosexual, but their article certainly succeeded in prompting a great deal of discussion about these issues.

To this point we have been discussing sexed and gendered bodies but it is important to keep in mind that bodies are always more than simply sexed and gendered. Other axes of bodily difference such as age, race, and abilities also determine who we are, what we do, and our interaction with others. For example, Annette Pritchard and Nigel Morgan (2005) explore discourses of tourism, fashion, place, and gender in the lifestyle magazine *Condé Nast Traveller*. They find that travel magazines tend to represent Asian and Eurasian women as hyperfeminine and sexually exotic: "The women are objectified and displayed in exotic silks and jade jewellery, recycling the racial and gendered stereotypes of the vulnerable oriental beauty (the exotic China doll) and the sinister oriental *femme fatale* (the dragon lady)" (Pritchard and Morgan 2005, 297). In this instance it can be seen that it is not enough to examine sexuality as just one axis of identity. Sexuality cannot be separated from gender, or from race, or from colonization.

Lawrence Knopp (1999) in describing some of his personal experiences as an "out" gay male academic who researches sexuality says that sexualization "is a process (or conjunction of processes) whereby identities are, in an ongoing and never complete way, constructed and reconstructed in terms of these [social and power] relations." Sexuality is not fixed. Nor are other axes of people's identities. It is important to keep this in mind as we put the spotlight on sex and gender. Being engaged in any kind of politics requires us to work out which axes of identity, which differences matter when and why. How can we construct alliances to create meaningful change? In writing this book we have in effect made a strategic decision to focus on sexuality and to treat sex and gender as *the* most significant differences but we also want to think about how other categories such as age, class, culture, well-being, disability, body size, race, and ethnicity intersect with sex and gender. It is these particular combinations of subjectivities that construct some bodies as attractive, powerful, and influential and others as disgusting, troublesome, and unimportant.

BODIES THAT DISGUST

Some bodies cause "gender trouble" by sitting outside normative constructions of masculinity and femininity. These bodies are sometimes considered to be disgusting or abject. Abjection is the affect or feeling of unease, repugnance, and abhorrence that the subject has in encountering certain matter, images, and fantasies—the disgusting—to which it can only respond with aversion, nausea, and distraction. Over the past decade we have taught university geography courses and modules on gender and sexuality. When talking with the students about people who do not fit the two-sex model or who choose to have sex with someone of the same sex/gender regularly or on occasion, one or two have registered their "disgust" by making comments such as "that's disgusting," "yuck," and "it's just plain wrong."

Julia Kristeva (1982) argues that the abject provokes dread and disgust because it exposes the border between self and other. This border is tenuous. The abject threatens to dissolve the subject by dissolving the border. Perhaps the students who publically register their disgust fear that part of themselves that desires someone of the same sex. The abject, however, is not only disgusting, it is also fascinating. It is as though it draws the subject in order to fend it off (see Young 1990a, 145). It is strangely compelling.

Much work on abjection is anchored by Mary Douglas's insights on boundary rituals and dirt. Douglas (1975, 47–59) argues that nothing in itself is dirty; rather, dirt is that which is not in its proper place and upsets order. The metaphorically "dirty" sexual body is the body which transgresses the borders of respectability and respectable places. It is the body that is constituted within brothels, alleyways, public parks, back streets, public bathrooms, "wrong" beds, dark, and illicit spaces. It is the sexual body that is "out of place." Douglas (1966, 5) claims: "Reflection on dirt involves reflection on the relation of order to disorder, being to non-being, form to formlessness, life to death." Dirt is essentially disorder—it is "matter out of place."

> If we can abstract pathogenicity and hygiene from our notion of dirt, we are left with the old definition of *matter out of place*. . . . Dirt then, is never a unique, isolated event. Where there is dirt there is system. Dirt is the by-product of a systematic ordering and classification of matter, in so far as ordering involves rejecting inappropriate elements. This idea of dirt takes us straight into the field of symbolism and promises a link-up with more obviously symbolic systems of purity. (Douglas 1966, 35; italics added)

Iris Young (1990a) argues that some individuals and groups in society are more likely than others to be constructed as abject or "ugly." Young (1990a, 145) claims that understanding abjection enhances "an understanding of a body aesthetic that defines some groups as ugly or fearsome and produces aversive reactions in relation to members of those groups." Young refers to the bodies of Blacks, Latinos, Asians, American Indians, and Semitic peoples in the United States, old people, women, gay men, lesbians, and fat people as occupying the position of "ugly, fearful, or loathsome bodies" (Young 1990a, 124). Bodies that operate outside of sexual moral norms are also constructed as abject or ugly.

Hubbard (2000, 211) examines how the boundaries between moral and immoral heterosexual identities are created and sustained but also challenged in particular urban contexts. Hubbard (2000) focuses on a red-light district in Birmingham, United Kingdom, and charts community protests against prostitution. The protesters used "moral narratives and discourses" in their attempts to put forward the idea of a community based upon the exclusion of "immoral" sex workers. Hubbard's research shows that understanding sexualized acts and spaces is multifaceted and contradictory since (hetero)sexuality does not stand alone but is entangled with gender, race, ethnicity, social class, age, and so on. It also shows that some sexual bodies are constructed as immoral, disgusting, dirty, and "matter out of place."

David Sibley (1995) also discusses forms of social exclusion arguing that society places "others," such as children, the elderly, gypsies, women, and the disabled, as outsiders. Sibley pays attention to spatial exclusion in relation to the routine practices of daily life. At the center of this marginalization is the drive of powerful groups to dominate and purify space. Undoubtedly these ideas about abject bodies and about the domination and purification of spaces are useful in relation to sexuality.

Sometimes people might be seen to choose particular subjectivities (although always within a bounded set of social relations) such as prostitutes or the lipstick lesbians and gay skinheads discussed earlier, but not always. Some people's embodiment is such that they challenge normative constructions of masculinity and femininity just by being. Take, for example, breasted men. They are commonly considered to be abject. Although it is rarely discussed publicly (including in the academy) it is reasonably common for adolescent men and boys to develop breasts that are more like a woman's than a man's. This condition is referred to as gynecomastia. *Gynecomastia* is a medical term that comes from the Greek words for "women-like breasts." Though this condition is rarely talked about, it's actually quite common. Gynecomastia affects an estimated 40 to 60 percent of men. It may affect only one breast or both. The website

EmbarrassingProblems.com claims that teenage boys sometimes notice that their breasts are enlarging and/or are tender. Man-breasts are related to the levels of estrogen and testosterone being produced in the body at different times and so approximately half of all boys at some time develop breasts. "It can start anytime after the age of about 10, and the breasts may be quite large by the age of 13 or 14. In the mid-to-late teens, they start to become smaller again, and will usually have flattened out by age 18 or 19. . . . By the end of the teen years most men no longer have enlarged breasts unless they are fat" (Longhurst 2005, 167).

Most men who experience breast enlargement (whether it be as a result of tumors, less testosterone being produced in old age, using drugs that have an estrogenlike effect on the breast, anabolic [body-building] steroids, aspartame found in many foods and drinks with artificial sweeteners, or antibalding scalp creams) face challenges reconciling their masculine subjectivity with their feminized body. Elizabeth Grosz (1994, 203) notes that "there are particular bodily zones that serve to emphasize both women's difference from and otherness to men." These zones are culturally determined rather than natural or biological. One such zone is the breasts.

"DISCIPLINING" SEXUAL BODIES

When bodies do not fit within prescribed sexual norms they tend to be "disciplined"—made to conform to these norms. Michel Foucault's work on bodies, in particular sexed bodies, and their regulation, has been highly influential in shaping the way that social scientists and others think about sex, sexuality, and the disciplining of bodies. Foucault (1978) traces how sexed bodies are socially constructed differently over time. Using a historical approach he has been able to ascertain that sexuality is not "natural" but rather socially constructed. It is created through discourses. Sexuality has changed through the ages.

> At the beginning of the seventeenth century a certain frankness was still common, it would seem. Sexual practices had little need of secrecy; words were said without undue reticence, and things were done without too much concealment; one had a tolerant familiarity with the illicit. (Foucault 1978, 3)

In the nineteenth century things began to change. Sexuality started to become confined to the home. Foucault (1978, 3) explains, "The conjugal family took custody of it and absorbed it into the serious function of reproduction." It became unacceptable, among the Victorian bourgeoisie at least, to talk about sex. The only legitimate space for sex it seems was parents' bedrooms.

Sexuality is a historical construct that is produced through discourse. Discourse plays an important role in shaping and controlling individual bodies as well as entire populations. Foucault (1978, 141 and 143) uses the term *bio-power* to describe the various techniques and institutions such as the family, army, schools, police, and medicine used to control populations socially and economically. Foucault is also interested in the ways in which individuals and populations are regulated through the power of a surveillant gaze. What Foucault means by this is that individuals often exercise self-surveillance and self-discipline simply because they know they are being watched. In *Discipline and Punish* (1977, 177) Foucault uses the example of penal reform to illustrate the change from private and public acts of torture used in the eighteenth century to control prisoners to "an inspecting gaze" used in the nineteenth century to punish and control offenders. Foucault (1977, 155) says: "There is no need for arms, physical violence, material constraints. Just a gaze. An inspecting gaze, a gaze which each individual under its weight will end by interiorising to the point that he is his own overseer, each individual thus exercising surveillance over and against himself." Simply being seen means that most individuals will exercise self-surveillance and self-control.

The inspecting gaze also functions in relation to sex and sexuality. Most (but certainly not all) people regulate their behaviors in accordance with social sexual norms. There are particular ways that individuals are expected to look and to act. In the late twentieth and early twenty-first centuries in affluent Western societies bodies have become important bearers of social and sexual meaning. A body's size, shape, firmness, fitness, and overall appearance have increasingly come to matter. Bodies are expected to fit idealized representations of what is desirable. They are supposed to be sexy (but not too sexy) adhering to society's exacting standards of size, shape, and appearance. Body makeovers, both surgical (e.g., breast or buttock augmentation, tummy tucks, face-lifts, and liposuction) and nonsurgical, have become big business. Bodies are "worked on." They have become projects (Shilling 1993, 5). Cosmetic surgeons, people in the diet, fitness, fashion, and beauty industries, retailers, advertisers, and the media are just some of those who have a vested interest in "improving" bodies.

Consider, for example, the athletic or "fit" body (which is seen to be sexually attractive). Derek McCormack (1999, 161) argues that constructions of fitness are created within "political and discursive economies." To make this point he focuses on NordicTrack home fitness products, which are marketed toward "well-educated, affluent 35–54 year olds" who want to "enhance their own and their family's well-being and enjoyment of life." McCormack (1999, 171) analyses NordicTrack's advertisements which depict figures "uncannily similar to that of the Nietzschean superman, striding confidently ever-forwards and ever-onwards with the arms outstretched. This well-sculpted, human-machinic, lean, muscular, masculinism signified control and solidity." McCormack points out that these hybrid human-machinic bodies "take their shape as racialised and gendered phenomena" (173). They also take their shape as sexualized phenomena. Bodies discipline themselves though the use of fitness machines to produce flesh that is lean and taut, adhering to contemporary Western standards of sexual attractiveness.

Sometimes bodies are disciplined by others rather than by the self. In October 2002 the media in New Zealand reported that a woman, known as Nikki, planned to be filmed giving birth for a pornographic movie (Longhurst 2006a). There was a public outcry. Birth is considered to be one of the most intimate of acts, a time when the birthing mother needs to be utterly focused on her labor and ensuring her baby's safe passage. In the West, births are usually attended only by health and medical professionals, a partner or a mother's nearest and dearest. It is not an event that is filmed for the purposes of the sexual gratification of strangers. As soon as Nikki's, and pornographic filmmaker Steve Crow's, plans were made public there were attempts by a New Zealand government department, the New Zealand Minister of Health, the High Court, journalists, midwives, doctors, social workers, and members of the public to discipline Nikki's and Crow's behavior. In the final instance the birth was not filmed. Nikki's body posed a threat to the supposed sanctity of the birthing ward. The sexualization of the birthing body lay outside of customary sexual and moral norms in New Zealand (Longhurst 2006a).

NUDE BODIES, CLOTHED BODIES

Being nude in public space also tends to fall outside of customary sexual and moral norms in most Western countries (Bell and Holliday 2000). This deters most from shedding their clothes beyond the walls of home. Nudism, however, has a long history—a history which varies from place to place (see Daley 2005 on nudism in Australasia and Toepfer 1997 on nudism in Germany)—and those who engage in it often argue that it has nothing to do with eroticism and everything to do with feeling healthy and at one with nature. Caroline Daley (2005, 149) quotes an article written in 1945 by a New Zealand nudist, Percy Cousins, who says, "There, in the midst of lovely surroundings, ourselves blending with the peace and quiet of it all, we recuperate and revitalize in Nature's own way." While sexuality was and still is often highly controlled in nudists' spaces, critics often find this hard to believe. In relation to nudism in Australia and New Zealand in the interwar and postwar period Daley (2005, 151) writes:

> While many could accept the benefits of exercising in the sun and fresh air, they saw no reason why people had to take off all their clothes to do so, especially in mixed groups. To nudism's many critics it was clear that the only reason nudists disrobed in public was because they were sex-crazed perverts. Claims about health were a front. All nudists really wanted to do was look at the naked bodies before them, and act on what they saw.

In September 2008 in New Zealand it was proposed that the Kapiti Coast (southwestern coast of the North Island) would soon become one of the world's longest (45 kilometers or 30 miles) nude beaches. The Kapiti Coast District Council's regulatory management committee endorsed a staff recommendation to allow nudity in its 2008 Draft Beach Bylaw so long as it is not deemed "lewd" in which case the behavior would be reported to police and people would be liable to prosecution. One of the beaches along this coast, Peka Peka, is already a nude beach and has been a sunbathing spot popular with gay men for the past ten years. "A local gay sunlover was worried gay people using Peka Peka beach could be targeted. 'Who is going to determine what is lewd behaviour? Will two naked men or two women lying on the beach together be slammed lewd?'" (Blundell 2008).

The act of sunbathing on beaches is still very common, despite the risks of skin cancer. People lie naked, or seminaked, on beaches to feel sexy both on and off the beach. Many also find the act of tanning to be transformative, as found in Lynda's study on suntanning on beaches in New Zealand (Johnston 2005b). Interviews with men and women, as they lay on the beach in the sun, revealed that Pākehā (white European New Zealanders) who actively seek brown skin negotiate a number of racialized and gendered truths as their suntan transforms their bodies. Participants expressed that they felt better about themselves when they are tanned. In particular, they felt healthy, attractive, sexy, confident, and younger when they are brown, not white (Johnston 2005b). On beaches in Aotearoa New Zealand, the practice of tanning is consistent with dominant forms of Pākehā femininity associated with youth, beauty, and leisure. For men, tanning is often deemed a by-product of active beach leisure practices, such as surfing or volleyball, and not the primary goal of beach leisure. Pākehā bodies that become "too brown," however, may be read as Māori, and risk losing privileges associated with being Pākehā (Johnston 2005b).

Still on the theme of naked bodies, in 2006 a television reality show was launched titled *How to Look Good Naked*. In the United Kingdom it aired on Channel 4 and the LifeStyle Channel. It is presented by fashion stylist Gok Wan (also see the accompanying book *How to Look Good Naked: Shop for Your Shape and Look Amazing*, Wan 2007). Each week Wan takes one woman who is dissatisfied with her body shape on a journey from loathing her body to feeling positive about her body. The program routinely involves the woman taking part in a naked photographic shoot and a fashion parade adorned not in street clothing but in lingerie. The aim is to encourage women to stop focusing on their stretch marks, bulges, cellulite, and saggy breasts and to instead celebrate the sexy female naked body in all its shapes and sizes.

Geographers Alison Bain and Catherine Nash (2006) also reflect on nakedness but in a different context. They consider their role as embodied researchers at a queer women's bathhouse in Toronto, Canada. As part of their preparations to carry out ethnographic research at the bathhouse, Bain and Nash had to decide what clothes, if any, to wear for the evening. In a frequently asked questions (FAQ) section of the bathhouse's website women are advised: "You don't have to be naked, if you don't want to be. We encourage you to bring something sexy to change into, mainly because we want you to symbolically leave behind the daily grind and get into a sexy mood, but you get to decide what is sexy for you—leather, lace, flannel, whatever!" (Bain and Nash 2006, 101). After a great deal of thought Bain and Nash decided to adopt casual attire—sandals, shorts, and for one of the researchers a tank top, and for the other a loose cotton T-shirt.

Thinking about the sexed, sexy, and naked body raises an obvious but interesting point, that is, that most of the time people are actually *not* naked. Most of us live our lives *not* as naked bodies but as "clothed bodies" (Banim, Green, and Guy 2001). Clothes perform an important material function by protecting bodies and keeping them warm but they also perform an important signification function. Douglas Kellner (1994, 160) says, "In modernity, fashion is an important constituent of one's identity, helping to determine how one is perceived and accepted." Currently there is a pervasive discourse, especially for women, that it is important to look and dress in a manner that is sexy. What constitutes sexy is time and place specific. It is discursively constructed rather than natural. While it is acceptable and even encouraged for some women to look sexy, others are discouraged from doing so. Some exercise self-discipline while others are disciplined by those around them.

Claire Dwyer (1999) and Robina Mohammad's (2005) research on young British Muslim women raises issues about the ways in which individual and community identity is constructed through clothing and behavior in different places. Mohammad (2005, 145–46) argues that Islamist discourses function to deny women's sexuality "by positing it as a threat to the Muslim family, the foundation of Muslim identity. In this formulation women's bodies are understood as endangering their own (hetero)sexual purity, which is key to marriage and the formation of Muslim families." The young British Pakistani women whom Mohammad interviewed told an array of stories about how they manage various aspects of their daily lives, dress, and identities, under the watchful gaze of family and community members. While some of the young women complied with community expectations to dress in a traditional and demure manner that concealed the contours of their bodies, others resisted. Mohammad (2005) reports that one respondent, Sharon, wore Western clothes, such as skirt, jeans, and crop top, as a way of distancing herself from the Pakistani community. In a discussion on the subject of virginity and marriage Sharon told Mohammad, "I started wanting guys at the age of ten." She then recounted her sexual history showing Mohammad photographs of her boyfriends. Women such as Sharon are highly likely to be subject to criticism by their communities and others.

Pregnant women who dress in a manner that is considered to be sexy are also likely to be subject to criticism. There have been interesting developments in maternity wear and in the sexualization of pregnant women since Demi Moore appeared naked and heavily pregnant on the cover of the glossy fashion magazine *Vanity Fair* in 1991. Until that time there had been a strong cultural taboo governing popular media representations of pregnant women (Tyler 2001). One of us—Robyn—has been conducting research on pregnant bodies and spaces for many years, focusing on the constitutive relationship between bodies and spaces. Pregnant bodies are a useful lens through which to think about space. They themselves are a space but also exist within various material and discursive spaces. This is not to suggest that space is merely a backdrop or container on/in which social processes unfold but that space actively constructs bodies in specific ways. Pregnant bodies illustrate that spaces are not abstract and discrete. For example, the pregnant body is a lived space. It is also a space that disrupts binary thinking in that it is both one and two (sometimes more)—mother and infant(s). Iris Young (1990b, 163) notes: "Pregnancy challenges the integration of my body experience by rendering fluid the boundary between what is within, myself, and what is outside, separate. I experience my insides as the space of another, yet my own body." The fetus is a space that is both separate from but also deeply part of the space of the mother.

Pregnant women, as "split subjects" (Young 1990b), have long been expected to be asexual (ironic given their condition), demure, modest, and maternal (Longhurst 2000). The phenomenon of the "hot mamma" is reasonably recent. While some pregnant women feel pressure to look sexy, dress well, and feel proud of their pregnant bodies others feel it is inappropriate for them to focus so much attention on themselves and/or to appear sexually attractive.

Mothers feeding infants have also experienced a shift in their subjectivity in recent years. In New Zealand in 2006 a new lingerie label was launched called HOTmilk. The creators of this new label, Lisa Ebbing and Ange Crosbie, thought there was a gap in the market for sexy maternity wear and lingerie. Ebbing had the idea when she herself was pregnant with her first child (she now has three children) and was not impressed with the maternity options available. The HOTmilk range is designed to empower women and "remind them that they are beautiful, confident and sexy" (Enting 2008). Ebbing was right. There was a gap in the market here. HOTmilk lingerie has grown into a global entity in just two years. It is currently available in four hundred boutiques worldwide including locations in Australia, Britain, Europe, China, Malaysia, Tahiti, and Singapore. They are about to launch in the United States. In 2007 HOTmilk won a number of business awards. Some, however, have seen their advertising (see figure 2.1) as rather risqué and inappropriate for mothers, but Ebbing says that "they are not our target market. We always portray the model in a strong, powerful pose. She is totally in control" (Enting 2008). Other maternity brands are now following suit and also introducing sexier lingerie into their collections.

This new trend of the hot mamma, it seems, is potentially both empowering and disempowering for women. It opens up new possibilities for pregnant and nursing mothers to also have a sexual identity, but not all want to and it can place pressure on women who feel they *have* to look and be sexy at a time when most of their energy is being channeled into caring for an infant. As many know from experience, it is not easy to look like a million bucks on three or four hours sleep and a limited budget. Photos and stories about celebrities outfitted in the latest designer maternity wear, or those who have lost all their gained pounds/kilos just weeks after giving birth, can set up unrealistic expectations. Over the past decade, celebrities such as Angelina Jolie, Nicole Kidman, and Jessica Alba have been photographed and filmed looking fresh-faced and fit in the latest designer maternity wear and this appears to influence public attitudes toward pregnancy and motherhood. Research indicates that some women find these media representations empowering, while others feel they set

**Figure 2.1.   Advertisement for HOTmilk linge-
rie. Figure appears courtesy of Lisa Ebbing.**

up unrealistic expectations. Some women may actually feel both these
things at different times and in different contexts (Longhurst 2005).

It is tempting to think that over the past fifteen years pregnant women
and new mothers have "come out of the closet." At last pregnant women
and new mothers appear to be free of the social constraints which formerly tied them to domesticity and private spaces, and yet, the debates
over representations of hot mammas tend to indicate that the regulatory
practices that shape maternal bodies have not disappeared entirely. Issues about morality, age, social class, ethnicity, religion, and culture are
deeply embedded in the discourses about hot mammas.

Fashion, of course, extends beyond lingerie and clothing to other dimensions of bodily grooming, modification, and adornment. Moving
from pregnancy chic to lesbian chic Jodi Schorb and Tania Hammidi
(2000) focus on bodily grooming, modification, and adornment, especially
hairstyles. In particular they examine "bad hair" and an unpopular cut
known as the sho-lo (sho-rt in the front, lo-ng in the back). Schorb and
Hammidi interviewed self-identified lesbian and bisexual women who
live in and around the Sacramento and San Francisco Bay areas. While

this cut was popular with lesbians in the early 1980s, in the late 1990s it emerged in the research as the "most disliked" lesbian cut or style.

To this point we have discussed bodies as though it is a fait accompli that all bodies are sexual. This tends to be assumed because many of us live in spaces and places that are highly charged with sexual imagery and expectation. Previous generations have fought for the right to be able to talk about sex and have sex with whoever and whenever outside of wedlock without guilt or shame. However, not everyone wants to have sex or even experience sexual desire. In this final section of the chapter on "the geography closest in" (Rich 1986, 211), therefore, we want to discuss the experiences of those who report experiencing no sexual attraction to either men or women, that is, those who are asexual (as opposed to those who are celibate—experiencing sexual desire but refraining from sexual activity).

ASEXUALITY

Recently the New Zealand media (Monk 2008, 16) reported the story of three people: Melissa Sinclair, who lives in Christchurch, is in her thirties, works as a biologist, and has never had sex; Chris Coles, who lives in Wellington and had sex for the first time when he was forty-one years old (he says he tried it out of intellectual curiosity); and Susan Matthews from the Waikato region who quit having sex five years ago because she found it "too unpleasant" and has since given birth to a child using donor insemination (see figure 2.2). None of these three people plan to ever have sex again. Chris Coles is the only one of these three who was prepared to use his real name in the story. There is a stigma attached to being asexual. It is not a phenomenon that is widely understood or accepted. The *Sunday Star-Times* reporter explains:

> They call themselves asexual and say they experience no sexual attraction to either males or females. They consider their indifference—or for some aversion—toward sex neither a problem nor a pathology, rather just another alternative on the sexuality spectrum. They are not straight, gay or bisexual—they are the Fourth Way. Being asexual is their sexual orientation. (Monk 2008, 16)

The Asexuality Visibility and Education Network (AVEN) website (www.asexuality.org) was founded in 2001 by David Jay from the United States. The website claims to host the world's largest online asexual community and a large archive of resources on asexuality. "AVEN strives to create open, honest discussion about asexuality among sexual and

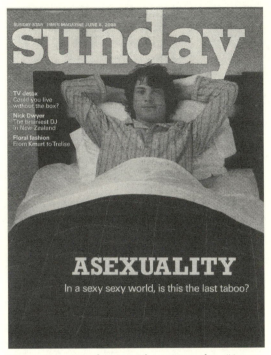

Figure 2.2. *Sunday Star-Times Magazine,* "Asexuality: In a Sexy Sexy World, Is This the Last Taboo?" Front cover, June 8, 2008. Reproduced courtesy of *Sunday Star-Times.*

asexual people alike" (AVEN 2008). Readers are told "unlike celibacy, which is a choice, asexuality is a sexual orientation. Asexual people have the same emotional needs as everybody else and are just as capable of forming intimate relationships" (AVEN 2008).

In 2005 Coles launched Asexuality Aotearoa New Zealand (AANZ). The site does not have many on its mailing list (only twelve according to Monk 2008, 18) but the issue has been getting press lately. In August 2008 a well-known and much-watched New Zealand television drama series which airs every weekday evening—*Shortland Street*—created a storyline around asexuality. One of the characters, Gerald Tippett, a hospital receptionist, stumbled across the concept of asexuality on the Internet and came out as asexual to his girlfriend. In the August 2008 News section of the AANZ website (www.asexuality.org.nz/news.htm) it is reported:

August is a big month for New Zealand asexuality as references to the Short-land Street storyline pop up in news services, blogs and bebo pages all over the Internet.

Great quotes from these include:

"New Zealand Wins Award For Most Asex-Friendly Country of 2008. Okay, there is no such award, but there should be! Probably the biggest news for the asexual community lately is the first ever explicitly asexual TV character."—The Gray Lady.

"He (asexual character Gerald) vehemently tells his parents something like, 'I'm not the only one! There's hordes of us!' and that just made me smile. (It's so bizarre how something you know well yourself becomes revalotory [sic] when you hear someone else saying it.) What a great thing for the youn-guns to hear, right?"—Asexy Beast

"The first EVER real media portrayal of asexuality!"—Emma Rainbow

"Why is New Zealand so much cooler than Canada/the US?"—Coleslaw

But New Zealand may not be quite as "cool" as this blogger assumes. Statistics New Zealand (2006) has recently been considering including a question on sexual orientation in future censuses but so far discussions have focused only on the need for information on gay, lesbian, and bisex-ual populations. There has been no mention of asexuals. This particular group of people remains invisible in most contexts.

To conclude this chapter, our sexual subjectivities are constituted within the body. Clearly there are many ways in which it is possible to think of the sexed body as a space in itself, and as a space that exists within other spaces and places at a variety of scales. It is the primary space in which and around which we construct our subjectivities. Our body shape, fitness, attractiveness, sexiness, sexuality, (a)sexual practices, comportment, naked-ness, clothing, hair, and adornment are the basis of our inclusion and exclu-sion from certain groups and spaces. "Access to our bodies, control over what can be done to them, how they move, and where they can or cannot go, are the source of regulation and dispute between household members, at work, within communities, at the level of the state, and even the globe" (Valentine 2001, 15). In a short experimental film *Salt, Saliva, Sperm and Sweat,* which was released in 1988, writer and director Phillip Brophy uses "storyboards" (represented as text on a computer screen) as well as visual images, dialogue, and sounds (especially sounds of dripping) to take view-ers on an extraordinary odyssey into the banalities of everyday life. His film focuses on eating, drinking, excreting, sex, masturbation, and violence. The main character, Phillip Dean, is an office worker who viewers follow to the office and cafeteria, to the same French restaurant each night, to the toilet, and to bed. This body has its basis in moisture—the consumption of and the excretion of salt, saliva, sperm, and sweat.

We began this book at the scale of the body—the seemingly banal and focus of Brophy's film. Traditionally geographers have paid a great deal of attention to other scales such as communities and nations but have paid little attention to the scale of bodies, especially the materialities of everyday (sexed) bodies. The words that make up the title of Brophy's film—"salt, saliva, sperm, and sweat"—remain largely outside of geography's disciplinary boundaries. We wanted to start, therefore, by thinking about "the geography closest in" (Rich 1986, 212). Our bodies including our health, the way we look, dress, move, our sexuality, and sexual practices all affect how we respond to others and how people respond to us. Bodies cannot be separated from experiences of spaces and places. In the next chapter we jump scale to think about homes, another scale of analysis that until the last decade has tended to be ignored by geographers.

3

❦

At Home with Sex

As a space of belonging and alienation, intimacy and violence, desire and fear, the home is invested with meanings, emotions, experiences and relationships that lie at the heart of human life. (Blunt and Varley 2004, 3)

Homes are important and complex places. They provide for people's material needs for warmth and shelter but they are also imbued with symbolic and ideological meanings. Homes have traditionally been constructed as private spaces but they are also subject to public rules and regulations. Mona Domosh (1998, 281) says that "the home is rich territory indeed for understanding the social and the spatial. It's just that we've barely begun to open the door and look inside." Andrew Gorman-Murray (2008) notes interest in the home and domesticity is rising in many areas of geography and other related disciplinary areas. He says a key focus in this work is the relationship between home, domesticity, and other categories of identity such as race, age, class, disability, gender, sexuality, and so on.

In the past, academics across the humanities and social sciences have not paid much attention to home. It has been characterized as a "woman's place" because it is women who have traditionally been responsible for making and looking after homes (Johnson with Huggins and Jacobs 2000). As a woman's place it has not been considered worthy of serious academic attention. This, however, has begun to change. Gorman-Murray (2008), in an attempt to create a new conceptual framework to understand the relationship between masculinity, domesticity, and home, examines three masculine identities: heteromasculinities, bachelor masculinities, and gay masculinities. This work breaks new ground given that in the past most research has tended to focus on women and home.

There has, however, been some research conducted on other aspects of home, for example, on the links between home, identity, and nationality (Blunt 2002), homelessness (Somerville 1992), domestic violence (Warrington 2001), identity, consumption, and the home (Reimer and Leslie 2004), kitchens (Johnson 2006a, 2006b; Llewellyn 2004; Floyd 2004), and diasporic homes (Asis et al. 2004). Much of this work is pulled together in Alison Blunt and Robyn Dowling's (2006) book simply titled *Home* (also, for a comprehensive review of research on geographies of home see Blunt 2005). In this chapter we focus on sexuality and home. We begin by examining heterosexuality.

HETEROSEXUAL IDENTITIES AND HOME

Gorman-Murray (2006a, 147; italics in original) notes that researchers of sexuality have shown convincingly that homes are *heterosexualized* spaces. "Over the course of the twentieth century, a combination of government policies, house design, and deeply ingrained social norms have conflated the nuclear family with domestic space across the 'West'" (Gorman-Murray 2006a, 147). Of course, within the West there are also huge variations. For example, some studies of home show that American parents tend to exclude the sexuality of teenagers from conversation and the family while Dutch parents accommodate culturally prescribed forms of teenage sexuality within the home (Schalet 2000). Victoria Robinson, Jenny Hockey, and Angela Meah (2004) interviewed men and women from three generations in twenty families from East Yorkshire, England. They found that family members experienced difficulties when trying to bring together their sexual and family lives. Even when family members were engaged in "hegemonic heterosexuality" it was difficult for some to discuss sexual matters within the family. There is a "respectability which family life accrues through maintaining a reserve or even coyness with respect to sexual talk and practice" (Robinson, Hockey, and Meah 2004, 419). For those who transgressed hegemonic heterosexuality in some way, it was even more difficult to discuss sexual experiences in the social space of the family.

But it is not just conversations about sex and sexuality that happen within the walls of homes that reiterate hegemonic heterosexuality; the design, structure, and layout of homes can also be seen to reflect and reinforce notions of hegemonic heterosexuality, nuclear families, and men's, women's, and children's gendered roles and relations. "Developers, architects and builders often assume that the occupants of houses are members of a nuclear family" (Longhurst 1999, 157). In many countries figures on household composition, however, indicate that over the past few decades fewer and fewer households have conformed to the traditional two-parent-families-with-children model. This means that many people now live in domestic spaces (which were designed for a nuclear family) that do not really fit their needs.

The standard interior of many suburban homes comprises a lounge or family room, dining room, kitchen (sometimes lounges, dining rooms, and kitchens are combined into one open-plan area), laundry, three or four bedrooms, and one or two bathrooms. The arrangement of these areas assumes a certain lifestyle and delimits the social relationships of the inhabitants. The labeling of the lounge as "family room" speaks for itself. This is designed as a room for all members of the family. Usually the kitchen comes off the family room, or in open-plan houses the kitchen is joined to the dining and family room, thus enabling the person in the kitchen (often presumed to be mother) to keep an eye on the children while cooking the meal. As Gorman-Murray (2008, 368) explains, "Men's identity at home is 'breadwinner' and 'master of the house' in a normative heterosexual nuclear family household" (also see Natalier 2004). In three-or-four-bedroom homes, one of the bedrooms tends to be larger than the others (it may also have an ensuite bathroom). This larger bedroom is often referred to as the master bedroom and is designed for a (presumed to be heterosexual) couple. The other smaller bedrooms are designed for children.

Such houses do not fulfill the needs of large or extended families, groups of young people sharing, single parents, elderly people sharing, couples who each want a bedroom, or almost any group other than a traditional nuclear family. For many people who share a house it would be more useful to have a number of medium-sized bedrooms (not one large and two or three small) large enough for carrying out social and/or sexual activities in their room. Assumptions about nuclear families and that their members will want to spend all their time together (in the family room), that couples do not want a room and/or bathroom for each partner, and that two or three rooms will be occupied by children are built into most homes. In this way, suburban homes are valorized as sites of heteronormative relations.

Real estate pages in the newspaper provide a useful example of this valorization. Advertisements for buying and selling houses often draw on assumptions about the way in which sexed and gendered relations are supposed to be constituted within domestic space. Many advertisements refer to "family homes," having lots of space for the kids, a great kitchen for mom, and a spacious garage for dad. Obviously assumptions such as these about the use of different areas of the home for different people do not always hold. Homes are complex spaces that are "both responsive to continuous interventions from 'outside' and shaped by agents whose identities are themselves in flux" (Floyd 2004, 61).

PRIVATE AFFAIRS OF THE HOME

Although homes have long been considered to be private spaces, the binary division between private and public is unstable. Geographers and others have been arguing for more than a decade that binary classifications do not hold. As David Atkinson, Peter Jackson, David Sibley, and Neil Washbourne (2005, 153) note, "Questions of liminality, spaces of uncertainty that resist binary classification, have now become an important focus of cultural geography." Home, like many other spaces, resists binary classification. It is not necessarily a haven or a private and secure space in which one can say and do exactly as one chooses as though the outside, public world does not exist. Even in that most private of spaces within the home, the bedroom, behaviors may be subjected to exterior monitoring and controls.

This is a theme explored by Craig Gurney (2000) in his research on "coital noise." Gurney conducted in-depth unstructured interviews with fifteen men and women who at the time of the research were postgraduate students at a British university. Respondents ranged in age from twenty-one to forty-six years, were all white, and identified as heterosexual. All had some experience of living in multiply occupied dwellings, often with poor sound insulation. All, therefore, had personal experience of overhearing sex noises such as "the ululations of satiation, uttered during solo or shared sexual activity and the accompanying sounds of squeaking mattress springs or banging headboards" (Gurney 2000, 39). Given the coyness that surrounds sexual talk and activity, it is perhaps not surprising that Gurney found that coital noise in the home can cause considerable anxiety both for other household members and neighbors. It is often perceived in a contradictory manner, as both "good sex and bad manners" (Gurney 2000, 45).

Gurney divides the results from the interviews into three themes: the incidence and experience of coital noise, responses to coital noise pollution, and the effects and etiquette of coital noise. In relation to the first, the participants all described the noise in similar ways referring to "moaning" or "banging." They were also all in agreement that the coital noise was aurally intrusive. In relation to the second theme, the participants' responses to coital noise varied greatly from anger and depression through to humor and sexual arousal. In relation to the third theme, it seems there are complex expectations and rules of etiquette surrounding sex noises. Some participants talked about forgiving or tolerating sex noises in exchange for reciprocity in the matter. Others went to great lengths to be quiet not wanting to transgress such a powerful taboo. Gurney (2000, 45) concludes:

> On the basis of the limited and partial data collected here it seems reasonable to argue that the experience of hearing coital noise is widespread. The impact of this noise was experienced unevenly among people interviewed for the purposes of this research, with occupants of houses in multiple occupation or flats and maisonettes with poor sound insulation suffering more than others.

Gurney then calls for further research arguing it would be useful to know and understand more about sexuality and privacy.

Another topic that often remains private—closeted—in homes is violence and sexual abuse. Violence and abuse that happens behind closed doors is not necessarily always overtly sexual, but it is about power and sex. Sexuality and gender cannot be extracted from understandings of violence and abuse in the home. "Home is a word that positively drips with association—according to various academic literatures it's a private, secure location, a sanctuary, a locus of identity and a place where inhabitants can escape the disciplinary practices that regulate our bodies in everyday life" (Johnston and Valentine 1995, 99). But of course home takes on very different meanings when it is a site where one is beaten, abused, or raped, away from the scrutiny of others. It is not secure; it is not a sanctuary but instead a space that poses considerable threat. Molly Warrington (2001, 365) states, "In England each year more than 50,000 are forced to leave their homes to find a place of safety." Nearly all of the time, the people fleeing are women and children and they are fleeing from a male perpetrator.

This is not to say that domestic or family violence does not occur in lesbian or gay households (it can and does) or that women don't sometimes abuse men (they do). As one of us has commented elsewhere, sometimes when lesbians withdraw from family and local life, putting up barriers against those outsiders, the increased privacy can become isolating and suffocate the relationship or enable one partner to emotionally or physically abuse the other (Johnston and Valentine 1995). However, the vast majority of domestic violence is carried out by men against women and children (Dobash and Dobash 1998). Family violence (which encompasses a variety of acts including physical harassment, assault, verbal abuse, emotional abuse, and intimidation) and sexual abuse (which also involves a variety of acts including voyeurism, fondling, sodomy, sexual exploitation, and rape) are difficult subjects for many to discuss. Any consideration of violence and abuse cannot be divorced from sexed and gendered relations but a myriad of other power relations are also involved. Family violence often occurs within the confines of the home (hence the name) and therefore tends to be considered as being outside of the concerns of public bodies. It occurs across all countries, social classes, ethnic groups, and ages.

Needless to say geographies of home change for women and children when they feel unsafe in their own private space. Often violence is represented as something that women and children are subject to outside rather than inside the home (see Valentine 1992 on how this "image of danger" is reinforced by the media). Fear and danger are associated with public space (Pain 1997). Girls grow up feeling more spatially restricted and in need of protection than boys (Longhurst 1999). Ironically, though, the biggest threat of violence comes not from outside the home from a stranger but from inside the home from someone we are intimate with.

Warrington (2001) asks why don't women leave home, why do they stay in these destructive situations? She suggests the answer is a lack of resources on which women are able to draw, their economic dependence on their male partners, and the powerful rhetoric of those who argue for family values. It is not always easy for women and children to find a place of escape from family violence and sexual abuse.

In the early 1970s in New Zealand, as well as in other countries, the Women's Refuge Movement mounted a campaign to raise awareness of domestic violence in an attempt to reduce it. Campaigners argued that private violence and abuse is of public concern and that it cannot be written off as part of the normal wear and tear of family life. The movement effectively challenged the privacy of the home, and male power within the home. They also exposed the brutal and destructive myth that violent and abusive relationships satisfy the masochistic (sexual) needs of women. Refuge workers argued that women and children endured the misery of violent relationships not because they enjoyed them but because they simply had nowhere else to go (Longhurst 1999, 168).

In New Zealand the first refuge opened in Christchurch in 1973. This was followed by the opening of a halfway house in Auckland in 1975 and the Dunedin Women's Refuge in 1976. They were inundated by women confirming that they had nowhere else to go. Over the next few years more refuges opened in provincial centers across New Zealand. Several decades later there is still a need for safe places for women and children, but in New Zealand the Women's Refuge Foundation continues to face financial difficulties and is forced to rely on donations and the unpaid labor of refuge workers in specific communities. The Women's Refugee Movement contests the privacy of the home by making family violence and sexual abuse a public concern. Whereas in the past individual women and children suffered violence and abuse in the privacy and isolation of their homes there are now safe places to go.

As mentioned earlier, family violence and sexual abuse is certainly not the sole preserve of heterosexual individuals, couples, and families, but heterosexual male perpetrators are the most common. We now want to change tack to consider lesbians' and gay men's experiences of home and family life. Over the past few years, an interesting literature has begun to emerge on this topic.

QUEER EXPERIENCES OF HOME

Andrew Gorman-Murray (2006b, 53) writes, "Geographic work on gay male spatiality has focused on gay men's uses of public spaces, and on their role in the gentrification of certain neighborhoods, while largely neglecting the ongoing importance of home to gay men." Gorman-Murray seeks to understand the role that home plays in constituting and affirming gay men's sexual identities. Drawing on Garry Wotherspoon's (1986) *Being Different,* a collection of autobiographical essays written by nine gay Australian men, Gorman-Murray concludes that these men use their home for rather "unhomely" (read nonheteronormative) purposes, which act to "queer" the space. *Unhomely* refers to the way in which gay men might open up their private home spaces to public parties to support gay subcultures. In one home a "garage had been converted into a fuck room—with walls of black plastic around a huge bed, towels and lubricant ready to go—to which a large circle of his men friends brought their illicit one-night stands" (Wotherspoon 1986, 165–66). Here the domestic space is reconfigured as an unequivocal homosexual site and usually not associated with the concept of "homely." In this way, private homes are sometimes more like public sites such as bars and beats. The home is "stretched." Sometimes public sites are also made more homelike.

An example of a public site that has been made more homelike is the gay venue, Family Bar, located on Auckland's well-known club strip Karangahape Road, or K Road as it is more commonly known. Family is a large gay bar offering regular entertainment including drag shows and karaoke. Adopting the name Family Bar for a very up-front gay venue shifts notions of family as being about blood ties, marriage, parenting, grandparenting, children, family planning, nuclear families, family values, and homes to being about something much broader. The notion of family is queered and reconstituted within a public space to mean people who have an affinity or connection with each other, in this case on the grounds of a shared queer sexuality.

Still on the theme of family, Gill Valentine, Tracey Skelton, and Ruth Butler (2003, 479) examine what is at stake in young people's decision whether to come out by thinking about the role that "families of origin" play in their lives. They uncovered diverse stories of young people's experience of coming out to families. For example, two of their participants who had been raised in single-parent households expressed that they "felt a duty to remain in the closet in order to protect their mothers from hurt, and to vindicate their mother's parenting skills" (Valentine, Skelton, and Butler 2003, 484). Others were motivated to come out for a variety of reasons such as feeling excited about falling in love and wanting to share that with family, and fear of the results of an HIV test. Valentine, Skelton, and Butler (2003) conclude that people "do" family differently in relation to coming out. The relationships between family members are complex and differentiated:

> It is only by understanding the nature of family members' interrelationships, the ways that individuals interact and jointly construct the experience of family life, how turning points in particular individuals' lives impact on others, and how individuals mobilise family dynamics that we can begin to understand the emotional functioning of the space of the family home. (Valentine , Skelton, and Butler 2003, 495)

As mentioned earlier Johnston and Valentine (1995) also make inroads into understanding the emotional functioning of the space of home in their examination of lesbians' experiences of living in and visiting the parental home. They found, among other things, that parental homes for lesbians are not always conducive to establishing a core or roots especially if they are not out to family. Since the publication of this research by Johnston and Valentine (1995) a number of other useful contributions have been made to the literature on lesbians and home.

Jacqui Gabb (2004) analyzes lesbian parent families in Britain. She conducted in-depth, semistructured interviews with eighteen lesbians and thirteen of their children. Informed by the psychoanalytical work of Sigmund Freud, Melanie Klein, and others, Gabb focuses on the passion and desire in lesbian mother-children love. Clearly there are numerous types of love that differ in character and expression but Gabb (2004, 399; italics in original) considers "the *physicality* of the mother-child relationship, the corporeal elements of sensuality and passion that constitute the embodied experience of maternal-children intimacy" for lesbians. She says the home is one of the few places where the sexual and maternal subjectivities of lesbian parents may be reconciled.

Sue Kentlyn (2008) wanted to find out about domestic labor practices of lesbians and gay men. To do this, she handed out fliers at Brisbane's annual Pride Fair Day which invited couples (who identified as lesbian or gay, had lived together for two years or more, and didn't have children living with them) to participate in semistructured, in-depth interviews. Kentlyn recruited twelve (six lesbian and six gay) couples. Each person was interviewed separately from their partner. Kentlyn (2008, 327) argues that "the queer home provides a *safe space* where people can cast off the constraints of heteronormativity and do varieties of gender and sexuality which would be sanctioned in other contexts; thus the queer home becomes a *subversive space*" (italics in original). In these homes, however, gendered divisions of domestic labor are still produced, yet not in the form of what might be understood as conventional understandings of femininity (woman) and masculinity (man). Kentlyn (2008, 332) noted that most of her research respondents viewed domestic labor as "closely aligned with femininity, low in status, and susceptible to power relations of dominance and subordination." Gay men seemed happy to engage in domestic chores, yet some lesbian couples had a "strong aversion to housework," so much so that they elected to be interviewed in a work space, rather than their "messy" apartment (Kentlyn 2008, 332).

Like Kentlyn, Sarah Elwood (2000) also used interviews to find out more about people's experiences of home. She conducted interviews with lesbians of various races, ethnicities, classes, and religions in the metropolitan area of Minneapolis and St. Paul, Minnesota. Homes for these lesbians held contradictory meanings. They were spaces of both liberation from dominant cultural norms and oppression where they encountered harassment and discrimination. Some felt under surveillance from neighbors, visitors, or straight members with whom they share a home. Some faced difficulty when searching for rental housing, not because of their sexual orientation per se but because of their gender and class positions, such as working inconsistently so as to take care of a young child, which were inseparable from their lesbianism.

In the context of Australia, Gordon Waitt and Andrew Gorman-Murray (both separately and jointly) have carried out research on gay men and homes including gay couples and the meaning of home (Gorman-Murray 2006a), homemaking for mature-age gay men (Waitt and Gorman-Murray 2007), and the role home plays in both constructing and affirming gay men's sexual identities (Gorman-Murray 2006b). Homes are potentially significant sites for gay men because they can foster difference, affirm and

sustain gay identity, and offer a place from which to resist heteronormative socialization (Gorman-Murray 2006b, 53).

Waitt and Gorman-Murray (2007) argue that geographers to date have
not paid much attention to older gay men's experiences of home and
yet this is an important area of research. Metropolitan bars, streets, and
beats—often the preserve of younger gay men—have received a great
deal of attention, but understanding other spaces beyond metropolitan
contexts that (older) gay men occupy also requires examination. Therefore they investigate homemaking for gay men over forty years who live
in the provincial center of Townsville (Queensland, Australia). Waitt and
Gorman-Murray were interested in "Townsville-as-home and house-
as-home." The aim was to provide insights on "non-heterosexual life in
provincial centres" (Waitt and Gorman-Murray 2007, 569) as opposed to
metropolitan centers such as Sydney. They conclude that Townsville is a
paradoxical space for older gay men. For example, some older gay men
thought the gay scene in Sydney is important in providing a range of opportunities to express same-sex desires but others "felt marginalised [by
the gay scene in Sydney] because their age or body shape did not confirm
to the *homo*normative script. For those older gay men who did not live
their lives through their sexuality, the gay scene was not always a place
of affirmation" (Waitt and Gorman-Murray 2007, 581; italics in original).
While we argued earlier that homes still tend to be hegemonically heterosexual, it is important to note that in the West there has been something
of a shift in recent years. Gay men have increasingly become associated
with home, especially the decoration of home. This is partly because of
the presence of gay men as designers and participants on lifestyle television shows such as the US *Queer Eye for the Straight Guy*, which has aired
in many parts of the world over the past few years (also see Gorman-
Murray's 2006c analysis of two Australian shows—*The Block* [2003] and
The HotHouse [2004]—that included gay male couples as participants).
Most people, however, still do not conceptualize domestic life in relation to "polyamorist" or polygamist relationships. This particular type
of queering of home space still assaults most mainstream sensibilities. In
the section that follows we change directions from talking about sex and
sexuality to talking about love.

"BIG LOVE": POLYAMORY AND POLYGAMY

Geographers are used to researching sex and sexuality but not many have
explored notions of love in relation to place. This omission is surprising

given that sexualized expressions of love infiltrate, arguably, every space. Western popular media suggests that love plays a vital role in constructing everyday—and extraordinary—social, sexual, and spatial relations. Polyamory and the US Home Box Office (HBO) television drama *Big Love*, which is about a polygamist family, are useful lens through which to examine both normative and nonnormative expressions of love, sexualities, and home spaces. The love expressed between multiple lovers and/or "sister wives" is complicated as it carries with it both possibilities and risks. To make sense of this love we draw on feminist and queer theorizing that posits love, on the one hand, as a means of subordinating women to men, yet on the other hand, as an embodied emotion with queer and nonnormative affects.

One reason why geographers have not paid much attention to love is because emotions—which are understood to be tied to the body—have long been constructed as Other in geography. Emotions may make bodies "volatile," "fluid" with "boundless desires" in contrast to the "dominant," "hard," "dry," "impenetrable," or "impermeable" ideals of Western culture (Lupton 1998). To devote academic time and resources to "bodies that love" would signal a challenge to existing "rational" and traditional geographical knowledge. Western philosophical frameworks have traditionally aligned particular forms of emotion with embodiment, femininity, irrationality, and passivity. "Women, it is commonly argued, are at the mercy of their bodies and their emotions, whereas men represent the transcendence of these baser features, mind to women's bodies" (McDowell 1999, 11). This binary division is implicated in the construction of geographical knowledge, as well as the social production of space.

Perhaps too geographers have deemed love to be a type of biological need which requires no explanation. Or, perhaps geographers are too cynical about love to conduct much research about it. Certainly it is time to question why geographers have paid little attention to actually explaining what romantic, passionate, or intimate love is. Perhaps geographers need to be more in touch with their emotions. Joyce Davidson and Christine Milligan (2004, 524) note that geographers have recently witnessed a "welling-up" of emotion. This work builds on the substantial contributions of embodied geographies as "our first and foremost, most immediate and intimately *felt* geography is the body, the site of emotional experience and expression *par excellence*" (Davidson and Milligan 2004, 524; italics in original). Emotions such as love and attachment have long been a focus of familial and intimate relationship studies (Jamieson 1998). Too often, however, many sociologists, feminists, psychologists, and others fail to appreciate that "bodies that feel love" cannot be separated from the places within which they are constituted.

Yet, even geographers—and sociologists (Jackson 1995a)—fall in love. Bringing some of these themes together, Deborah Thien (2004) starts to sketch out a feminist geography of love and Jaqui Gabb (2004) examines the complex boundaries between mother-baby and adult lesbian sexual love. David Bell and Jon Binnie (2000) try to rethink their love and discuss romance as a codification of love for the sexual and global citizen. Geographers first got "hot and heavy" about love back in the early 1990s. Robert Hay (1991), David Bell (1992, 1994b), and M. E. Robinson (1994) engaged in emotionally charged epistemological debates about love and place, particularly around the topic of heteronormative understandings of love that pervade both the spaces of the academy and beyond. This is where geographies of sexualities—and geographers concerned with sexualized subjectivities—can make a significant contribution to geographies of emotions.

As feminist geographers whose work for many years has focused on sexuality and space, we too are guilty of not taking love seriously as an academic pursuit. Our colleagues have heard us say on several occasions "I love my job" but not "what has love got to do with geography?" until now. Radical feminists in the 1980s and 1990s made heterosexual love a feminist issue. The dominant scripting of love has been in terms of long-term monogamous heterosexual pairing, which is legitimized in the institution of marriage. Feminists have argued that love is an invention of patriarchy and that marriage is the bedrock of patriarchal domination. Some have tried to think about love beyond the couple form, as Lauren Berlant (1998, 285–86) notes:

> Desires for intimacy that bypass the couple or the life narratives it generates have no alternative plots, let alone few laws and stable spaces of culture in which to clarify and cultivate them. . . . To rethink intimacy is to appraise who we have been and how we live and how we might imagine our lives that make more sense than the ones so many are living.

Notions of love need not be completely scorned, as Stevi Jackson (1995b, 50) argues "[i]t is not necessary to deny the pleasures of romance or the euphoria of falling in love in order to be sceptical about romance ideals and wary of their consequences." Scholars interested in charting geographies of love find themselves in paradoxical spaces. Critically examining the social construction of love (and the discourses of romance) involves being both skeptical and open to possibilities of love outside limited and limiting discourses (Bell and Binnie 2000). It is from this paradoxical position that we think that the geographies of polyamory and *Big Love* are indeed queer.

Polyamory, according to the New Zealand Polyamory Group (see New Zealand Polyamory Group 2008), is

> the desire, practice, or acceptance of having more than one loving, and intimate relationship at a time with the full knowledge and consent of everyone involved. People who practise polyamory respect a partner's wish to have [a] second or further meaningful relationship and to accommodate these alongside their existing relationships.

Polyamory is different from swinging. It is not casual sex with strangers, which some polyamorists tend to view as impersonal and mechanical; rather, it tends to be based on love, commitment, and domesticity. Nor are all polyamorists Mormons, as depicted in the aforementioned TV series *Big Love*. Some polyamorists live in what they consider to be nonpatriarchal relationships. There are many different polyamorous configurations. Sometimes one or both partners have another partner. Sometimes the group is exclusive, sometimes it is more causal, allowing outside lovers. In an article in a daily newspaper Emily Watt (2008, E5) explains, "People take on the lifestyle for numerous reasons—one or both are bisexual, the couple have a libido mismatch, one has an insatiable appetite for variety, or one falls in love with someone else but still loves their partner." The article reports the story of Zachary, Mary, and Anna—a "ménage à trois—a household of three." Zachary and Mary have been married nearly six years. When they met Anna a year ago they invited her to move in. Both women are bisexual. They say it is an interesting household with "never a dull moment." Polyamorists Zachary, Mary, and Anna argue that in a society where monogamy is the norm but in which adultery is commonplace, polyamory makes sense.

The aim here is not to engage in a detailed discussion of polyamory but simply to highlight that it is important when considering sexual relations in the home to think outside of heterosexual and homosexual binary categories. Notions of femaleness, maleness, being single or being a couple (whether straight or gay) are constructed within sexually, socially, politically, historically, and geographically specific milieus and yet bodies continually contest and resist these prescribed identities. Individuals, couples, and groups perform a vast range of sexed and gendered identities, some that do not fit within prescribed norms. These bodies cause "gender trouble" (Butler 1990). In the aforementioned newspaper article about Zachary, Mary, and Anna it is worth noting that none of the people interviewed for the story wanted to be identified because they were concerned with how they might be perceived.

> They say those they have told about their lifestyle were mostly supportive. But few had told everyone they knew. Zachary says his local library refused

to display the support group's leaflets. He likens the reaction to the attitude towards homosexuals three decades ago and thinks it will open up as the life-style becomes better known. "There's an opening in society for non-traditional relationships. It's honestly the logical next step," he says. (Watt 2008, E5)

Polygamist families also often live their lives shrouded in secrecy, sensing that others will find their loving and sexual relationships difficult to com-prehend. This is at the heart of the series *Big Love,* which first aired March 12, 2006. In the second episode Margene (third wife) finds Nicki (second wife) having sex with Bill (the only husband) in Margene's bedroom. Later, Margene confronts Nicki saying, "Second wives can't sleep with third wives' husbands, in third wife's own bedroom" ("Viagra Blues" episode, first season of *Big Love,* 2006). The complex relationships, sex schedules, and rosters of this polygamous family are at the heart of *Big Love.* HBO is producing new kinds of critical drama programming, with an emphasis on quality production, innovative scriptwriting, explicit sex and violence, complex structure and plot with contemporary social and cultural political themes. HBO programs such as *Six Feet Under, Sopranos,* and *Big Love* are aimed at adult audiences on cable or satellite television (but free to air in some other countries). The genre of *Big Love* fits with ele-ments of family saga and soap opera drama. Bill Hendrickson, the main male character, his three wives (Barb, Nicki, and Margene), and their seven children live in Salt Lake City. As the owner of a growing chain of home improvement stores, Bill struggles to balance the financial and emotional needs of his wives. Barb, Nicki, and Margene live in separate, adjacent houses with a communal backyard and husband. Their polyga-mous arrangement is a secret as it is illegal in Utah and banned by the mainstream Church of Latter-day Saints.

Salt Lake City is well known as a city dominated by Mormons. In 2000 there were forty religious denominations represented in Salt Lake City, but Mormons composed 82 percent of its adherent population (Warf and Winsberg 2008, 422). In Salt Lake City, religion has long been a potent social force and plays an important role in city politics.

At first glance, this representation of love may be understood as hetero-normative family values, *tripled.* There are, however, subversive readings of *Big Love* which may queer normative family formations and sexualized subjectivities. Not surprisingly, expressions of love pervade much of *Big Love.* While love—like all emotions—may not be directly observable, it can be analyzed through the ways in which it is talked about and through the institutions that support it. *Big Love*'s sister wives Barb, Nicki, and Margene spend a great deal of time talking about love and their love is not always directed to their husband, Bill, or their children. They claim to love each other, and often express this directly. Barb says: "I love you Nicki," to which Nicki replies: "I love you too, Barb."

These expressions could be simply dismissed as platonic sister love, yet the repetition and intensity of these expressions invites another reading. Their love appears to be felt deeply. Romantic and intimate love tends to hinge on the idea of "falling" in love. "Falling" seems to be a means for establishing an intimate and deep relationship (Jackson 1995b). While Barb, Nicki, and Margene do not confess to being or falling in love with each other, they claim *passionately* to love deeply not only Bill but also each other. Western ideas about love are premised on notions of individualization where two people come together "each of whom should be the only one of the other" (Jackson 1995b, 51). In *Big Love*, three women and one man love each other causing us to rethink love and subjectivities. However, and at the same time, this kind of love may serve to conceal, legitimate, and render palatable gendered power relations of subordination and domination. It is both normative and nonnormative.

Big Love was created by Mark Olsen and Will Scheffer, who, from the outset, intended to challenge normative family constructions. They wanted *Big Love* to showcase the "values of family that are worth celebrating separate of who the people are and how they're doing it" (Kurtz 2006). Hence the subversive nature of *Big Love* is to critically engage in (non)normative constructions of family. To take this further, subjectivities such as sister wives are not coherent or consistent, rather they are contradictory, as shown in this next example from the show.

During a visit by Barb's disapproving biological sister Cindy, Nicki gives her a tour of their communal backyard, and while doing so, Nicki delights in shocking Cindy further about their polygamist arrangements:

> Nicki: So this is the backyard. Look how big. . . . So it goes me [pointing to houses], Margene, and Barb at the far end. Three sister wives in a row. No fences. Kind of a metaphor for sisterhood, working together, bringing down the walls, acceptance, love. My goodness, stop me, I sound like a greeting card!

Barb's biological sister Cindy is highly critical of the way in which the children are being raised by three mothers. After removing Cindy from their house, Nicki comforts Barb; Nicki: "I can't just stand by and watch somebody hurt you" ("Happy Baptism," *Big Love*, 2006). Their expressions of love may be a reaction to outsider disapproval creating a feeling of marginalization as a result of their love. Sister wives' love may be regarded as queer because it is outside the normative constraints that apply in Western contemporary family formations. The sister wives are marginalized as a result of their relationships.

The communal backyard and three houses is the private space where sisters can express their love to each other. Away from this domestic space—even in their husband's hardware stores—they must hide their relationship. Some similarities may be drawn here with other sexual dissidents such as lesbians and gay men who negotiate public space and sometimes conceal their sexual subjectivity.

There are numerous occasions on which the sister wives feel the need to defend their familial relations to outsiders (and outside their home). In particular, the youngest and third wife, Margene, becomes friendly with a neighbor. The neighbor gradually suspects that Nicki (but not Margene) is part of a polygamist arrangement and calls all polygamists "cockroaches." Margene takes this opportunity to defend Nicki, saying, "Nicki's a good person. She's not a cockroach and I wouldn't do anything to hurt her. I'm sorry if I led you to believe that I would" ("Happy Baptism," *Big Love*, 2006). Clearly, Margene's allegiances are with her sister wives. Her love involves a kind of ethics of care. Toward the end of the same episode in which Margene had been questioning her role in the family, she becomes euphoric about her love for her sister wives.

> Margene: When I married into this family I guess I must of thought I was just marrying you [Bill] and now I realize I was marrying all of you. I was marrying sisters. My sisters. That was my choice and I'd make that choice all over again right now. I know I've made a lot of mistakes lately and, alright, maybe always, but I can get better. I will be 'cause (looking at Barb and Nicki) I want to be with you guys forever too. I love you guys and I need you and I never ever wanted to not be in this family here or in heaven. Now, I'm ready.

Bill looks at each wife (all have tears in their eyes). Barb and Nicki smile at each other and Nicki reaches out to hold Barb's hand. Bill baptizes Margene in their communal backyard swimming pool ("Happy Baptism," *Big Love*, 2006).

The love expressed between sister wives in *Big Love* may provide opportunities to think of love as (post)homo/heteronormative, in that it goes beyond the constraints of normative sexualized subjectivities. Yet, this love and the subjectivities that are constructed in *Big Love* are paradoxical—sister wives are part of a strong patriarchal tradition that binds particular people into polygamous arrangements.

Polyamorist love and love as depicted in the TV series *Big Love* provide a window through which to understand the contradictions of romantic love and sex. What can be taken from these kinds of relationships conducted often within the confines and privacy of the home is the need to reformulate what love and sex mean. Research on this subject can potentially make a significant contribution to queer, emotional, and feminist geographies. We have put forward some of the possible reasons for the lack of attention paid to love in geographical writing and research. We have chosen to think about love and its links to sexuality because the desire to love is often translated into bounded sets of (normative) usually heterosexual relationships and spaces, and because love is often expressed, understood, felt, and represented as natural, essential, and compelling. Love, therefore, may legitimize specific forms of sexualized subjectivity because love itself is felt to be natural. The queer "home" geographies of polyamory and polygamy subvert and reassert these norms.

HOMELESS: SEX ON THE STREETS

Thinking about love, sex, and sexuality at the scale of the home raises questions about those who do not have a home, those whose home is on the street, or those who sleep rough. There is now a reasonably extensive geographical literature on homelessness (e.g., Somerville 1992), much of it addressing the social and political relations surrounding homelessness. Our aim here is not to relay the findings of this research but to raise issues about sex, sexuality, and homelessness. Not having the ability to control other people's entry into one's space results in a lack of privacy to conduct one's intimate relationships. People who are homeless remain continually under the surveillance of others who are homeless, members of the public, and the authorities. This is an important issue but one that to date has received little attention in the geographical literature.

Tim Cresswell (1999) is one of only a handful of geographers who have had much to say about sex and homeless people. Cresswell examines "female tramps and hobos" in the United States between 1869 and 1940. Some women dressed in men's clothing (knickers or pants) in order to pass as men and move more freely from town to town, state to state. They committed a "kind of gender treachery" (Cresswell 1999, 186). Cresswell notes that women were supposed to be scared of and protected from tramps, not *be* tramps. He continues, "In fact, many commentators during the period 1875–1939 referred to female tramps and prostitutes in almost the same breath, often making the assumption that the two were more or less equal" (Cresswell 1999, 186). Some female tramps did sell sex for money. Others were raped. These categories were not mutually exclusive. Cresswell (1999, 186–87) sums up:

> Female tramps constantly had to negotiate their positions vis-à-vis men while on the road. Strategies adopted included travelling with a male companion, working as a prostitute and disguising their bodies in men's clothes.

Occasionally women would also travel in groups, and there are accounts of a secretive lesbian subculture amongst female tramps.

Alan Radley, Darrin Hodgetts, and Andrea Cullen (2006) take up the question of what it means to be a woman who lives on the streets and in hostels in the context of London. They explore the circumstances of three homeless women, Mary (aged 42), Rose (aged about 60), and Jean (aged between 50 and 60). Only one of these women, they say, admitted to having a sex life that she attempted to arrange as best she could by meeting up with particular men. Jean pointed out to the interviewers that she was not a woman who traded sex as a commodity (although she said in the past she had traded sex for food) but that sometimes she would be induced to have sex if it was safe. Radley, Hodgetts, and Cullen (2006, 447) quote Jean:

> You don't think about sex a lot but when it stares you in the face, you know, when somebody says, "come on, you know I could do with a session," well, I'm clean, you know, I go to the clinic every week, but I still insist that you wear a condom. "Oh I haven't got any." So I say, "well it's no good, I won't have sex." I'll do it like in the hand you know, but I said "I'm not having intimate sex without a condom." A lot of the homeless people, I notice, they do not carry condoms because sex seems to go from your mind. You're too busy trying to survive.

There are many issues that emerge in relation to sex and homes when one does not have a private home or is transient. Being homeless does not automatically mean that sex is missing from a person's life but that it is likely to be experienced in more public settings such as hostels, public parks, or on the streets (we acknowledge of course that homeless people are not the only ones having sex in such places—some people for whatever reason choose to have sex in public places).

Ironically, while some people, such as those who are homeless, are expected to not have sex in public places, others, such as sex workers and clients, are expected to not have sex in homes or domestic places. Over the past decade or more in New Zealand, and in a variety of other countries that implement town planning processes, it has been hotly debated as to where sex premises ought to be located. For example, some signs for sex premises have been deemed offensive and concerns have been voiced about the location of sex shops and massage parlors in residential areas. In New Zealand these debates were given new life in 2003 when Parliament passed the Prostitution Reform Act, which decriminalized prostitution and allowed territorial authorities to make bylaws and/or use its district plans to control the location of brothels in its district. Over the next few years, following the passing of this act, it became evident through media reports, protests, and court actions that people are squeamish about sex being for sale in residential, homely, areas (see NZPA Images 2006).

The issue of whether brothels ought to be located in residential areas illustrates that there is nothing inherent in the space of homes, or in public spaces, that makes them appropriate or inappropriate for sexual activity, but it is ideological constructions about specific bodies—the bodies of homeless people or sex workers—that dictate where those bodies are seen to belong or be "in place." As this chapter shows, home is a rich and important site for understanding sex and sexuality. By paying attention to the design, symbolism, and social functions of home we can deepen our understanding of the relationship between place, space, and sex. The domestic has often been represented as mundane and boring—unworthy of academics' attention and yet "geographies of home influence, and are influenced by, social relations not only within, but also far beyond the household" (Blunt and Varley 2004, 4). It is just as important to understand the construction of sexed bodies at home as it is to understand them nationally or globally. Jumping scale yet again, in the next chapter we focus on communities as a platform for thinking about specific kinds of sexual-social activities. As mentioned previously, we are not wanting to reify these different scales as fixed entities but use them as a way of opening up a variety of positions from which to talk about the fluidity (both metaphorically and materially) of sexual relations.

4

Communities

A Sense of Belonging

Communities are about being on the inside, which means they are also ultimately about being on the outside. They are about belonging, which means they are also ultimately about being excluded. This chapter is about being on the inside and outside, about belonging and being excluded from groups who share or are interconnected through a sexual identity or practice.

The term *community* has been subject to an enormous amount of critical debate. As Valentine (2001, 105) notes, it "has a very long and complex history within the social sciences, being defined, researched and theorized in very diverse and contradictory ways at different times and by different academics." Traditionally communities tended to be understood as groups of people who are interconnected socially. They tended to be people who lived, worked, or socialized in close proximity to each other, maybe in a village or small town. Such communities are sometimes referred to as "neighbourhood communities" (Cater and Jones 1989). These communities still exist in some places but over the past few decades many people have instead begun to form communities based on common interests or beliefs rather than on geographical proximity. Benedict Anderson (1983) makes the important point that communities are often not based on territory or physical closeness but on shared mental constructs. He is not implying that communities do not have real or material consequences—they do—but that people can be pulled together with others whom they have never met but feel a shared sense of identity. Anderson uses nationalism as an example saying that the emotional pull of the nation is so powerful that people are prepared to fight and die for their "imagined community."

People in contemporary Western societies are often highly mobile. Perhaps more than ever before a sense of belonging is no longer necessarily bound to being born somewhere, or even living somewhere, but rather to social structures such as feeling part of an imagined community or of a particular organization. More than four decades ago Melvin Webber (1963, 23) termed communities which are not bound to a particular place as "communities without propinquity." More recently John Silk (1999, 8) called them "place-free" or "stretched-out" communities (for more discussion on this issue see Valentine 2001, 119–22). People often forge physical and online connections with others with whom they share similar subjectivities or opinions.

Communities are both sites of social action and produced by social action. They are spaces that both reflect and reinforce particular sets of social relations. Sometimes groups of people come together to form communities over particular issues such as fighting injustices, campaigning for social or political rights, or protecting or gaining access to something or some place. Being united on one issue may well conceal many individual differences among group members. For example, in May 2003 the Civil Union Bill was put before the New Zealand Government Cabinet. The purpose of the bill was to establish civil union for same-sex couples (and for different-sex couples if they preferred this to marriage). The government's primary objective was to provide a mechanism for same-sex couples to formally solemnize their relationship, providing legal recognition of their loving and committed relationship. Many, especially Christian, groups opposed the passing of the Civil Union Bill, but the lesbian and gay "community" mobilized nationally to argue the case for passing the bill. In April 2005, after many protest marches, petitions, and angry calls to talk radio shows from those on both sides of the debate, the bill was finally passed (see chapter 7 on gay and lesbian marriages).

While people do not usually see themselves or are seen by others as being part of the heterosexual community (because heterosexuality is hegemonic—the unmarked norm) references to "the" gay, lesbian, transsexual, and queer community are common. Testing the limits of "the" gay community (who is in and who is out) Dawne Moon (1995) examines the term *fag hag* to think through how the rhetoric of community is used to mobilize gay men. Fag hags are heterosexual women who spend extensive periods of time socializing with gay men. Their motivations are numerous and varied depending on the particular women. Moon (1995, 507) explains the term *fag hag* "is located at the nexus of discourses of gender and sexuality within gay male culture. As such it also resides at a point where hierarchies of difference in gender and sexual identity may be used to define the boundaries of 'gay community.'" Fag hags raise the question of who is considered an insider and who is considered an outsider in gay culture.

It is not surprising that the notion of community has been subject to much debate and critique over the past few decades. While we do not want to recount here all these debates, we do want to point out that we have been influenced by Iris Marion Young's work on community, in particular *Justice and the Politics of Difference* (1990a). To summarize, Young (1990c, 302) argues that communities "overlap, complement or sit at acute angles to one another." Often people may feel both inside and outside of a community depending on numerous different factors. Young criticizes the notion of community on the grounds that it privileges an ideal of unity over difference. This encourages people to suppress the other ways in which they may be different from the group, such as their class position, gender, age, or race in order that there be a single rallying factor. Young also points out that communities are often founded on excluding some individuals. In an attempt to create and build a sense of camaraderie, boundaries are drawn between those who are seen to belong (insiders) and those who are not (outsiders). Affrica Taylor (1998) provides a useful example of how building a community can generate exclusions. She explains:

> On the surface, the innocent idea of purchasing some "lesbian space," of becoming part of the rate-paying public with a stakehold in inner-city Sydney real estate, does not deviate far from the standard Australian dream, of home ownership. But a community project in the first half of the 1990s which set out to do just that stirred up a political storm of property and propriety within diverse sectors of Sydney's lesbian community. (Taylor 1998, 129)

Taylor continues, noting that cracks soon appeared in "the community" when partway through the fundraising stage the question of lesbian-identified transsexuals' use of space emerged. Some wanted to exclude this group arguing that they were not "real" lesbians (for other research on lesbian communities see Valentine's extensive corpus—Valentine 1993, 1994, 1995a, 1995b, 1996, 2000).

By way of another example of how communities group and regroup at different times and in different spaces, when we were writing this chapter (February 2008) we received an e-mail via the listserv Sexuality and Space Specialty Group of the Association of American Geographers (sxsgeog@lsv.uky.edu). It invited "professors and grad students of all ages, ranks, and disciplines" to the next meeting of the Academic Circle, which is "a group for gay academics." The meeting was to be held at the Lesbian,

Gay, Bisexual and Transgender Community Center in New York. Often professors and graduate students are careful to avoid talking about their sexual identities. It is seen by many to be inappropriate. In this instance, however, professors and graduate students were coming together to talk openly about topics such as being out in the academy, the pros and cons of professors coming out to students, and how to come out to students. For at least the duration of the meeting, professors and graduate students could be seen as becoming part of a community that orientated around a shared identity—"gays occupying the space of the academy."

It is perhaps often more difficult for secondary school students than for tertiary students (who are a little older) and professors to be open about their sexual identities. An article in a daily Hamilton, New Zealand, newspaper reports: "Pupils are being prevented from taking same-sex partners to school balls unless they sign contracts confirming they are homosexual" (*Waikato Times* 2008). The New Zealand Human Rights Commission states it is aware of policies barring pupils who choose to take same-sex ball partners, and excluding someone on the grounds of sexual orientation is potentially unlawful. Serafin Dillon, education officer for Rainbow Youth (an Auckland-based group that supports homosexual young people), is reported as knowing at least four Auckland colleges which do not allow same-sex gender ball partners unless pupils sign contracts stating their sexual orientation. Dillon notes, "It's a mechanism for social exclusion. If this was in the workplace it would be discrimination and it would be unheard of" (Hannah 2008, 3). In this example, gay and lesbian pupils are included in the school community but only if they follow a set of rules that heterosexual pupils are not expected to follow. Also, it becomes difficult to take as one's partner a friend with whom one is not romantically involved. The school community becomes fractured as various members of that community find themselves included or excluded on the grounds of sexual orientation and/or who they might want to take as a partner to the school ball. A pupil at Rongotai College, Joshua Wright, aged sixteen, said that "policies which discriminated against gay pupils were cruel and unfair." He planned to take a male ball partner. "If (the school) ask[s] me to sign a contract, I'm going to say 'no' and just go anyway" (*Waikato Times* 2008). Rainbow Youth held the Alternative Ball where attendees were free to bring same-sex partners (Hannah 2008, 3).

This chapter has opened by briefly theorizing the notion of community. *Community* is a hotly contested term and one that probably ought to be put in quotation marks throughout the chapter. We now proceed by providing four examples of the ways in which communities can revolve around or be unified by sex and/or sexuality. We begin by focusing on the Gay Games, which were first held in San Francisco in 1982, last held in Sydney in 2002. We then discuss the gay church, followed by gay gardening. The focus then shifts to cyber or online communities, for example, the Queer Sisters in Hong Kong. It will hopefully become apparent as the chapter unfolds that off- and online (or a combination of both) interactions and communities that form around sex and sexuality are diverse and complex.

GAY GAMES

The Federation of Gay Games (FGG) has become increasingly popular since the first event, organized by Tom Wadell (a decathlete who participated in the 1968 Mexico Olympics), was held in 1982 (Waitt 2004; also see Federation of Gay Games 2008 and *Wikipedia* 2008). The games are held every four years. They have been hosted in San Francisco (1982 and 1986), Vancouver (1990), New York (1994), Amsterdam (1998), Sydney (2002), and Chicago (2006). In 2010 they will be held in Cologne. The aim of the FGG is to provide a sports environment in which all athletes can be celebrated as winners. Anyone can enter but the emphasis in on gay, lesbian, bisexual, transgender, and intersex (GLBTI) participation "in order to enable opportunities for GLBTI sexualities to experience an affirming and empowering sports environment" (Waitt 2004, 42). The Gay Games (many would argue unlike the Olympic Games) aim to be free of heterosexism, elitism, racism, and nationalism. This was Tom Waddell's vision. The Gay Games aim to be a space of "celebration," "affirmation," "belonging," "acceptance," and "diversity" (FGG 2001 cited in Waitt 2003, 168) that is free from prejudice. Traditionally, sport has been a "training ground in heteronormative masculinity" (Waitt 2004, 42). Sport produces spaces that are oppressive for many gay men. The FGG aims to disrupt the heteronormativity of sport and instead positions all competitors as winners who can take pride in challenging the dominant form of masculinity that so often underpins sport. Consequently, the Gay Games are often

> pitched in the language of the American politics of gay pride. The FGG imagines the Games as creating an inclusive sports community through which marginalized social groups attempt to challenge cultural norms of sport that are oppressive and which constrain the bodily performances of those who identify as gay, lesbian, bisexual, transgender, and intersex. (Waitt 2004, 42)

It is useful at this point to probe in a little more depth the notion of community since the Gay Games are clearly made up of a wide variety of people who occupy multiple gendered and sexed subjectivities. In the 1970s gay liberation was founded on a reasonably narrow notion of people sharing similar sexual identities in order to counter oppression. Some people found this limiting and even worse alienating. Obviously not all gay men or lesbians see themselves as fitting within some consensus of what it means to be gay or lesbian. The Gay Games, therefore, have spread their net wide to embrace rather than deny people an opportunity to be part of the Games. As Waitt (2003, 168) points out, reappraisals of ideas about community have been propelled by "queer theory," which has sought to embrace rather than deny contrasting identities within social groups. Social groups or queer communities are forged across difference rather than assumed sameness. People do not have to be the same in order to be unified.

Despite the rhetoric of unity and inclusiveness at the Gay Games, Waitt (2003, 172) points out that the community of athletes is very selective:

> Participants have been predominantly North American males, from white, middle-class backgrounds. Important constraints over participation are leisure time and disposable incomes for sports, registration fees and travel costs. Equally, the sports disciplines represented are exclusionary, almost solely of European and North American origin. Tensions are created because orthodox understandings of competitive sports persist. Despite emphasizing personal best performances, national participation rates, record keeping and medal ceremonies imply that values of faster, higher, stronger and winning are still prized.

Waitt argues that the Gay Games are in a sense a paradoxical space of community. On the one hand they contest and resist hegemonic sporting practices but on the other hand they reinforce them by rewarding such practices. Waitt (2003) carried out thirty in-depth interviews with self-identifying gay men four months prior to the Sydney Gay Games in November 2002. Not all were in support of the Gay Games. While some saw them as a wonderful community event offering many opportunities for transgression, others saw them as unnecessary and/or "retrogressive" or "passé." One of Waitt's participants, Luke, says, "I think it's weird. . . . There's no sense in which being gay or lesbian affects your capacity to perform in sport." David says:

> Part of me doesn't understand why the whole need for it . . . why we have our own special games often eludes me. . . . Like I knew once upon a time they had it, like you know, because it's a challenge to homophobia, but like I just don't think it does the same thing anymore, like, I just don't think that's the way to challenge homophobia anymore. (Waitt 2003, 176)

Although not everyone feels part of the Gay Games, they do represent an interesting example of the way in which communities can and do form around sex and sexuality. The games are not fixed in one place—every four years a different venue and country is chosen to host the event—and yet people come together as a collective to be part of an international GLBTI community or citizenry. This community participation creates a queer space that has the potential to destabilize heteronormative space. Yet another form of community participation that can create queer space is faith.

FAITH-BASED QUEER SPACE OR THE "GAY CHURCH"

Sure, I mean [being gay and Christian] is the big thing that religious gay people grapple with isn't it? There's homophobia in there, and there's fear of divine retribution, there's all of those things. What if I'm wrong? What if there's a Hell and I'm going there because I'm a faggot, and I have sex with men?

Eric Rodriguez and Suzanne Ouellette (2000) use this quote from a research participant to open their essay on "Gay and Lesbian Christians" in which they explore the ways in which individuals integrate two different parts of their identities—their sexual orientation and religious beliefs. They explain that there are at least four different strategies gays and lesbians use for dealing with being both homosexual and religious. One is to reject a religious identity. Another is to reject their homosexual identity. A third is to put these two parts of their identity into separate compartments in order to avoid them conflicting. A fourth is to integrate these two parts of their identity and it is this strategy that Rodriguez and Ouellette are most interested in.

Jenell Williams Paris and Rory Anderson (2001) argue that faith is underanalyzed in studies of queer space and yet it can have a powerful effect including affecting some queers' choice of residential neighborhood. "There is a queer presence within mainstream denominations of US Christianity, but it is often closeted or marginalized" (Williams Paris and Anderson 2001, 149). Often marriage is seen as the only legitimate venue for intimate sexuality. Williams Paris and Anderson focus on a specific residential space in Washington, DC, where Christian queers are working with others to shape a neighborhood called Mount Vernon Square. There are a number of markers of queer space including queer people, a queer-affirming church, and rainbow stickers and flags on some houses and cars. Williams Paris and Anderson (2001) explain that the

Universal Fellowship of Metropolitan Community Churches (UFMCC) is a Christian denomination based in West Hollywood, California. It has more than three hundred member churches and was founded in 1968 by Rev. Troy Perry. The church defines itself as having a special ministry to the "Gay, Lesbian, Bisexual and Transgender Community." It is seen by queers as an important part of the Mount Vernon Square community and is unusual in having a significant number of both gays and lesbians.

W. Bernard Lukenbill (1998) examines another local congregation associated with the UFMCC, the Metropolitan Community Church of Austin, Inc. (MCCA) in Texas. Lukenbill carried out participant observation of this congregation for three years. The aim of Lukenbill's research was to find out more about the "corporate culture of a gay and lesbian congregation." He concludes that most members come to MCCA concerned for their individual needs that grow out of their sexual orientation. They see the church as a "safe haven."

> Recognizing these needs, MCCA makes considerable effort to meet not only the spiritual needs of its members, but also to satisfy their social and community needs, and to help them function better in the world at large. Members soon learn that if they are to continue to benefit from the functional aspects of the church they must compromise some of their personal expectations. (Lukenbill 1998, 450–51)

What Lukenbill means by this is that individual members put aside some of their own aspirations to instead find common goals with others in order to become partners in one of the congregation's basic goals of community building.

Eric Rodriguez and Suzanne Ouellette (2000) also examine the Metropolitan Community Church—the New York (MCC/NY) church located in midtown Manhattan. They employed qualitative and quantitative research methods to reveal that MCC/NY played an important role in helping its forty participants integrate their homosexual and religious identities. The study revealed, however, that lesbians were less likely than gay men to report feeling conflict between their homosexual and Christian identities; in other words, they appeared to be more able to effectively integrate these two aspects of their lives. The authors suggest that maybe this was because lesbians also reported attending more worship services and church ministries and activities than gay men.

Even these reasonably minor differences between lesbians and gay men who are members of the same church indicate that communities are not always as inclusive as they may seem. To return to the story of Mount Vernon Square (the queer Christian neighborhood in Washington) Williams Paris and Anderson (2001) found that some sexual identities are privileged over others. In the 1970s, Ridge Street was known for its leather scene and drag queens. Many older African American families also lived in the area. Williams Paris and Anderson (2001, 158) explain, "These sexual minorities are not present in the church membership, and if present in the neighborhood, have reduced their public visibility." The church's membership is mostly gays and lesbians rather than those who are part of the leather scene or drag queens (not that these are necessarily mutually exclusive). Williams Paris and Anderson (2001, 158) report queers often move to the neighborhood because it is quiet and lacks a party scene—they described "fitting into the neighborhood because they behave, for the most part, like their straight neighbors." As with the Gay Games, clearly not everyone feels part of the Mount Vernon Square faith and spiritual community. Communities include some but not others. Both these examples, however, illustrate that communities can and do form around sex and sexuality and often intersect with other factors and activities such as athleticism or faith.

"OUT IN THE GARDEN"

Home gardening is perhaps a somewhat more unexpected activity that sex and sexuality can coalesce around to form community. By home garden we mean "an area of enclosed ground cultivated or not, within the boundaries of the owned or rented dwelling, where plants are grown and other materials [are] arranged spatially" (Bhatti and Church 2000, 183). They are physical locations, that is, places, but they are also discursive spaces that are constituted by a myriad of social relations. Elsewhere (Longhurst 2006b) one of us has explained that it is useful to think about home gardens because, first, over the past decade home gardening has become incredibly trendy in many places. Bhatti and Church (2000, 183) note: "It has been described as 'groovy' by *Vogue*, and 'the new sex' by *Tatler*." Gardening, it would seem, has become fashionable over the past few years. "Such media hype ought to alert social scientists that something important is going on" (Bhatti and Church 2000, 183). Television programs, such as *Ground Force*, have aired in many countries including the United Kingdom and New Zealand. Second, although gardening has become a major leisure activity there is very little investigation of how contemporary home gardens and gardening speak to wider social, economic, and cultural processes (Bhatti and Church 2000). Third, in New Zealand gardening is a very important activity. Homeowners often speak of "spending the weekend in the garden." Outdoor living (which includes cooking on a barbecue and eating outdoors, usually on a deck or patio) especially in the warmer northern temperate zones is very popular. Geddes and Brewis (1986, 7) claim: "New Zealanders love their gardens and sometimes gardening takes on an almost religious fervour" (also see Longhurst 2006b).

In many Western contexts home gardens are important sites of leisure and homemaking (Bhatti and Church 2000). Research has been carried out on the ways in which gardens reflect and reinforce complex gender relations (see Bhatti and Church 2000). Some of this research is historical (see Martin [2001] on nineteenth-century domestic gardens in Australia and Goldsmith [1994] on "Mexican women gardening in the American Mesilla, 1900–1940"). There is also a range of useful research that pursues themes of culture and migration in relation to gardens and gardening practices such as Gerda Wekerle's (2001) work on the experiences of first generation immigrants who garden in both private and community spaces in Toronto and its suburbs and Ieti Lima's (2001) work on Samoan immigrants in Auckland growing flowers to decorate churches. Cultural identities often revolve around gardening practices.

Much less work has been done on sexual identities and gardening practices. The dream home and garden in the suburb has long been associated with nuclear families (moms look after the flower beds while dads dig the vegetable patch) but many gays and lesbians (especially those with high disposable incomes) are also tilling the soil (see Hanly [2000] and Heroic Gardens [2006]). In a documentary called *Out in the Garden* produced by Television New Zealand and aired on January 25, 2004, the narrator, Simon Miller, explains that he is an arborist in Auckland, which means he gets to see a lot of gardens. Miller continues that lately he has seen a lot of "stunning" gardens that all have one thing in common, that is, "that the gardeners are all gay." The documentary features the gardens of and interviews with gardeners who explain what their gardens mean to them. Making this documentary is one of a long list of projects on gardening undertaken by gay men and a few lesbians in Auckland.

Almost a decade before *Out in the Garden* aired, in 1995, a group met to discuss the idea of organizing a Heroic Gardens Festival. The group envisaged the event as being part of the Hero festivities, which included an annual gay pride parade (which has since stopped but the Heroic Gardens Festival has continued). The first festival took two years to come to fruition and the proceeds (NZ$8,000—approximately US$4,700) were presented to Herne Bay House (Hanly 2000, 7). The Heroic Gardens' website (www.heroicgardens.org.nz/) explains:

Co-founded by The Fifth Season [garden group for gay, lesbian, bisexual and transgender people] and GABA [Gay Auckland Business Association],

Heroic Gardens was started as a fund-raiser for Auckland City Mission's Herne Bay House, a respite and treatment centre for people living with HIV and AIDS. The festival has become an annual event ever since. Over the last eleven years Heroic Gardens Festival has given over $415,000 to two charities who assist those living with or affected by HIV. In the first ten years $375,000 was donated to the Auckland City Mission for this purpose. Herne Bay House has since closed and since 2007 and beyond the organizing committee [have] decide[d], in conjunction with input from the gardeners themselves, who to direct the funds to.

The Heroic Gardens Festival has also been commemorated in a book *Heroic Gardens* (2000), which contains photographs by Gill Hanly and entries from eighteen writers on twenty-eight gardeners (some individuals, some couples—just one lesbian couple feature in the book; all the other gardeners appear to identify as gay men).

The Fifth Season garden group is also made up of gay, lesbian, bisexual, and transgender gardeners. The objective as stated on its website is: "To promote the enjoyment of plants and gardens amongst people of similar interests. To foster an interest in learning about plants and appreciating their value. To develop a supportive environment" (Fifth Season 2008). This hive of activity around gardening—garden tours to raise money, garden groups, making a television documentary, publishing a book that celebrates the gardens and gardeners of the Heroic Gardens Festival—creates a sense of community. The well-known and openly and committed gay New Zealand writer Peter Wells (2000, 109) comments after visiting Geoffrey Marshall and John Hayward's Auckland garden:

> Gay men have often been leading proponents of style, be it in gardening or in other imaginative spheres. It seemed to me, as I closed the garden gate and left behind this magical world, that part of the reason could be that gay people have historically had little control over wider aspects of society, and indeed small control over laws which affected our lives so directly. To create a small kingdom—an area of sovereignty—has been an essential survival strategy. More than this, it is, in some sense, a triumph. Creating—as in this case, gardening—is how we stay sane.

ONLINE SEXUAL COMMUNITIES

Up to this point we have paid attention mainly to communities that are founded on members having at least some kind of proximity, that is, face-to-face social networks with each other, such as competing at the gay games, meeting at church, or touring a garden together, but as mentioned earlier increasingly people are also members of communities that have little proximity. They are members of stretched-out communities. That is, people form social relationships which are based on shared subjectivities or interests rather than as a result of intentional choices. People do not simply form a bond because they occupy the same place; instead, they seek out others with whom they share something in common. In the remainder of this chapter, therefore, we explore the formation of various online communities predicated on a shared sexual identity or a desire to engage in some kind of shared sexual activity.

Academic literature on online communities that revolve around sex and sexuality has exploded over the past decade. A sample could include research on sex tourism websites (Chow-White 2006); online queer communities in Japan (McLelland 2002); the significance of the Internet for queer, lesbian, bisexual, and transsexual women (Bryson 2004); the use of Internet chat sites by gay men in Sydney and Melbourne (Murphy et al. 2004); cyber community support for "tranny boyz" (Gautheir and Chaudoir 2004); online dating and intimacy (Baker 2000; McCowan et al. 2001); and intermarriage or foreign bride websites (Angeles and Sunanta 2007) such as Planet Love.com (www.planet-love.com). Figure 4.1 shows

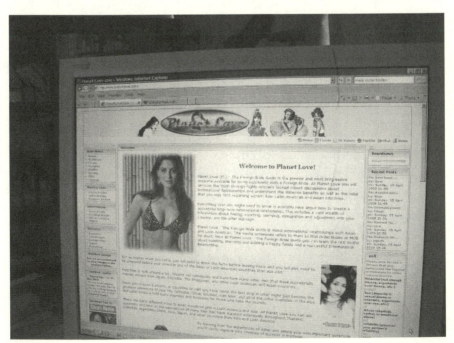

Figure 4.1.   Planet Love website. Photograph by Lynda Johnston.

the Planet Love website (see also chapter 8 on global intimacies for a full discussion of mail-order brides).

There are many ways in which people conduct online sexual relationships. Some examples described by Monica Whitty (2005) in her research on cybercheating include cybersex or "net sex" as it is sometimes referred to (describing the sexual act while typically masturbating), hot chatting (a type of erotic talk that moves beyond lighthearted flirting), emotional disclosure, pornography, and meeting for sexual intercourse. Sometimes the sexual discourse of the Internet may extend to an offline physical and/or emotional relationship.

Michael Ross (2005, 342) in "Typing, Doing, and Being: Sexuality and the Internet" says: "The increasing salience of sexuality on the internet, whether cybersex or use of the internet to make sexual contacts, has focused interest on how internet-mediated sexuality informs social theory." Ross (2005, 342) is interested in the "development of intimacy, the association of texts with sexual scripts, the emergence of cybersexuality as a sexual space midway between fantasy and action." He sees the Internet as being an important "sexual marketplace" but also important in creating sexual communities, particularly where sexual identity or behavior is stigmatized or marginalized.

Sometimes online and offline communities are posited as being in opposition to each other and yet interactions that occur in cyberspace can and do have real impacts on people's lives. Although there are no material bodies online, actions can still have real and lived consequences. Cyber communities and cyber sexual relations, even if people do not meet face-to-face, matter because online and offline communities and interactions are intimately interconnected. An example of this can be found in Gill Valentine and Sarah Holloway's research on "cyberkids" aged eleven to sixteen. They examined the incorporation of children's real and virtual worlds and found that children use online activities to reconfigure offline relationships. They also use information and communications technology (ICT) to find information about their offline hobbies and interests and make virtual friends who may then become offline friends (Valentine and Holloway 2002). Cyberkids' online identities are constructed within the offline context of their classrooms—spaces which are dominated by heteronormativity. Their online identities are commonly constructed in ways that are imagined to be heterosexually desirable (Valentine and Holloway 2002). Monica Whitty (2005) also illustrates how online and offline communities and interactions are intimately interconnected in her research on "the realness of cybercheating." She found that the majority of her total of 234 participants saw Internet infidelity as real betrayal that had a serious impact on the couple's traditional offline relationship.

Given that so many people in the West now spend so much time online perhaps it is not surprising that we often hear warnings about people increasingly ignoring those they live next door to while leading increasingly virtual lives. Participation in online communities is seen by some to draw people away from offline communities. Joyce Nip (2004) argues, however, that there is little evidence to substantiate this claim. As argued above, online communities are not necessarily autonomous from offline communities. People's sexual subjectivities, and the communities of which they are a part, are constituted within both online and offline spaces. They are both real and discursively constructed.

Paula Rust (2001), realizing this, sets out to examine the ways in which bisexual people, and bisexual men in particular, define and experience online community. She explains that for many individuals the form of community based on geographic proximity is perhaps no longer as important as online communities. Rust begins by posing the question "is there a bisexual community and, if so, what makes it a community?" When we conducted a Google search in October 2008 of the phrase "bisexual discussion groups" it resulted in approximately half a million hits. There are undoubtedly numerous bisexual online discussion groups but whether these online interactions constitute a bisexual community is an interesting question. Rust draws on findings from an international study titled "Sexual/Bisexual Identities, Communities, and Politics" involving over nine hundred bisexual men and women. Data were collected using in-depth interviews, participant observation, and self-administered questionnaires in the United States, United Kingdom, France, Germany, Belgium, Canada, Australia, and New Zealand. She concludes that there is an incredible variety of beliefs about what a community is or should be. Feelings of both isolation and belonging surfaced among the bisexual men in the study.

On a similar theme, Joyce Yee-man Nip (2004) examines an online bulletin board created in 1998 by a women's group in Hong Kong called the Queer Sisters (although the Queer Sisters group itself formed in 1995). "Like other organizations in new social movements, the Queer Sisters organize themselves around a collective identity and therefore are likely to use the bulletin board for such a purpose" (Nip 2004, 412). Nip says that an indication of the size of participation on the board can be seen through a survey posted by the group on its home page. They asked what new features people would like to see on the site. Over a six-week period May–June 2000, one thousand people responded. It is not the only Hong Kong online site for lesbians but it is clearly a popular one. Nip's research revealed that "a sense of belonging was found among participants on the bulletin board, even though some disagreed with the board for various reasons" (2004, 413), such as a concern that too many personal feelings were being expressed on the board.

Over the past few years there has been substantial growth in research on the significance of Internet technologies for sexual community participation. For example, Mary Bryson (2004) investigates "queer women and the net." She says that the Internet helps "scaffold" the lives of QLBT (queer, lesbian, bisexual, transsexual) women by creating a relatively safe space for interaction with other queer women, providing opportunities to experiment with sexual identity and learning how to be queer and accessing culturally relevant knowledge and technological know-how.

DeAnn Gauthier and Nancy Chaudoir (2004) examine cyber community support for "tranny boyz." They argue that female-to-male transsexuals (FTMs) are highly cognizant that manhood is not just about anatomy, it is about fitting socially. Failing to fit, or to pass the test of manhood, means possible stigmatization as a deviant for having attempted the feat of passing as a man. Many tranny boyz, therefore, are using the Internet to form support groups, study groups of sorts, to help them pass. Themes for online discussions include "'passing,' surgical worries, legal avenues and blockades, and social support" (Gauthier and Chaudoir 2004, 375).

But what about "straight" online communities? Much of the academic literature focuses on online dissident sexualities. That which is considered the norm is more likely to be overlooked or invisible. While straight people do not necessarily go online to find other straight people to share their stories or experiences of marginalization, it is nevertheless their sexual identities that are the basis upon which they may form a community of sorts. Advances in technology have generated numerous possibilities for electronic attachments or intimacies (Agathangelou 2004). The most obvious example is the availability of pornographic websites (not that these are all straight). Sex is now a global commodity. Cyberspace is fertile ground for fantasy. Some people have their own favorite sites and reconnect with the same partners and images to which they feel attached and/or a sense of community.

Internet dating is another example of people using the Internet to connect sexually. Seduction, desire, and intimacy are sought not just in the real world. Some seek more than one-off sexual encounters. They seek ongoing relationships (online, offline, or a combination of both) that involve both friendship and sexual intimacy (McCowan et al. 2001). In New Zealand, there are sites such as matchfinder.co.nz, nzmatch.com, nzdatezone.com, and findsomeone.co.nz. A site called Internet Dating Protocols advises:

Face it, our society is one in which there is very little human contact, at least compared to how life used to be. We are more likely now to meet and "talk" to our future husbands or wives on a web page than at a barn dance or even a nightclub. It is pretty common to start "dating" before you have even seen a person—and some very successful relationships begin this way. So, how to go about it? Well, there are a few rules to internet dating, unspoken as they may be. Their importance differs depending on the dater and on the site, but in general the following can be seen as giving some pretty solid guidelines. (Nzgirl 2008)

The site offers a number of strategies for online dating such as how to write your profile, post a photo, make cyber contact, and make real contact. Judy McCowan, Diane Fischer, Ryan Page, and Michael Homant (2001) explain the Internet has become a popular medium for forging friendships and personal relationships, some of which move beyond virtual communication to face-to-face encounters, usually after talking on the phone. The Internet, e-mail, instant messaging, and chat rooms are just some of the technologies people have been using since the early 1990s to establish and maintain interpersonal relationships, including romantic and sexual relationships with others. Jo Barraket and Millsom Henry-Waring (2004) claim that in the United States in 2003, forty million users made use of websites dedicated to dating. In 2004 nearly one million Australians used formal online dating services and there were more than sixty major commercial online dating sites available to Australians.

The Internet, however, is used not only to make romantic and sexual contacts but also to wed. While this might not (yet) be the norm, Douglas Groothuis (2003) has documented the case of a couple—Karen Bray and Keith Prior—who were married in cyberspace (they were both in different cities at the time). A small group of people watched a video monitor while a minister sat next to the bride and typed in the wedding vows, which were mailed to the groom. Groothuis (2003, 1) is not a fan of online weddings, describing them as "a disturbing trend in our technological culture." Regardless of whether one thinks it is a ridiculous or a fantastic idea the point remains the same—that in thinking about sex and sexuality it is important to consider not only real space but also cyberspace. Cyberspace is not just a space for those who want to engage with pornographic material but also for those who want to strike up friendships, be involved in communities, and share their lives in a myriad of ways with others.

Clearly, communities are no longer based just on proximity between people. People having feelings of sharing some sense of common identity or purpose with people who live some distance away used to be rare. The Internet, however, has dramatically changed the way in which we approach and construct relationships with others. Communication methods have changed notions of community. While communities can still be found in workplaces, churches, clubs, and so on, the Internet has given us more ways of meeting people with whom we share things in common. The advent of discussion boards, listserves, e-mails, chat rooms, and instant messaging means that we are no longer bound by geographical borders or time. We have access to increasingly large numbers of people who we want to form bonds with. No longer are we restricted to a small circle of likeminded people who we would come into contact with in our daily offline world. We can establish relationships with people whose physical embodiment we have never experienced. Communities can be configured, both short-term and long-term, across distances and time zones. Clearly this is important when thinking about sexual identities, activities, and practices.

5

❦

"Sex and the City"

In the popular US cable television sitcom *Sex and the City* (*SATC*) Carrie Bradshaw and her tight-knit group of women friends—Miranda, Samantha, and Charlotte—talk frankly about sex and life in New York City. Their bawdy sex talk and sex action may be the reason that *SATC* became one of the most watched and discussed television series in recent times (Gerhard 2005). Carrie, Miranda, Samantha, and Charlotte have New York at their fingertips and, if they so choose, can work, talk, shop, and have sex "like men" while still maintaining all the privileges associated with being attractive women. The space of the city affords the women the ability to fulfill their sexual fantasies, to date men, and to enjoy sexual and romantic attention. While men are their objects of pleasure, what is particularly transgressive about *SATC* is that "these women's girlfriends are the most valued people in their lives. And indeed, the show insists that these relationships are more lasting and trustworthy than those with men or potential husbands" (Gerhard 2005, 43). Carrie, Samantha, Charlotte, and Miranda could easily be a family of four, without husbands and babies, and still be happy.

The everyday act of wandering city streets—shopping, lunching with girlfriends, meeting and dating—has a long history and reflects the role of capitalism in producing new spaces of consumption such as malls, boulevards, cafés, and arcades in the city. Some cities have developed reputations in relation to sex. For example, in New York it is now possible to take a tour to visit locations featured in *SATC*. The New York streets allow a certain kind of freedom for the women characters in *SATC*, and tourists are interested in this kind of freedom, yet such freedom has not always been the norm, as this chapter will show.

Cities are spaces that offer possibilities but they are also spaces that produce tensions and conflicts. Millions of people across the globe live in cities. This makes them extremely significant places. The size and density of urban populations mean that cities are places where all sorts of people with different views and values live together in close proximity. The anonymity of large cities has made them spaces of illicit sexualities and nonconformist gender practices, yet they are also spaces which inscribe, or enforce, gendered and sexualized norms. Often this happens at the same time and in the same spaces. Cities, therefore, offer a concentrated view into the materialization of sexual identity, politics, performances, and paradoxes.

There are three sections to this chapter: the first section, Cities as Spaces of Dread and Delight, draws on fiction and nonfiction texts to document some of the histories of urban sexualities. It emphasizes how cities are spaces of both freedom and constraint. The second section, Queering City Spaces, considers the spatialized politics of traditionally marginalized groups such as gays, lesbians, bisexuals, and transgenders. We provide a number of protest and celebration examples to highlight the ways in which cities' heterosexual spaces are disrupted and subverted. Following this, in the final section, we draw readers' attention to the ways in which rezoning cities may exclude "undesirable" bodies and activities from city centers in order to fashion cities into cosmopolitan spaces.

CITIES AS SPACES OF DREAD AND DELIGHT

Cities have often been regarded as spaces of social and sexual liberation because of a perception that they offer anonymity and escape from the familiar and community relations of small towns and villages. The rise of capitalism produced city spaces such as cafés and boulevards, which tended to be associated with male freedom, as derived from the nineteenth-century figure of the *flâneur*. The *flâneur*, usually associated with the writings of the poet Charles Baudelaire, was assumed to be a man. Mike Featherstone (1998, 913) explains:

> On the one hand, the flâneur is the idler or waster; on the other hand, he is the observer or detective, the suspicious person who is always looking, noting and classifying. . . . The flâneur seeks an immersion in the sensations of the city, he seeks to "bathe in the crowd," to become lost in feelings, to succumb to the pull of random desires and the pleasures of scopophilia.

It is easy to understand why the *flâneur* is a masculine figure when one considers that during the nineteenth century respectable middle-class women were assumed to be at home and not to have the freedom to stroll around the city.

In the nineteenth and early twentieth centuries, however, women did have more freedom in cities than in rural spaces where traditional gendered roles were more strongly defined and policed (Wilson 1991). At this time rural to urban migration was common for women seeking economic and social independence. Similarly, and as documented in *City of Dreadful Delight* (Walkowitz 1992), some urban spaces in Victorian England enabled bourgeois young men to transgress the oppressive codes of morality of the time. The East End of London became a site for gambling and illicit heterosexual and gay relationships.

To probe further the role of urban spaces in constituting gay sexual identities during the late nineteenth and early twentieth centuries it is useful to turn to George Chauncey's (1994) *Gay New York: Gender, Urban Culture, and the Making of the Gay Male World 1890–1940*, which brings together a number of fascinating sources in order to understand how urban space operated as a network of mostly working-class neighborhoods. Neighborhoods such as Greenwich Village, Harlem, and Times Square became the "public gay world" for gay men (which included a number of gay identified queers, effeminate men sometimes known as fairies and men who identified as heterosexual but had sex with men). Activities such as drag shows, dances, and beauty contests were held in a range of spaces such as cafés, restaurants, bathhouses, and speakeasies (a shop or a bar where alcohol is sold illegally). This networked gay male geography facilitated the development of gay men's cultures and relationships between 1890 and 1940. Toward the end of this period, however, these spaces became less and less publicly visible as police attempted to crack down on so-called undesirable behavior, and, one would need to add, undesirable bodies.

Alongside Chauncey's (1994) work other American urban historians such as Gayle Rubin (1993) also demonstrate that US capitalist development led to the formation of what might be commonly associated with a modern gay consciousness. Some commentators argue that homosexual identity in the West is a product of modernity and that "the city is the key site in the production of that identity and modern gay consciousness" (Binnie 2000, 167).

In *Odd Girls and Twilight Lovers* Lillian Faderman (1991) draws on various historical texts as well as interviews with 186 women in order to document lesbians' creation of a cultural space. Faderman makes links between contemporary urban lesbian identities and US war efforts. During the recruitment for World War II single women composed a large proportion of the substitute bodies required by each state to meet the accelerated industrial needs of war and reconstruction. This undoubtedly created the conditions for women's entry into the paid workforce and professions in the United States. Faderman charts the rise of lesbian subcultures, and during the 1950s and 1960s the bar scene was important for young working-class lesbians.

Urban novels are another useful way to understand the city's gendered and sexed spaces. At first read, novels often portray cities as men's spaces. While male authors have included women as subjects in their novels, they are often depicted as whores (Boswell 1950), thieves (Defoe 1978), and generally "odd" women (Gissing 1980). (Gissing uses the metaphor of "odd" women to think about society as a whole.) Classic fiction by women often portrays city spaces as full of both perils and thrills. In these novels the city is sexually exciting, yet it is also a place where women's actions and identities are often misconstrued, as Elizabeth Wilson (1991) notes, to be a woman—that is an individual and not part of a family or kin group—in the city is to become a public woman, a prostitute. The big city of Victorian London features prominently in the novel *Tipping the Velvet* (Waters 1999) where diverse public and private lesbian subcultures unfold. The main character—Nancy King—emerges from a provincial and working-class background to pursue her passion for music-hall acts and songs. Nancy becomes besotted with a singing and dancing male impersonator—Miss Kitty Butler—and soars in status from a fan in the crowd, to an acquaintance, to an assistant, to an erotically obsessed friend. When Kitty leaves to perform in London she takes Nancy with her as her dresser. In London they perform in many seedy music halls. When they finally become lovers their new relationship is reflected in their popular stage performances—audiences are drawn to the spectacle of two cross-dressing young women provocatively frolicking together. The transgressive gender performance does not last and when Kitty panics, Nancy leaves. While the spaces of music halls afforded the women some freedom (and income), Nancy finds that being alone in London without an income seriously restricts her ability to move around in public spaces. Drawing on her gender-bending knowledge, she survives as a rent boy (a young male street prostitute) in London's gritty and dark back streets. When she must convincingly pass as a boy, picking up men amid the bawdy street culture, Nancy laments that there is no one to applaud her excellent performances:

> My one regret was that, though I was daily giving such marvellous performances, they had no audience. . . . I would long for just one eye—just

one!—to be fixed upon our couplings: a bold and knowing eye that saw how well I played my part, how gulled and humbled was my foolish, trustful partner. (Waters 1999, 206)

We get a sense of embodied place through reading historical novels such as *Tipping the Velvet*. Traditional images of cities construct these spaces as masculine yet *Tipping the Velvet* is an excellent example of the ways in which women step beyond the gendered and sexualized norms of Victorian London.

In the London-based novel *Night and Day* (Woolf 1919) the main protagonist, Katherine Hilberry, wanders the streets looking for a more creative path for her life. Indeed, Virginia Woolf (1924) needed to create her own space—"a room of her own"—in London. Woolf discusses the sights, sounds, and smells she encountered as she walked the streets of London. In her search for creativity the streets would engage her imagination by "withdrawing to some duskier chamber of being" (Woolf 1984, 249).

Literature is an excellent source through which to explore the ways in which cities are racialized, classed, gendered, and sexualized. Drawing on some key authors, we have shown that cities may represent freedom and possibilities despite obstacles. The very act of exploring different parts of the city may become a metaphor for self-definition. These literary geographies provide for a multilayered analysis.

QUEERING CITY SPACES

Currently in many Western cities queer residential and commercial zones have become increasingly visible and attract a diverse population. Part of the visibility can be attributed to the success of gay rights movements and the economic recognition of the queer market. Political progay activism has undoubtedly contributed to the changing spaces of cities, and alongside this there has been a steady rise in the commercialization and commodification of queer lifestyles. Pat Califia explains:

The city is a map of the hierarchy of desire, from the valorized to the stigmatized. It is divided into zones dictated by the way its citizens value or denigrate their needs. . . . In the city there are zones of commerce, of transit, of residence. But some zones of the city cannot be so matter-of-fact about the purposes they serve. These are the sex zones—called red-light districts, combat zones, and gay ghettos. . . . [T]here is no city in the world which does not have them. In part because of these zones, the city has become a sign of desire: promiscuity, perversity, prostitution, sex across the lines of age, gender, class, and race. (Califia 1994, 205)

More commonly associated with gay urban spaces is the emergence of visible gay neighborhoods within cities. The development of gay suburbs dates back to 1967 when, on the night of June 27, 1969, police raided a gay bar called the Stonewall Inn in Greenwich Village, New York. For many, the famous Stonewall riots signaled the beginning of the gay liberation movement. The anniversary is marked, in most Western cities, by gay pride parades. The Stonewall riots also represent the first time in US history when gays and lesbians openly protested and resisted police harassment. The assertion and creation of a new sense of identity was produced, one based on being proud of being gay (see Adam 1995 *The Rise of the Gay and Lesbian Movement* for more information on Stonewall). A mixture of pride, defiance, and visibility came to eventually dominate public gay and lesbian neighborhoods.

In 2001 we both visited Greenwich Village and the Stonewall Inn. It felt like a pilgrimage of sorts—an important space that we had long read about and that was important to our lives albeit in different ways. A gay and lesbian monument (by sculptor George Segal) consisting of four figures—two male and two female—has been erected in the small park—Christopher Park—outside the inn (see figure 5.1). This gay lib-

Figure 5.1.   George Segal's Gay Liberation Monument in Christopher Park, Greenwich Village, New York. Photograph by Robyn Longhurst.

eration monument stands as a positive symbol of queer lives and marks the site of violence against homosexuality. Yet the park is a much more complicated space than just a marker of nonheterosexuality. This park is indeed a space where queer identities are accepted, yet there are also some constraints about the expression of queer identities due to factors such as time, other park users, the placement of monuments, and even park furniture like bench seats. Homeless park users share this space with Western tourists like us. The homeless men (and sometimes women) in Christopher Park disrupt and subvert norms associated with public and private boundaries. Alongside this, the soliciting of men by male prostitutes and the expression of same-sex desire in Christopher Park all profoundly upset the illusion of heterosexual space.

Public rituals surrounding heterosexual sex are usually acceptable in cities, for example, a man and woman marrying in a public park, or a straight couple kissing on a bus. Other sex, such as homo-, trans- and bisexual is usually less acceptable. Certainly city authorities have tried to govern, control, and understand various sexualities through a vast array of competing discourses. Ideas and practices associated with law, popular culture, religion, economies, and politics guide understandings of which sexualities are considered normal, virtuous, and healthy and which are deemed to be deviant, bad, and associated with disease (Foucault 1978; Knopp 1995, 1998). It is clear that a very small proportion of human sexuality has been deemed to be seen as natural, safe, normal, healthy, mature, legal, and sanctified—for the most part, only heterosexual monogamous relationships (Foucault 1978; Warner 1991). Yet of course, these ideas are not stable and what is considered acceptable is always contingent upon time and place. The governance of sexuality may take the form of: social control; elimination of particular sexualities from urban spaces; and management of sexualities and sexual institutions through various ways such as persuasion, incitement, inducement, and encouragement. The overall effect is a type of moral cleansing of city streets depending on particular anxieties of the time.

In response to the marginalization of gays, lesbians, bisexuals, transgenders, and other sexual minorities most cities in the West hold gay pride festivals and parades. Recognizing the anniversary of the Stonewall riots, gay pride parades and festivals transform streets into queer sites of celebration and protest. Drag queens, dykes on bikes, leather bears, buff boys, marching girls, gay parents with their kids, gay and lesbian school children, and many more "queer" bodies *queer* city streets. Discourses of pride, defiance, visibility, and celebration dominate these public gay and lesbian political landscapes (Johnston 2005a). One of us—Lynda—has been researching pride organizations and activities for many years and has recently started working with a newly formed group called Hamilton

Pride Incorporated (see Hamilton Pride 2007a). This group was established in 2007 when the New Zealand AIDS Foundation called together members of Hamilton's queer communities in response to a recent rise in numbers of people living with HIV/AIDS in the Waikato region. Hamilton Pride had its first festival in 2007, and figure 5.2 shows the advertising leaflet "Hamilton Pride 07, 1st to 9th December."

Being out, proud, and public has, Jon Binnie (2000) argues, increased visibility of mainstream queer sexual cultures, yet some queer sex—such as the leather scene—has been further marginalized. Binnie (2000, 166) says: "For example, it is hard to envisage brewing, leisure

Figure 5.2.   Flier for Hamilton Pride 07. Appears courtesy of Hamilton Pride Inc.

and retail industries opening up a chain of leather bars, whereas coffee shops, and café bars can be marketed at both straight and queer markets." Dereka Rushbrook (2002) argues that queer space is often popular with nonqueers and that parallels can be drawn with the emergence of a kind of ethnic diversity in cities. Queer space is "tentatively promoted by cities both as equivalent to other ethnic neighbourhoods and as an independent indicator of cosmopolitanism" (Rushbrook 2002, 183). Rushbrook turns to an article titled "The Geography of Cool" in the *Economist* which outlines the growing numbers of gay clubs and neighborhoods. The *New York Times* published an international club scene tour guide to cities such as Paris, Berlin, Madrid, and Amsterdam (Cohen 2000). The article informs readers that these "cool places" are frequented by gays and straights. For example, the Greenwich Club in Berlin is a place where

> cowhide adorns the padded walls and a certain animal intensity is definitely in the air as couples, heterosexual and homosexual, admire each other over some of the best martinis and whiskey sours in the city. This establishment, full of Asian-Germans and African-Germans, gives a real sense of new Berlin, a city whose population is an exotic mix. (Cohen 2000, 91)

The establishment's desire for diversity stands in for what might be understood as "sophisticated allure" (Rushbrook 2002, 184) as nonwhite and/or queer bodies provide cultural capital for the assumed cosmopolitan city dweller. Rushbrook (2002) notes that Asian and African are offered as Other to whiteness, and homosexuality is offered as Other to heterosexuality. This example highlights the consumption of cosmopolitan queers and queer space by a broader, but not necessarily queer, public.

Cosmopolitanism is a notoriously difficult concept to define. It can be understood as "first of all an orientation, a willingness to engage with the Other" (Hannerz 1996, 103). This definition puts the emphasis on possessing knowledge about diverse cultural experiences with the goal of becoming comfortable with traversing between and within different cultural spaces and contexts. Isin and Wood (1999) examine the rise of the new cosmopolitan class of professionals and managers, who tend to identify more with their occupation rather than any other identity. Beck (2002) argues that the formulation of cosmopolitan spaces is always contested and that cosmopolitanism is not available to all. In other words, in order to be cosmopolitan it is necessary to exclude others. Binnie (2004a, 127) unpacks the notion of cosmopolitanism and queer urban space by asking if cosmopolitanism offers a way forward in terms of "thinking though the relationships between globalization (queer) desire and the production of (urban) space."

Contrary to this idea of cosmopolitanism we return to a story discussed in the opening chapter of this book—the story of the gay bar, at the Peel Hotel in Melbourne, Australia, that recently won the right to ban heterosexuals and lesbians. The Victorian Civil and Administrative Tribunal granted the pub an exemption to the Equal Opportunity Act, which put into effect the right to prohibit entry to nongay men. The deputy president of the tribunal, Ms. McKenzie, gave the following reasons:

> This would undermine or destroy the atmosphere which the company wishes to create. Sometimes heterosexual groups and lesbian groups insult and deride and are even physically violent towards the gay male patrons. Some women even booked hens' nights at the venue using the gay patrons as entertainment. To regard the gay male patrons of the venue as providing an entertainment or spectacle to be stared at, as one would at an animal at a zoo, devalues and dehumanizes them. This exemption seeks to give gay men a space in which they may, without inhibition, meet, socialize and express physical attraction to each other in a non-threatening atmosphere. (Doran 2007)

The owner of the bar, Tom McFeely, told reporters that the hotel predominately markets toward homosexual males and his main concern was to protect the integrity of the venue as well as making the space comfortable for gay men. He also noted that the aim was not to ban all straight patrons and lesbians but to limit their numbers so that gay men could freely express their sexuality ("Gay Aussie Hotel Wins Right to Ban Heterosexuals, Lesbians" 2007). The bar has been popular for hen nights and stag parties, which have created friction for the gay male clientele. What is primarily understood as gay male space becomes contested when the bar contains clientele that are so openly heterosexual. Gay bars are deemed by many to be cool, sexy, or just fun for mainstream consumption. The presence of straights in queer spaces may dilute the queerness of these bars or reappropriate bars as straight. Gay bars can be seen to be part of the broader commodification of gay cultures. There have been a number of scholars who have picked up this issue of straights in gay bars (Matejskova 2007; Rushbrook 2002; Skeggs 1999; Whittle 1994). The expansion of heterosexual customers in gay venues is often discussed alongside the production and consumption of symbolic cultural economies in late capitalism.

In an attempt to understand nongay patrons' desire to spend time in gay bars Martin Holt and Christine Griffin (2003) interviewed heterosexual customers in Birmingham's (UK) "gay village." They found that like gay and lesbian customers, many straight customers went to gay bars so that they too could be "themselves." They found that the gay scene is attractive to straight customers who wished to escape rigid and traditional gendered roles. This seemed particularly salient for women such as Diane.

> I think you have a perception that you're just not going to get hassled, I don't, like I've never been hassled by . . . say a lesbian or anything like that, I never ever, I've had people come up and chatting, but never in a sort of way that, say if you go to a heterosexual bar, a drunken man [Laughs] decides he wants to dance with you and wraps his arms round you no matter how many times you tell him to "piss off," they just don't take no for an answer, so I think in a way you just feel more. . . . I feel more relaxed almost, you just be yourself, be whatever. (Holt and Griffin 2003, 414)

For Diane she found the space of the gay bar to be liberating. It is a space where she can feel free from heterosexual men that "hassle" her. Away from the objectifying male heterosexual gaze, women like Diane have positive experiences in gay bars. Gay men are seen as safe and nonthreatening. It is important to remember, however, that in "what is supposed to be lesbian and gay space, the mutually appreciative relationship between dressed-up heterosexual women and gay men can leave lesbians feeling sidelined and excluded" (Holt and Griffin 2003, 416).

Holt and Griffin's study found that straight men that frequent gay bars were generally positive about the scene and liked the "lack of rules." One of their participants, James, comments:

> My first impressions of the gay places were there were less rules of what you can and can't do, again I say the people seemed a lot more open, and a lot more honest, whereas in most sort of straight sort of pubs, the men are very manly, very stand-offish, and the girls are always really giggly in the corner sort of thing, not wishing to be stereotyped. [Laughter] But it did seem, yeah that's right, seems you could be a lot more yourself in those sort of places. . . . Mm, yeah, like I saw blokes, I mean I know it's gay, but blokes were sort of putting their arms round other blokes, and, it just generally seemed a lot more . . . open, and a lot less sort of blokes standing there sort of being big men sort of thing. (Holt and Griffin 2003, 416)

Although these straight customers clearly felt comfortable in Birmingham's gay village, Holt and Griffin's research revealed that there were some negative impacts on gay and lesbian customers. Some participants in this study said that the scene might function as a "freak show" or a space for "heterosexual tourism," that is, straight customers wishing to gaze on queer bodies and spaces. One respondent commented: "Y'see, you've got to care for the fact that, because you can say that The Palace, 'oh let's go and have a laugh and look at the freaks' that's kind of the attitude that's easy to develop about it" (Holt and Griffin 2003, 417). Going to the gay bar may, therefore, involve surveying and consuming the performance of queer sexualities.

In keeping with the findings of other scholars such as Rushbrook (2002), Holt and Griffin (2003) found that gay bars are deemed to be cosmopolitan spaces and straight customers often want to be, or at least want to be *seen* to be, cosmopolitan. Some straight customers, it seems, go to gay bars for the kudos attached to taking part in contemporary queer culture.

> There's a bit of a, an association now, I don't know how old it is, but being gay is almost cool, isn't it, sort of, and, and you wonder how many people dabble in the scene, because of the credibility, and I don't mean sexuality necessarily, 'cos the credibility is the association with it . . . because the, it's the fashion, and not so much musically, I don't think necessarily, but definitely from a fashion point of view, it's sort of leading the way. (Holt and Griffin 2003, 417)

The rise of television shows such as *Queer as Folk* and *Queer Eye for the Straight Guy* have started to (re)present lesbians and gay men as cool, knowledgeable, and superconsumers with plenty of disposable income to spend on clubbing and fashion-centered lifestyles (see chapter 3). These idealized images of lesbians and gay men as exciting may have lifted the profile of gay bars. What has become apparent is that in urban spaces some performances of sexuality and sex are deemed to be cool and cosmopolitan but others, such as prostitution, are not. The next section highlights the moral panic connected to spaces of sex work and the ways in which city officials try to control these activities.

PLANNING FOR, AND ZONING, SEX IN THE CITY

New York provides a useful example of a city in which officials have tried to regulate certain sexual activities. When Mayor Giuliani put in place new zoning laws he radically altered the sexual geography of the city (Binnie 2000). The new laws were an attempt to regulate sex businesses and as a consequence, purify city spaces. Businesses were prohibited from operating within five hundred feet of one another and also from operating close to residential buildings, churches, and schools. Binnie (2000) argues that these laws were an attempt to drive sex establishments out of downtown Manhattan and into the outskirts of the city (see chapter 3 on selling sex in the suburbs). Lauren Berlant and Michael Warner (1998, 562) note that the new zoning laws have major consequences for public spaces of intimacy in the city.

Because the heteronormative culture of intimacy leaves queer culture especially dependent on ephemeral elaborations in urban space and print culture, queer publics are also peculiarly vulnerable to initiatives such as Mayor Rudolf Giuliani's new zoning law. The law aims to restrict any counterpublic sexual culture by regulating its economic conditions.

In New York the sexual geography of streets is changing. For example, Christopher Street, which is located in the West Village neighborhood in the borough of Manhattan, has been at the center of New York's gay rights movement since the late 1970s but is now becoming a site for queer tourism. Berlant and Warner (1998) explain that New York's zoning laws assume the desirability of a defined and coherent neighborhood as the basis for a thriving city. One of the major difficulties with the zoning scheme is that it assumes that people share similar interests simply because they live in the same neighborhood. Berlant and Warner (1998) argue that the ideology of "neighborhood" needs to be challenged. It is important to think not just about the residents who make up communities but about the full range of people. In relation to Christopher Street, Berlant and Warner explain that on any one day there are likely to be thousands of nonresidents occupying the space.

> Those who actually live in the West Village should not forget their debt to these mostly queer pilgrims. And we should not make the mistake of confusing the class of citizens with the class of property owners. Many of those who hang out on Christopher Street—typically young, queer, and African American—couldn't possibly afford to live there. Urban space is always a host space. The right to the city extends to those who use the city. It is not limited to property owners. It is not because of a fluke of politics of zoning that urban space is so deeply misrecognised; normal sexuality requires such misrecognitions, including their economic and legal enforcement, in order to sustain its illusion of humanity. (Berlant and Warner 1998, 563–34)

It can be argued that the new zoning laws are an attempt to contain unruly or deviant behavior and turn New York into a respectable global city. The attempt to cleanse sex industries in Manhattan has been likened to the attempt to cleanse the supposedly unsightly blue collar industries also in Manhattan, shifting them out to less "respectable" suburbs:

> As anyone who has followed policy decisions in the city for the past few decades will affirm, New York markets itself as the "Global City" *par excellence,* and has become an information-based economy that pushes the atavistic *materialismo* of industry and manufacturing out of Manhattan and into the lowly, ethnic, blue-collar outer boroughs and suburbs. (Serlin 1996, 50; italics in original)

There are parallels here between the treatment of the commercial sex industry and the industrial and manufacturing industries—both are constructed as polluting and unsightly and therefore need to be contained. David Serlin (1996) argues that in rezoning, both these industries and "areas where minority groups live and work" are targeted. These neighborhoods are then converted into "purified, gentrified zones" (Serlin 1996, 51).

Public sexual dissidents challenge the naturalization of heterosexual norms. Faced with this challenge, many cities have tried to purify their streets by using zoning in an attempt to eradicate or move red-light districts in favor of gentrified family spaces. Hubbard (2004) notes that red-light districts have long been a characteristic feature of Western cities. He examines several forms of "moral cleansing and purification enacted by the state and law" (Hubbard 2004, 1687).

Punitive policing and public order acts are designed to displace prostitutes in cities such as Paris and London (Hubbard 2004). In particular, women sex workers are being targeted as threatening Others, and many cities are adopting a zero tolerance stance against sex workers. Hubbard (2004) argues that in cities such as London and Paris policymakers are seeking to assert a moral order by reclaiming red-light districts from sex workers. This expulsion of sex workers from the city is intended to maximize capital accumulation based on family-oriented gentrification. Faced with being pushed out of cities, sex workers have been engaging with public forms of activism, such as going on strike and marching in streets.

There have been continued attempts by London's Westminster City Council to displace sex workers and reclaim sex work sites from Soho "through the compulsory purchase of properties that the authorities claimed were being used for immoral purposes" (Hubbard 2004, 1687). Female sex workers, some who have lived and worked in the area for as many as twenty years, are being evicted from Soho. A spokesperson for the International Union of Sex Workers made the following comment:

> We organised a carnival in Soho, because not many people knew that there was going to be a prostitutes' strike. We wanted to make people aware of it and to think about the issues . . . so we marched through the streets of Soho on the evening of International Women's Day, the day of the strike and it was brilliant, because it was a good opportunity to celebrate what it is to be a sex worker. Although the action was firstly in support of those sex workers who were angry at being evicted . . . it had a positive side. So it was a fun celebration, and that's very important—because it's important that sex workers feel pride in themselves, and pride in what they do. (Sex Workers Pride 2002)

Properties that were suspected of being used for prostitution were being purchased by Westminster Council and Metropolitan Police, who conducted an eight-week crackdown at the end of 2002 resulting in the arrest of thirty-one women (Hubbard 2004). Hubbard notes that while this was happening in London, there was similar action taking place in Paris. On November 5, 2002, approximately three hundred sex workers protested outside the French Sénat in Paris (Hubbard 2004).

These protests are highly significant and have occurred in response to attempts to displace sex workers through the use of blatant, and often brutal, zero tolerance policing. The public rhetoric encompasses notions of spatial cleansing and purification, which is often layered with fears of Otherness. Furthermore, such policies gain a great deal of public support, which means opposition to these new policies remains muted. Hubbard (2004, 1688) argues: "Female sex workers are currently being identified as a threat to national values in an era when nebulous anxieties about difference and diversity are prompting the state to instigate 'public order' legislation which serves to criminalise specific groups (rather than particular offenses)." The removal of commercial sex workers and Others such as vagrants, "gypsies," homeless, teenagers, and street performers (see Fyfe 2004; Mitchell 2001; Sibley 1995) is designed to reinvent city centers as safe, middle-class, and heteronormative family spaces of consumption. Sibley (1995, xi) puts it like this: city centers are becoming shopping spaces aimed at "white middle-class nuclear families, the kind of public which populates architects' sketches." Alongside a desire for urban gentrification is the desire to marginalize those who threaten the moral values of the state. Sex workers are often identified as criminal Others as part of a dual strategy for both displacing them from city centers and "reasserting the moral values that lie at the heart of the nation-state" (Hubbard 2004, 1699).

This chapter has discussed a number of different city spaces in an attempt to show the complexity of sexualized identities in urban areas. No two urban spaces are the same, although sometimes patterns exist across a range of cities. Furthermore, gendered and sexualized norms change over time. We have argued that most (but certainly not all) social practices surrounding heterosexual sex are acceptable in cities, for example, a man and woman stroking each other tenderly on the cheek in public, but Other acts of intimacy between, for example, gays or lesbians still tend to be less acceptable. This chapter has explored the idea that cities can be understood as sexually contested urban spaces where there are attempts to "clean up" city streets but there is also resistance to this. In the chapter that follows we change tack to consider sex practices as constituted within rural societies and spaces.

6

❦

Rural Erotics

The relationship between sexual identities and rural spaces has come under more scrutiny in recent years than in the past (e.g., Cloke and Little 1997). Rural spaces are often represented as natural or pure spaces, contrasted with urban spaces which are often represented as unnatural and impure. Rural spaces are frequently epitomized as tranquil and have long being associated with those who wish to be "closer to nature." Life in the country is commonly characterized as providing a space of refuge away from the oppressive spaces of the city. There is also a history, in the West, of radical communities establishing alternative living arrangements in utopian rural spaces. In addition to this, rural spaces have been commodified for tourists engaging in outdoor activities such as whitewater rafting, skiing, and climbing. Rural spaces are also spaces of agricultural production. In short, they are sites of both consumption and production, and of leisure and work. In this chapter we examine the construction and performances of sexualities as constituted within rural spaces.

Geographers have illustrated the ways in which sex—from farmers "wanting a wife" campaigns to bestiality and naturism—is "played out" within the countryside (Bell 2000a, 2000b; Little 2003, 2007). Valentine (1997) has explored some of the ways in which rural space is transgressively eroticized. Her work on "lesbian lands" as utopian space in the United States highlights a Western idealization of rurality as supposedly different from urban space. Engaging with popular culture also provides opportunities to explore the relationship between the rural and sexuality.

FARMER WANTS A WIFE

For many years now research by rural social scientists on understanding gender has highlighted the importance of the nuclear family and the uncritical acceptance of rigid and stereotypical gender roles and relations within rural households and rural communities (Little and Leyshon 2003; Little 2003, 2007). This work has identified that constructions such as rural womanhood and the associated gendered domestic and nurturing roles are very durable (Hughes 1997). Social relations in many rural communities are founded on a set of hegemonic gendered relations in which male and female roles in families and at work remain unquestioned. The persistence of highly traditional attitudes and expectations about masculinity, femininity, and family formations means that heterosexuality has become the dominant norm in many rural spaces.

Research on gender roles and relations has dominated much of this rural scholarship, that is, until recently. An interest in difference and Otherness has prompted a focus on rural sexualities and identities. The examination of rural heterosexuality—specifically the ordinary and benign forms of family-based heterosexuality—is becoming more prevalent. The performance of rural heterosexuality is now under the lens of rural geographers such as Jo Little (2003, 2007). Little (2007, 852) focuses on a number of themes in her research, including "the importance of the survival of the farm-family household to the agricultural business and rural community; the role of marriage and permanence in rural society; and the maintenance of traditional values in rural social relations and individual identities." Sexuality is evident in all of these themes. Little's research puts the spotlight on the more familiar practices and commonly held views surrounding gender, sexuality, and rural society, particularly in relation to households, families, and the reproduction of rural communities. For this reason, it is worth focusing on her research in some depth.

In order to highlight various dimensions of rural heterosexuality, Little (2003, 2007) draws on two sources—a UK campaign called "The Farmer Wants a Wife" and a New Zealand event called the Middlemarch Singles' Ball (see Middlemarch 2008). The Farmer Wants a Wife campaign ran for many years in association with the UK magazine *Country Living*. The campaign was first established in 1999 and it was designed to introduce single rural men (the majority of which were farmers) to partners with a view to establishing a permanent relationship. The rural men who were selected to participate in the campaign wrote a short personal biography which featured in the magazine. This campaign went on for many years and the magazine reported on the progress of farmers and wives. Another spin-off from the 2002 campaign was a television program that featured the participants. Little (2003, 2007) analyzed these sources and material gained from interviews with farmers in order to elicit their views and attitudes toward sexual relationships, family, and rural life. She adopted a similar methodology to examine the New Zealand annual event—the Middlemarch Singles' Ball, which first began in 2005. Little (2003, 2007) draws on media reports and interviews with organizers and members of the Middlemarch farming community.

Little's research discovered that one of the dominant themes shaping the construction and performance of rural sexualities is the survival of the rural community. In both the United Kingdom and New Zealand people interviewed were concerned about population decline as well as a desire to preserve the rural community idyll. Farmers participate in these events because they want to settle down, start a family, and reproduce the farm-family household. One of the farmers, Nigel, remarked: "I'd love to meet a permanent partner, that's my aim. In the countryside it's mostly families, no single people—either young couples with children or elderly couples" (Little 2007, 856). The organizer of the Middlemarch Singles' Ball was concerned about the depopulation of the area: "We are just trying to find additions to the community and we know there's a lot of bachelors around. . . . If we can get some of the bachelors to start a family, all the better" (Little 2007, 856). When interviewed by Television New Zealand, the organizer reinforced this point saying, "The locals organized the event because unless they get the bachelors married off, in 20 years time, they won't have a rugby club" (TVNZ 2001).

Stable and long-lasting relationships were preferred and despite some participants saying they were out to have a bit of fun, they also claimed to be serious about finding a permanent partner. Some men had motivations that went beyond personal expectations and reflected on the nature of rural relationships:

> Oh yeah, it's a lot more traditional, it's a lot more, you expect to get married in a church, you expect to have your kids after you got married not before. . . . Our family are well known in the village cos they've been there for generations and they've done you know parish council whatever and everything and it's all kind of like you've got a name that you, in the village as, as being you know good reputation you don't want to bugger that up. (Little 2007, 856)

The identity "country girl" was deemed an appropriate type of femininity for women who would make suitable partners. They would need to understand the countryside and the farmer's responsibilities, be emotionally stable and "low maintenance," be tolerant of problems that may arise from rural living, as well as being home-loving and family oriented (Little

2007). Many of the farmers' advertising in the Farmer Wants a Wife campaign specified the importance of farming knowledge: "I'd like a woman who understands the fun and problems of farming" (*Country Living* 1999, 52; cited in Little 2007, 857). "Down-to-earth," "low maintenance," "a good sense of humour," and an ability to "muck in" were qualities held in high regard. Richard says:

> I know that I've got to meet someone who would understand that way of life really, it's not going to work if I go out with someone who likes mini skirts and high heels and make up, they're not going to fit in to my lifestyle really . . . living on the farm . . . the reality is you don't live that life. (Little 2007, 858)

The appearance and presentation of women impacted upon farmers' decisions as to whether the women were suitable potential partners. Hyperfemininity was deemed "unsuitable." Some farmers commented that their date "wouldn't be used to the mud. And she didn't look very country at all, in black leggings and a black coat" (*Marie Claire* 2004, 156; cited in Little 2007, 858). Another farmer commented, after his date with a woman from the city: "She didn't have enough clothes on—you can't wear skirts all the time in the country or you'll freeze. And you'd have to ride side saddle . . . she was more intellectual than a rural date" (Little 2007, 858). Appearance is assessed in terms of practicality. If a woman is to understand the countryside, she must dress in a manner that is seen to be appropriate for the countryside. Little (2007) notes that these concerns also point to the need to distance the rural body from any sign of urban sexuality, which may be thought of as more risky and transgressive and a potentially more deviant form of feminine sexuality.

Popular representations and discourses of rurality center on narrow and deeply conservative views of the family (Little 2003). Family, in idyllic constructions of rurality, is a heterosexual formation with traditional gender identities and is based on the moral superiority of procreative sex. "The practices that sustain the dominance of such heteronormativity can be seen strongly articulated through the wider currency of rural relationships—specifically through the moral rejection of a clearly identified 'urban' sexuality" (Little 2007, 858). Hence, rural relationships and identities need to be set apart from urban relationships and this is achieved by linking rural relationships with values and personal qualities that are felt to be missing from urban life. Idyllic constructions of rurality extend to representations of sexuality associated with such traits such as honesty, plainness, an ability to endure, and rurality. In contrast, urban relationships are portrayed as "temporary, possibly exciting but usually confusing and unfulfilling" (Little 2007, 858). Little's research (2003, 2007) shows the urban-rural division is most evident in the knowledge, experience, and even appearance of women.

"City girls" are unlikely to make good partners, whereas "country girls," according to farmers, are more relaxed and easygoing. One farmer discusses his date with city girl Debbie.

> I've never dated anyone from the city before. I have been there though and it's very different from the countryside. They're out almost every night in bars and stuff. We go out a lot but it's not that frenetic. They're nutters! I think country girls are probably less aggressive than city girls, too. City girls can really stick up for themselves. (*Marie Claire* 2004, 156; cited in Little 2007, 859)

At New Zealand's Middlemarch Singles' Ball a train, dubbed by the media "the love train," was hired to transport city girls from Dunedin (a city with a population of approximately 120,000) to Middlemarch (a small rural town). Television New Zealand (2001) reported on the first Middlemarch Singles' Ball:

> Romance is in the air after a singles dance intended to partner off 35 southern bachelors was held at Middlemarch in Otago. Some 200 women from around Otago travelled to the Strath Taieri A and P [Agricultural and Pastoral] show dance, many making the trip on what was dubbed the Love Train. (TVNZ 2001)

Middlemarch rural men were described as shy, a bit old-fashioned, honest, and hardworking. They needed assistance to develop relationships with women. "Once in a real relationship with the 'right' woman they could become presentable both as husbands and as figures of the community" (Little 2007, 859).

Ideas about nature are vitally important in Little's (2007) research. She found that the linking of rurality to nature is used to uphold heteronormativity, which acts as a powerful defense of existing sexual identities and performances of rural sexual relationships. The countryside allows people to be closer to nature, which in turn supposedly enhances social well-being, reduces stress and friction, and allows couples to focus on each other. The so-called natural rhythms of the countryside imply healthy relationships and are contrasted with the "unnatural" pace of the city (Little 2007). The magazine *Country Living* quotes a relationship counselor about the benefits of the countryside: "People underestimate the effect of peace and quiet and beautiful scenery. To sit by a flowing stream or walk through the countryside in different seasons makes people relaxed and happy, which produces the same chemical in the body as that released when you are in love" (*Country Living* 2004, 45). One of the farmers that Little (2007) interviewed made explicit connections between nature, biology, and country girls as the most appropriate partners or wives to farmers. Nurses, it seems, are more in tune with the rhythms of nature, making them ideal farmers' wives. One farmer comments: "The fact that she is a nurse is quite a compatible thing in many ways, a lot of farmers do end up marrying nurses actually because I think they've got the same hands on attitude to life and they're not frightened of a bit of blood and guts" (Little 2007, 826).

The heterosexual ordering of rural space constructs a particular type of rurality. We have focused at length and in some depth on the examples put forward by Little (2003, 2007) because they illustrate effectively particular hegemonic forms of heterosexual identity which are embodied and embedded in rural society. This identity is sustained and re-created through repeated tactics and strategies yet it maintains its superior status through discourses of nature and naturalness. Other sexual identities, however, are also performed in rural spaces and we explore these later in this chapter. First, we turn to an event called Fieldays as another example of the mutual constitution of heterosexuality and rurality.

"FIELDAYS' RURAL BACHELOR OF THE YEAR" COMPETITION

Fieldays (see Fieldays 2008) is a New Zealand agribusiness event which aims to bring together both buyers and sellers to create a type of agricultural hypermarket. It is tipped to be the largest agricultural event in the Southern Hemisphere. In 2008 sales generated by the show reached NZ$330 million or US$205 million and there were more than one thousand exhibitors (*Otago Daily Times* 2008). Apart from viewing farm machinery, animals, and tractors, spectators can also attend the Fieldays' Rural Bachelor of the Year competition. The organizer of the event explained the search is for "an honest, reliable, sensitive yet masculine, genuine Kiwi bloke, who wasn't married, but had personality, and could cook dinner and sing" (*New Zealand Herald* 2003).

Bachelor "heats" have become a big attraction at Fieldays with approximately eight men competing to show off rural skills and bachelor eligibility in a range of events involving chainsawing, fencing, dancing, a race involving pushing a cheerleader in a wheelbarrow, and using a barbeque to cook breakfast. There are three days of competition and the winner of Fieldays' Rural Bachelor of the Year receives a Golden Gumboot (in New Zealand the gumboot, or Wellington/wellie as it is called in the United

Kingdom, is often used to symbolize rural life) trophy as well as prizes worth approximately NZ$30,000 or US$18,000.

The competition has prompted contestants to elaborate on their ideal date. The kinds of women who are seen to make suitable dates are women who can have fun and be "one of the boys," are "down-to-earth," and have a strong sense of humor. One Rural Bachelor of the Year contestant—Charlie Taituha, aged twenty-two, a former rugby player for a provincial club and currently employed as a veterinary technical field representative—describes his perfect date as "having a few beers while listening to stories from All Black [New Zealand's representative rugby team] legend Colin Meads at his local rugby club, Waitete" (Ihaka 2008). The date would also include a trip to a local restaurant in Te Kuiti for a steak dinner with his ideal woman, who is described as "a chick who isn't scared to eat a [meat] pie, or have a handle of Waikato [beer] at 10am with the boys on Sunday" (Ihaka 2008).

The relationship between masculinity and New Zealand's drinking culture has been addressed by anthropologist Hugh Campbell (2000) who engaged in eighteen months' participatory ethnographic fieldwork at two pubs in a South Island village in the Canterbury region (also see Campbell, Law, and Honeyfield 1999). Campbell returned to live in one of the South Island villages for three years. He notes that in small communities there is a high degree of networking between pubs, clubs, and other associations. These are spaces occupied largely by men. Rural pubs are spaces where knowledge is generated and meaning is negotiated and legitimated. They are not isolated spaces where small groups of men form opinions that carry little weight or influence; rather, they are key sites for maintaining the legitimacy of hegemonic masculinity in the wider community (Campbell 2000).

It is within the space of rural pubs that Charlie (the aforementioned Fieldays' Rural Bachelor of the Year contestant) is likely to have formed his strong views about women. He believes that "they [women] should really be themselves, not too girly but not too manly either, there should be a good balance" (Ihaka 2008). The coconstruction of gender is important to the success of a rural heterosexual relationship. In this instance "chicks" have to be tough in order to withstand rural life, but not too tough and masculine so as to transgress traditional notions of femininity. Charlie reflects on the tasks that he will face in the Fieldays' Rural Bachelor of the Year 2008 competition. "We have to make a dress for a cheerleader—I think it's a farm orientated dress, so that should be interesting" (Monahan 2008). According to one media report Charlie hadn't had a girlfriend "for a couple of months at least" (Monahan 2008). He is not too worried about the tasks he has to perform and tells a reporter: "We have to cook a meal too. Anything to do with barbecues and I should be sweet. I'm not too flash on wine selections though" (Monahan 2008). The contestants are judged on their chainsawing abilities, fencing prowess, and their ability to maneuver an earth digger. Charlie seems confident: "I think we have to use the digger to place an egg in a cup or something like that. . . . I had a bit of practice at a mate's place with his digger and a few beers over the weekend. Should be sweet, mate" (Monahan 2008).

Fieldays, according to spokeswoman Nicole Foster, are "really popular, especially with the ladies. . . . We've noticed their attendance has crept up and up over the past few years to the point where they're almost half of all attendees" (Monahan 2008). Within this wider rural region there is a "man-drought" (Monahan 2008). The New Zealand 2006 census indicates that there were 96,708 more women than men in New Zealand (Statistics New Zealand 2006). In Hamilton—the closest urban center to Fieldays—there are 6 percent more women than men in the "30-something" age group, and this is similar to national trends. Demographer Ian Pool thinks the term *man-drought* is rather loaded and suggests "it's better to look at it as a particular deficit at certain age groups" (Pool, cited in Monahan 2008).

> [The gender imbalance] depends on whether you are looking at downtown Auckland or if you are looking at the Mackenzie Country. . . . In that case, the situation may be reversed. In metropolitan areas there has been a trend in recent decades that affluent women are moving to cities, are well qualified, are pursuing careers and putting off when they are going to meet Mr. Right and settle down. Rural areas tend to be the opposite. (Pool, cited in Monahan 2008)

It is not surprising then that farming men often lament that they find it hard to meet women, living in isolated areas, working with other men, for long hours on the farm. Charlie, the aforementioned finalist in the bachelor competition, says: "Down where I live, you don't see many girls out at the disco in Piopio" (Monahan 2008).

Charlie did not win the 2008 Rural Bachelor of the Year competition (although he was given the People's Choice Award). Mark Woodcock took the top title. Mark's views on gender relations and what makes a "good" rural woman are similar to Charlie's. Mark believes that women want "a man that's a man and not someone whose namby pamby [soft]" (Downey 2008). Mark's ideal woman is someone who is "not too sensitive . . . someone who's real, someone who can pull the calf out while I'm home lighting the fire. Nah just kidding," he laughs when speaking to a newspaper reporter after his win (Downey 2008). The reporter notes, however, "The calf situation is perhaps not too far from the truth because whoever becomes Mrs. Woodcock will need to be into the rural scene because that's where Mark intends to continue his career." Mark emphasizes a rural-urban division when it comes to thinking about the ideal woman: "I don't think a Remuera [a well-to-do suburb in Auckland] girl would hack it in Pouto [a small rural coastal community in Northland]" (Downey 2008).

Fieldays are another way through which it is possible to examine the relationship between sexuality and space, focusing on the construction and performances of heterosexuality in rural societies. The Fieldays' Rural Bachelor of the Year award is an articulation of a particular form of normative heterosexual identity, with a heavy reliance on hegemonic masculinity and its associated values and characteristics in rural societies. Heteronormativity, however, is not the only expression of sexuality in rural spaces.

OTHERS IN NATURE, QUEERING NATURE

In recent years geographers such as Bell (2000a, 2000b, 2006); Fellows (1996); Little (2007); and Phillips, Watt, and Shuttleton (2000) have begun to document the ways in which the trope of nature is not used exclusively in support of family-based heteronormativity. In this section we provide an overview of work on sexual activities that queer rural or nature spaces beginning with Bell (2000a, 84–85) who concentrates on "white-trash erotics, bestiality, and naturism," and his "own archaeology of sex in the middle of nowhere" to argue that the rural occupies a very particular and complex location in the economy of desire. Bell (2000a) illustrates the ways in which sexualized notions of rurality are complex clusters that vary dramatically from place to place (and time to time). Marginalized rural Others, such as southern US poor white people, are often described disparagingly as "crackers, rubes, hayseeds, hicks, hillbillies, bumpkins, peasants, rednecks, yokels and white trash" (Creed and Ching 1997, 17).

Films such as *Pulp Fiction* and *Deliverance* provide examples of eroticized rurality and "hillbilly horror." *Pulp Fiction* makes an explicit reference to *Deliverance*'s well-known rape scene of Bobby who, while being sodomized, is made to squeal like a pig. Both films mobilize a particular construction of poor white country folk. Creed and Ching (1997, 23) note that "rustic expression often takes the form of homosexual rape" in US movies. *Deliverance* also carries signifiers of in-breeding "with the deformed, imbecilic figure of Lonnie, the boy who plays 'Duellin' Banjoes' with Drew" (Bell 2000a, 87). This "hillbilly horror" genre is full of characters whose sexual identities are constructed through popular notions of rurality—that of "in-breeding, animalistic passions and polymorphous perversions" (Bell 2000a, 87). White trash erotics and bestiality has the potential to upset idealized notions of nature by "showing the country's underbelly: a site of unwholesome—maybe even *unnatural*—existences and activities" (Bell 2000a, 85; italics in original).

Seemingly "unnatural" (but not bestial) acts, this time of homoerotic love and sex, are also depicted in Annie Proulx's (1999) story *Brokeback Mountain*, which was released as a film in 2005. It is the story of two cowboys whose intense relationship is multiply textured by beauty, cruelty, and sex. Their interactions, for the most part, are constituted within the wild and spectacular spaces of Wyoming, and span two decades—1963 to 1983. Social conservatives were upset by the film's depiction of these queer cowboys in what appears to be a natural and pure landscape.

Another polymorphous perversion in the countryside—"'dogging"— also challenges the idea of normative family-based hegemonic heterosexuality, as already described in the above examples of the Farmer Wants a Wife campaign, the Middlemarch Singles' Ball, and the Fieldays' Rural Bachelor of the Year competition. *Dogging* is a "complex set of practices which centre on forms of public sex, voyeurism and exhibitionism, 'swinging,' group sex and partner swapping" (Bell 2006, 387). It usually takes place in dog-walking sites in rural or semirural locations and involves heterosexual couples driving to secluded sites in the countryside to engage in sex acts in or outside their cars. The sexual encounter may be casual and might involve others either watching or joining in. There are known dogging sites where people will meet after advertising via the Internet or texting using mobile phones. This alternative rural heterosexuality is Other to the dominant and accepted constructions and practices of rural heterosexuality. Dogging, of course, may be an urban practice that is mobilized in the rural, involving urban people meeting in the countryside. Dogging transgresses legal and/or moral sexual practices and may be policed or contested as inappropriate by local people actually walking their dogs (Little 2007, 863).

Little (2007) reminds us that the coconstruction of rurality and heteronormativity may be contested also by the notion of rural space as a place of relative freedom for sexual experimentation and expression among young people. Early sexual encounters in the countryside are sometimes imbued with "an innocence that renders them harmless—at least in relation to similar encounters in the city" (Little 2007, 863). While ideas of idyllic countryside childhoods abound in popular discourses, Owain Jones (1999, 118) has observed that "the 'natural' state of childhood is a wild, innocent maleness. Tomboyism can be seen as a resistance to narrow and strict gender delineations, but also reveals the gendered basis of constructions of childhood." Boys are seen as part of nature, as clearly illustrated in the popular saying "slugs and snails and puppy dogs' tails" yet they grow into adults who become aligned to culture. For girls issues of sexuality, reproduction, and motherhood are critical in shifting their identities from tomboy (in other words, not aligned with nature) to being aligned with culture and "made of sugar and spice and all things nice."

Perhaps the most common expressions of Other ruralities, however, are when gay men, lesbian, bisexuals, and transgender people live in the country. It is common for dissident sexual identities in Western countries to be frequently spatialized through a rural/urban binary (Gorman-Murray 2007). As noted in the previous chapter large cities are often understood as sites of homosexual freedom, affirmation, and inclusivity and places where same-sex desires can be enacted openly. Rural spaces, however, tend to be understood as sites of gay, lesbian, bisexual, and transgender oppression and absence where same-sex desires remain hidden. The urban-rural spatialized imaginary suggests that queers belong in the city, and hence are rendered invisible in the countryside. In terms of population mobility, the primary form of migration for gay men and lesbians is rural-to-urban to escape the constraints of small town life (Binnie 2004a; but see Gorman-Murray 2007). As Gorman-Murray, Waitt, and Gibson (2008) note, this normative binary is prevalent in many Western countries. For example, in Australia, the outback is posited in opposition to Sydney, which is marketed as the "gay capital of the South Pacific" with its famous Gay and Lesbian Mardi Gras Festival, which has become an international tourist event (Johnston 2005a; Markwell 2002; also see chapter 8).

It might be tempting to assume therefore that a small town such as Trinidad in Colorado is closed to sexual Otherness but this is not the case. Once again, it is not possible to offer any simple reading of urban-rural space. The saying "taking a trip to Trinidad" in Colorado has come to mean that one is about to undergo sex reassignment surgery, not something that one immediately associates with most small towns. Trinidad, with a population of ten thousand, is located in the Rocky Mountains of southern Colorado. It is a frontier and socially conservative town. Mayor Joe Reorda says it is a "live and let live" kind of place (Doane 2008). Trinidad has become a mecca for people who are seeking sexual reassignment surgery and has become known as the "sex change capital of the world" (Doane 2008).

This world fame can be attributed to physician Dr. Stanley Biber. As a general practitioner, Dr. Biber fitted his sex change surgery in between procedures such as tonsillectomies, delivering babies, and setting bones. He is known to have performed over five thousand sex change operations in his career. Dr. Biber was among the first doctors in the United States to perform sex changes and for years was one of only a handful to offer them. He steadily became one of the United States' most prolific providers of the operation. It is currently estimated that about three hundred people have sexual reassignment surgery each year in Trinidad (Doane 2008). Across the United States there are twenty-five surgeons who will perform the operation but fewer than six who regularly perform the surgery (Doane 2008). Stanley Biber originally intended to become a rabbi. He interrupted his studies to work for state intelligence services during World War II. After the war, he studied at the University of Iowa, where he earned a medical degree in 1948 (Fox 2006).

During the 1970s to early 1990s some local residents resisted the town's reputation while many others embraced it. Dr. Biber's work brought economic benefits to Trinidad and transformed it from a former coal-mining town to a tourist destination. "It's a boon to business here," Dr. Biber told the *New York Times* in 1998. "They come with families, they stay in the hotels, they eat in the restaurants, they buy at the florists" (Fox 2006).

Most of Dr. Biber's patients were men seeking to become women, though he also performed female-to-male sex changes. His patients came from all over the world and from all walks of life.

> There were three brothers who became three sisters. There were an 84-year-old train engineer, a 250-pound linebacker and an American Indian medicine man, all of whom emerged as women. . . . Movie stars, judges, mayors . . . I have had everything except a president of the United States. (Fox 2006)

The local pastor, Dick Valdez, is blasé about the town's reputation. When journalists arrive he responds:

> Well, let's put it this way, I heard that you [CBS News] were in town yesterday. And, you know, it immediately clicks, "Well, they're gonna be doing the *transgender reassignment whatever* deal again." And it's like, "Okay, we've had Geraldo here, and we've had Oprah here, you know? I think we get a little tired of that being our claim to fame." (Doane 2008)

By 2003 Dr. Biber had stopped performing sexual reassignment surgery altogether. He maintained a small general practice until his death in January 2006. His practice has been taken over by a protégée, Dr. Marci Bowers, who herself made the transition from male to female several years ago (Fox 2006).

As can be seen, it is not possible to simply conflate urban spaces with dissident sexualities, and small town and rural spaces with straight sexualities. There are a growing number of gay men and lesbians who choose to live outside the city and their experiences are being documented (Bell and Valentine 1995b; Cody and Welch 1997; Kirkey and Forsyth 2001; Phillips, Watt, and Shuttleton 2000). Fellows (1996) and Wilson (2000) outline the experiences of those gay men and lesbians born and raised in rural America who have chosen not to make the trek to the big city. Valentine (1997) and Bell (2000a, 2000b, 2003), meanwhile, discuss those gay men and lesbians who actively choose to move *from* the city *to* the country to escape the urban expectations placed on gay and lesbian communities in the city. Some social scientists have specifically examined (semi)rural localities that are increasingly associated with the visibility and acceptance of gay and lesbian populations. For example, Gorman-Murray, Waitt, and Gibson (2008) draw on the work of Anne Forsyth (1997a, 1997b) to think about the concentrated number of lesbians who are intimately involved in public life in the town of Northampton, Massachusetts. Forsyth (1997a, 57) argues that the public presence and involvement of lesbians has created a well-recognized "'out' territory in terms of visibility, community activity and organization." Newton (1993) has written about the extensive contribution of gay men and lesbians to the development of Cherry Grove, in New York, since the 1930s, describing it as "America's first gay town." The phenomenon of lesbian migration to the small town of Hebden Bridge, United Kingdom, has also been examined (Smith and Holt 2005, 318) and it was found that lesbian identities and relationships were "openly performed in publicly visible ways" and were "widely accepted and embraced" by the community. There is evidence in these studies that resists the standard spatialization of gay men and lesbians' lives and demonstrates the ways in which queers have cultivated a sense of belonging in and to rural spaces (Gorman-Murray, Waitt, and Gibson 2008).

SEX, ANIMALS, AND NATURE

Geographers are now also exploring questions about the role played by animals in constructing identities and places, and about the binary division that is often drawn between people and animals and animals' subjectivity and agency. For interesting examples one can look to Kay Anderson's (1995) work on zoos and Heidi Nast's (2006) work on pets (also see Davies 2000; Elder, Wolch, and Emel 1998; Lynn 1998; Philo and Wilbert 2000; Woods 2000). Some geographers have taken up questions of animal subjectivity in explicitly urban contexts. One only has to think of the movie *Best-in-Show*, which parodies, with plenty of humor, famous dog shows such as New York's Madison Square Garden's Dog Show and the British Crofts' Dog Show. As Jennifer Wolch (2002, 726) notes:

Anyone who has seen either the movie or the dog show itself can hardly deny that certain sorts of animals are intimately tied up with stereotypical urban identities: suburban white trash; urban gay couples; preppy, neurotic DINKS (double income no kids) as well as rural good ol' boys steeped in the wisdom of coon dogs. Moreover, the dogs in question clearly took things into their own paws (so to speak), ingratiating themselves with their handlers as well as "resisting" human domination by, in one case, biting the judge!

Geographers are increasingly seeking to understand the role of animals in the development of multiple subjectivities that urban or rural residents adopt or have ascribed to them (Wolch 2002). These identities are time and place specific or can even relate to imagined communities such as nations. Adopting critical race, gender, sexuality, and postcolonial theories have helped highlight the connections between race, gender, nature, and representations of "animality."

This work has prompted a questioning of broad categories such as human, animal, politics, and practices. And so, we might ask, are there any limits to what animal geographers study? The territory is broad. Perhaps it is not surprising, therefore, that animal geographies have also become a focus for some queer geographers who continue to explore topics that have been taboo in geography (see Bell 2007; Binnie 2007; Brown and Rasmusssen 2009; Browne 2007; Oswin 2008). This focus on animals, sexuality, and space is carving out new territory that has previously made (and still does to some degree) geographers and others squeamish. One topic that most sexuality and space researchers have been avoiding, until recently, is animal-human sex. A useful place to start exploring the topic of bestiality and erotica with animals is rural spaces. There are two studies in geography that are worth noting. The first focuses on dolphins, the second on horses.

Viewing and swimming with dolphins is a popular activity which usually takes place in wild, marine, natural, or nature spaces. Where we live, in New Zealand, swimming with dolphins fits comfortably with the country's "100% Pure" advertising campaign (New Zealand Tourism Board 2002) which is directed at tourists. The nation has a reputation as a world premiere natural destination, with plenty of adventure and ecotourism activities (Cloke and Perkins 1998). Tourist activities such as whale watching and swimming with dolphins have grown rapidly over the past decade (Cloke and Perkins 2005). In 1983 it was estimated that only twelve countries participated in whale and dolphin watching but by 1998 approximately one hundred countries and nine million participants were involved (Hoyt 2000). Within this global ecotourism market, New Zealand is an important destination for viewing and swimming with dolphins. According to New Zealand's Department of Conservation there are fifty-six companies permitted to allow dolphin swims, with twenty-two of them selling dolphin swims as the main attraction.

This captured our imaginations and prompted us to think critically about the embodied activity of swimming with dolphins (see Besio, Johnston, and Longhurst 2008). Interestingly, we found that "sex talk" dominated tours to watch and swim with dolphins. Promotional materials (such as postcards, brochures, Internet websites, and advertising), participant observation on dolphin tours, and interviews with tour operators reveal "that dolphins are constructed paradoxically as sexually polyamorous and promiscuous sexy beasts and as loving and maternal devoted mums. These seemingly contradictory narratives about dolphins and nature perform different functions" (Besio, Johnston, and Longhurst 2008, 1212). We found that the act of viewing and swimming with dolphins, in part, rests on polyamorous heterosexual and homosexual discourses. It is commonplace for dolphin ecotourism operators, and for publications and Internet sites on dolphins, to not only mention dolphin sexuality but also to be explicit about dolphin sexual activity. Promiscuous dolphins make this nature space "wild" and exciting. Dolphin sexuality and its diversity are part of the dolphin tourism experience. One possible reason why ecotourism operators emphasize dolphin sexuality and sexual activity is that sex as Other sells. Dolphin tourism operators often represent dolphins as sex crazed and engaging in same-sex behavior. One dolphin swimming tour guide told us that "not only do dolphins have sex up to forty times a day (or, as he put it, sex is not just for birthdays and Christmas) but also they will have sex with anyone—that is, both same sex and opposite sex" (Besio, Johnston, and Longhurst 2008, 1225).

The connection between dolphins, sexuality, and humans is complex. Queer or polyamorous dolphin sex is represented as an amusing oddity that stands outside of so-called normative sexuality. Nonreproductive and nonheterosexual behavior, however, runs counter to ideas of nature and procreation, or, in other words, the natural order. Rather than saving sex for reproduction, it seems that dolphins are "playfully erotic" and androgynous (Bryld and Lykke 2000, 18). For dolphin tour operators to apply their own meanings to dolphins, dolphins must be sufficiently similar to humans to allow a sense of connection yet sufficiently different to be wild and Other. The dominant sexual discourses that connect dolphins, sexuality, and humans is reinforced when one considers the ways in which sex toys—such as dildos and vibrators—are sometimes created in the shape of dolphins (d.vice 2008). It seems that dolphin swimming excursions in the open ocean or in bays around New Zealand rely on tropes of "sexy beasts" within wild nature in order to sell their ecotourism product.

Animal lovers of a different sort are at the heart of research undertaken by Michael Brown and Claire Rusmussen (2009). They map out an incident, and the subsequent furor, following the death of a man after he had sex with a horse. A widespread moral panic ensued because there was no law against human-animal sex.

> On July 2, 2005, the body of 45-year old Kenneth Pinyan was wheeled into the emergency room of the community hospital in Enumclaw, Washington, a rural working-class farming community some 35 miles southeast of Seattle. Doctors pronounced Pinyan dead, and the friend who brought him had fled. Police later identified that friend as James Michael Taitt, 44, who owned a farm with horses on it in town. The cause of the death was acute peritonitis due to a perforated colon. The authorities furthermore discovered that Pinyan had suffered the injury after being sexually penetrated in the rectum by a male horse. (Brown and Rusmussen 2009)

Further investigation into the incident uncovered that the farm in Enumclaw was a place where you could pay to have sex with animals. A "bizarre sex panic" (Brown and Rasmussen 2009) spread across the United States when it was established that Taitt could not be charged because bestiality was legal in Washington State. There were no laws against human-animal sex. The political arguments for an antibestiality law, and the way in which they were represented, suggest a moral outcry based on concepts of both disgust and fascination. Legislation was passed—within six months—that criminalized bestiality in Washington State (Woodward 2006).

As Brown and Rasmussen (2009) note, this story of rural bestiality gained an extraordinary level of attention and became the most read online story for the *Seattle Times* in 2005 (Westneat 2005). They examine the way in which this case played out in the media and found that nearly everyone agreed that bestiality should be prohibited. Brown and Rasmussen (2009) also bring to our attention that the event "provoked near universal disgust and disapproval, a feeling that the state of Washington felt needed to be codified in law." But how do we make sense of the fascination this case caused and what do the arguments reveal about constructions of sex and rural spaces?

One of the arguments used to justify a law against bestiality was linked to place. It was deemed that without a law against bestiality Washington State would attract people who wanted to have sex with animals. Pam Roach, state senator at the time, said "I found out that Washington is one of the few states in the country that doesn't outlaw this activity. This has made Washington a Mecca for bestiality. People know it isn't against the law, and so they come from other states to have sex with animals" (quoted in Smith 2005). Taitt's farm was known as a place for people to have sex with livestock and it was also known in Internet chat rooms, but it would be difficult to label the farm as a mecca. Furthermore, the three men in the Enumclaw case were all locals. The senator's remarks are consistent with notions that rural spaces must be protected from outsiders and that sexually promiscuous urban dwellers might invade Washington State's chaste and pure rural communities.

Spatial imaginations structured the moral panic in Washington State in a way that differed from historical constructions of space and bestiality. Bestiality as an act has been associated with rural spaces, and in particular with rural boys (Dekkers 2000). "In the public imagination, bestiality has often been associated with rural settings explained away by male curiosity, the lack of sexual outlets (for boys), opportunity, and the lack of 'civilized boundaries' in agricultural settings" (Brown and Rasmussen 2009). In Enumclaw the public debate reflected a concern that rural and urban boundaries would be crossed. Urban corruption was seen to be the motivating factor for why men were having sex with horses on the farm. Idealized notions of rural moral purity were held up against the so-called dangerous morally degenerate outsiders from the city. The gendered and sexual subjectivities which reinforce queering of the boundary between human and animal serves a valuable role in reconsidering our relationship to animals, which has previously hinged upon human and animal differences and a hierarchy. It also may help us to reconsider the binary relationship between rural and urban.

In concluding this chapter, the myths and actualities of "animal loving" and "hillbilly horrors" construct distinct forms of rural erotics which are at odds with normative expressions of heterosexuality and countryside. Campaigns and events such as the Farmer Wants a Wife, the Middlemarch Singles' Ball, and the Fieldays' Rural Bachelor of the Year reproduce hegemonic gendered and sexualized bodies and rural spaces. These constructions are challenged by Other heterosexuals who might engage in what are seen to be more dissident activities such as sex changes and dogging. The existence of lesbians, gays, and transgendered people living in rural areas also challenges dominant ideas about nature and the countryside as straight space.

7

Nations and National Identity

A nation is "a community of people whose members are bound to-gether by a sense of solidarity rooted in an historic attachment to a homeland and a common culture, and by a consciousness of being different from other nations" (Johnston et al. 2000, 532). It is difficult for most of us to imagine a world that is not divided into nations, but this way of organizing human society only came to dominate the globe in the late 1700s. The politicocultural systems which predated nation-states were religious communities (sacred languages and hierarchies linking clergy to heaven) and dynastic realms (monarchical states expanded by warfare and sexual politics). The cultural traditions and symbols through which national identities are produced can create an illusion that nations are a natural or timeless entity. Nations are often assumed to be the primary axes of identification for their populations. However, they are not natural. Nations are socially constructed. Benedict Anderson (1983, 6–7; italics in original) argues they are also "imagined."

> It [the nation] is *imagined* because the members of even the smallest nation will never know most of their fellow-members, meet them, or even hear of them, yet in the minds of each lives the image of their communion. . . . The nation is imagined as *limited* because even the largest of them, encompassing perhaps a billion living human beings, has finite, if elastic, boundaries, beyond which lie other nations. No nation imagines itself coterminous with mankind [sic].

Today, globalization, information communication technologies, and the burgeoning of transnational companies and organizations are, some argue, making the boundaries of nation-states increasingly irrelevant. In some nations there are attempts to dissolve the sovereign state from within (nationalist movements) by those who want to create their own independent nation-states, breaking away from the larger social, economic, and political unit. Nationalism arises when the political and territorial spaces seem incongruent to members of its population. Some people today feel less loyalty than earlier generations to their country and more to their social group with whom they share an identity based upon, for example, ethnicity, disability, gender, and/or sexuality. In this chapter we consider how some people come to be excluded from nations on the grounds of their embodied sexual difference. They are not seen as fitting the national identity and are not offered full rights of citizenship.

RIGHTS OF CITIZENSHIP

National identity can be thought of as a historical process of collective identity built on ideologies of political parties, stories about the nation, sentiments about the nation, information released from government, and mass media reports. Imagining a nation depends upon a process of self-awareness toward contemporary notions of rights and responsibilities that are attached to being a good citizen. Being a good citizen means conforming to and performing particular types of sexual identities—ones based on normative ideals of heterosexuality.

In this section we examine sexual citizenship as a form of social identification, which some writers claim is replacing traditional and dominant forms of national identity. Citizenship is usually regarded as the legal expression of membership in a bounded territory or state, carrying with it obligations for its defense and welfare. For more than a decade now activists and academics have debated issues of sexual politics using the notion of sexual citizenship (see for example Bell and Binnie 2000; Binnie 2004a; Evans 1993; Hubbard 2001; Richardson 2005; Weeks 1998). These debates stem from discussions of the notion of citizenship and the figure of the citizen in late modern Western societies. Being a citizen means balancing one's rights against one's responsibilities.

When certain people are excluded from the rights and duties of citizenship, for example when gays and lesbians are denied the right to marry, adopt children, or are banned from the military, they tend to feel little or no responsibility toward, and even ostracized from, the nation-state. Not surprisingly, therefore, there are often attempts to redress the systematic exclusion of such groups. In fact, the progressive expansion of gay rights has been the result of much gay activism and visibility not just at the scale of the community but also the nation. For example, the organization Queer Nation was founded in 1990 in New York City by AIDS activists who were outraged at the escalation of antigay and antilesbian violence on the streets, homophobia, and discrimination in the media. Queer Nation sought to redefine sexual citizenship using what were considered by some to be militant tactics (such as outing people, reclaiming the word *queer*, and adopting slogans) to extend rights to all members of the nation-state.

Foucault reminds us in *The History of Sexuality* (1978) that in the eighteenth and nineteenth centuries European society increasingly embraced a monolithic norm of heterosexual monogamy. This bourgeois norm translated into laws that restricted sexual behavior and forced the diverse sexual identities of Europe into the closet. As Foucault (1978) demonstrates, these identities were painstakingly enumerated in law, which regulated extramarital sex, premarital sex, incest, sodomy in all its forms, miscegenation, prostitution, and so on. Thus a category of moral degenerates joined a number of other social categories such as women, the landless, Jews, gypsies, and others as legally excluded from the full benefits and privileges of citizenship. The persecution of what Foucault called "peripheral sexualities" (1978, 40) shares a common heritage with the persecution of these other minorities (Sengupta 2002). For example, the AIDS crisis sparked a significant backlash against lesbians and gay men and countries such as the United States and United Kingdom were criticized for failing to appropriately respond to and assist people who needed help (Isin and Wood 1999). It became readily apparent that individuals who do not fit into the nation's self-construction are marginalized.

The modern state assumes citizens to be heterosexual men or women who engage in particular kinds of sex. In many states of the United States, sodomy, oral sex, and "unnatural sex acts" are criminalized (Isin and Wood 1999). Since 1995 the US federal government has attempted to legislate so that gay marriage and civil unions do not take the same form as "real" marriage (Adam 2003). The idea of homosexuality as culturally subversive is popularly held. Queer bodies have long been thought of as a threat to social stability and public order. As Binnie (1995, 189) points out, legislation in Britain has "served an important ideological purpose as part of the wider Conservative family value agenda in which homosexuality was seen as one root of moral decay of the nation." This legislation, however, has been significant in the mobilization of gay activists and allies, assuring sexualities remain a crucial focus of debate and struggle in nations such as the United Kingdom.

Homosexuals have been, and still are, constructed as being in need of external control and regulation.

The recent emergence, however, of a new category of citizenship in public discourse—"the normal gay citizen"—is worth considering. Diane Richardson (2005) highlights the shift in the political agendas of social movements concerned with gender and sexuality. She states that rather than critiquing social institutions and practices that have historically excluded queers, the dominant discourse of mid-1990s to mid-2000s has been that of seeking access to mainstream culture through demanding equal rights (Richardson 2005). Integration and assimilation strategies have been employed by groups to achieve social change. Gay and lesbian struggles over, for example, the civil recognition of domestic partnerships, the right to marry, and the right to serve in the military are at the forefront of debates within lesbian and gay groups (Phelan 2001; Richardson 2000). At the heart of these struggles is a desire to be seen as "normal," "ordinary," and "good" gay citizens. Gay Pride Parades and queer celebrations may be understood as enabling new forms of neoliberal cultural citizenship, which queers may want to "buy into." The commercialization and commodification of gay and, to a lesser extent, lesbian communities over the past ten to fifteen years has fostered the emergence of new commercial and professional gay identities (Richardson 2005).

To unravel this issue of seeking access to and citizenship through mainstream culture we examine in the next section the right to marry. Arguments about same-sex marriage have taken center stage in many queer rights movements over the past decade. Some see arguments for the right to marry as detracting from useful critiques of institutions and practices that have traditionally denied queers particular rights. Others see it as an important politics of inclusion—to be afforded the same human rights as any other citizen.

GAY AND LESBIAN MARRIAGES

Pitched as the biggest celebrity union when California legalized same-sex marriage, Ellen DeGeneres, aged fifty, and Portia de Rossi, aged thirty-five, wed on August 16, 2008, in a small ceremony at their Beverly Hills home (GayNZ.com News Staff 2008b). Both wore white outfits: Ellen DeGeneres was in a suit, while Portia de Rossi wore a billowing gown.

DeGeneres is arguably the most (media) famous lesbian in the United States, as well as commanding a large international audience. While there have been other well-known lesbians on television, none have been as accessible. DeGeneres is unique in that she has an incredibly high media profile and is likely to be remembered in years to come as an important part of popular cultural history. For more than a decade she has been involved in two sit-coms, hosted network awards shows, performed stand-up on the US Home Box Office channel, and regularly appears on talk shows and, of course, her own extremely successful daytime talk show *Ellen*, which won four Emmy awards in its first season (Reed 2005).

Perhaps DeGeneres has become a fixture on television because she is so likeable. There is nothing threatening about her; she is funny, nice, and "easily consumable," which makes her a perfect television personality (Reed 2005). But lesbians, and particularly lesbians who marry, are supposed to be a threat to the very core of heteronormativity. DeGeneres's wedding to de Rossi challenges the supposed norm of marriage and notions of proper citizenship. DeGeneres, however, seems a welcomed presence in nonqueer people's living rooms. It is through the relatively safe medium of television where viewers may learn about Others. According to John Hartley (1999, 32), television is a "teacher in the best sense," through its use of cross-demographic communication. Mass media, he argues, has cultivated a type of citizenship. For Hartley, television teaches in an "anthropological" not a "schooling" (1999, 45) sense of the word, as it can explore "the way in which different populations with no necessary mutual affinity . . . produce and maintain knowledge about each other, communicate with each other, stay in touch" (1999, 32). Furthermore, the teaching that happens on television may be influential because it allows for a reasonably high degree of societal coherence. For Hartley, television "teaches the formation of identity and citizenship in a society characterized by the unknowability of its nevertheless sovereign populations" (1999, 46). It is the primary way various populations understand the differences between people.

Taking this notion further, Hartley (1999, 157) contends that citizenship "needs to be seen in historical rather than categorical terms; it is an evolving and cumulative concept adapting to changes in western development." The complex debate about who and what denotes citizenship can be broadly summarized as arising from the Enlightenment period in the form of civil citizenship which involved ideas of individual freedoms, through political citizenship that centered on voting rights in particular to social citizenship issues such as rights to social welfare. Cultural citizenship is another step in this process and is dependent on mass media. It also applies mostly to what Hartley (1999, 163) calls the "disenfranchised or unenfranchised" of so-called minorities, and it is citizenship that recognizes distinct identities.

Gays and lesbians, along with many others who are marginalized, are allowed "among the 'masses' both to participate freely as audience along with all the other people in the mediasphere, and to observe an official culture that was not comfortable with their presence" (Hartley 1999, 170). Hence DeGeneres obtains the status of citizenship through her various media roles and through her marriage.

Arguments about same-sex marriage, particularly for those of us who do not have celebrity status, have been a focal point in many lesbian and gay rights movements. Marriage is often held up as the necessary element—a rite of passage—into proper, successful citizenship. Bell and Binnie (2000, 53–54) note, in relation to

> sexual citizenship, marriage is often focused on as a necessary element of the politics of recognition—in this case, the recognition of same-sex union. The question is of course, also one of equality: heterosexuals can marry, so it is wrong that lesbian and gay couples cannot enjoy the same privilege.

Currently the federal government of the United States does not recognize same-sex marriage although it has long been a contentious issue. In 1993 gay litigants challenged Hawaii's marriage laws arguing that the state's judiciary could extend marriage rights to same-sex couples. The Hawaii Supreme Court, however, ruled that a state law restricting marriage to opposite-sex couples was at odds with the Hawaii state constitution (Cherlin 2004). Hawaii then passed a state constitutional amendment making same-sex marriage illegal. Following this, the US Congress passed the Defense of Marriage Act in 1996 thereby allowing states to refuse to recognize same-sex marriages that had been licensed in some states (Cherlin 2004). In 1999 the Vermont Supreme Court passed a law legalizing civil unions for same-sex couples. Three years later the Massachusetts Supreme Court decided that there is no rationality for distinguishing between heterosexual civil marriages and homosexual civil unions. They mandated identical legislative treatment of straight and gay couples seeking marriage status.

The same-sex marriage debate took center stage in 2004 when then President George W. Bush announced his support for an amendment to the US Constitution defining marriage as only allowable between one man and one woman. This proposal became a dominant issue in the national presidential race. In November 2004, eleven states (Arkansas, Georgia, Kentucky, Michigan, Mississippi, Montana, North Dakota, Ohio, Oklahoma, Oregon, and Utah) voted on and passed constitutional amendments outlawing same-sex marriage (Hester and Gibson 2007).

The right to marry in the United States is touted by many liberal-reformist activists as a cornerstone for attaining full citizenship. Indeed for some the right to marry is seen as a "basic human right" and "constitutional freedom" (Wolfson 1996, 79). It is not just about a recognized relationship, the benefits are deemed to be far-reaching "because literally hundreds of important legal, economic, practical, and social benefits and protections flow directly from marriage . . . exclusion from this central social institution wreaks real harm on real-life same-sex couples every day" (Wolfson 1996, 8). While marriage represents a publically sanctioned avowal of a relationship and commitment, it also allows couples access to benefits such as health care, insurance, and inheritance. The right to marry, therefore, has been at the forefront of gay and lesbian activism.

On May 15, 2008, the Supreme Court of California overturned that state's ban on same-sex marriage, hence allowing Ellen DeGeneres and Portia de Rossi, and many other couples, to wed. Not long after, however, on November 4, 2008, Proposition 8—the official ballot to eliminate the "right of same-sex couples to marry"—was voted in to restrict the definition of marriage to a union between a man and a woman. Legally, now only marriage between a man and a woman is valid or recognized in California. DeGeneres was reported as saying that the Californian voter ban on same-sex marriage (a ban supported by 52 percent of voters) has left her feeling "saddened beyond belief. . . . Here we just had a giant step toward equality [with the election of Barack Obama as President] and then on the very next day, we took a giant step away" (Silverman 2008).

Having considered the rights of gays and lesbians to marry, in the next section we look at another, sometimes related group, who also agitate to be treated as equal citizens. Like gays and lesbians, transsexuals and transgenders often find themselves excluded from the nation. Calls for trans equality revolve around the desire to establish civil identities as a basis for equal rights including full recognition of the acquired gender, the right to marry in the acquired gender, and arguments for birth certificates to show the new gender (Munro and Warren 2004). The forms, details, and politics of exclusion differ from place to place and are dependent on the intersection with other identities such as age, ethnicity, gender, and class positions.

EXCLUDING TRANSSEXUALS FROM THE NATION

"Transgender is like a refugee without citizenship" (Bird 2002, 366). Awareness of transgender citizenship is emerging out of a coalition of trans activist and support organizations. Mapping out the connections between transsexual and transgender rights and nationalism has become a focus in a number of nations including Hong Kong (Emerton 2006), United Kingdom (Aizura 2006; Munro and Warren 2004), Australasia and the Pacific Islands (Alexeyeff 2000; Besnier 2002, 2004; Mageo 1992;

Schmidt 2001, 2003), and the United States (Currah and Minter 2000; Kirkland 2006) to name but a few. At the heart of all of these studies is the reality that transsexual and transgendered people are excluded from full citizenship. Let us now look at a few in more detail.

There are several new trans social movements in Hong Kong including TEAM, which stands for Transgender Equality and Acceptance Movement. Robyn Emerton (2006) traces the objectives and aims of TEAM, which formed in 2002. TEAM emerged after two transgender women committed suicide within days of each other. A strong desire to create something positive out of the loss of two Hong Kong transwomen prompted a series of activities. TEAM aims to act as a support group and an advocacy group to allow transgendered people to be treated equally in law and society; encourage the formation of a transgendered community in Hong Kong; and assist in the provision of social activities (Emerton 2006).

Transgenders tend to remain invisible in Hong Kong for a number of reasons including that there is no transgender entertainment, beauty, or sex industry in Hong Kong where transpeople might feel comfortable openly making a living out of being transgendered. Also, recently the small number of transsexual workers who do work in these industries have largely been replaced by Thai and Filipino transgender sex workers (Emerton 2006). The media tend to consistently produce negative images of transgenders, which tends to fuel prejudice and discrimination against this group in Hong Kong. TEAM is assisting Hong Kong's transgendered community to fight for legal recognition. There are, however, a number of culturally specific factors—such as a fear of publicity and negative social attitudes—which prevent a court challenge.

Further south, transgenders in the Pacific Islands region—specifically Tonga, Cook Islands, and Samoa—face other culturally and ethnically specific transgender issues. Niko Besnier (2002, 2004) draws on ethnographic material to illustrate patterns of inequality directly and indirectly related to Tongan transgendered citizenship. Besnier (2002, 2004) highlights the importance of the Miss Galaxy beauty pageant held annually in the capital Nuku'alofa. The pageant showcases transfemales who Tongans refer to as "fakaleitī or leitī, who form a small but visible minority in Nuku'alofa. . . . The word leitī is borrowed from the English word lady and is applied only to transgendered males, whereas faka- is a polysemic prefix ubiquitous in Tongan. In this context it means 'in the fashion of'" (Besnier 2002, 534; italics in original). The beauty pageant appears, at first glance, to be a show of transgender "camp" glamour and it is through the Miss Galaxy pageant that most Tongans form knowledge of fakaleitī identity. The pageant is also a display of what Besnier (2002) calls "translocality." Translocality is a way to understand the formation of sexual citizenship that is formed within Tonga and moves beyond the borders of Tonga.

The name of the pageant itself—Miss Galaxy—plays on some of the more camp aspects of "real" beauty pageantry. In one of the events, contestants are required to appear in national costumes representing foreign countries (such as Miss Rarotonga or Miss South America) even though contestants have no connection to these places. The desire to emulate international beauty pageant practices enables contestants to reach beyond the confines of their local spaces. Besnier (2002) argues that through the Miss Galaxy pageant Tongan leitī have opportunities to transcend or dislocate from Tongan life while at the same time they remain in place geographically and socially.

Besnier's (2002) analysis of the pageant relates to a number of debates about international transgender identities and Tongan transgender identities. Transgenderism in Tonga is intertwined with another type of crossing based on Otherness, as noted:

> The pageant, and leitī identities in general, are only partly concerned with gender. When Tongan traditionalists make fun of straight overseas Tongan men by calling them *fakaleitī* (because they do not have full command of Tongan), they are putting their fingers on the fact that the embrace of Otherness (as indexed through language choice among other things) may be as central to *fakaleitī* identity as the claim that one is of another gender. (Besnier 2002, 599; italics in original)

Nearly nine hundred kilometers away, in the islands of Samoa, lies another expression of transsexual citizenship. As mentioned in chapter 1 "Samoan Fa'afafine are biologically males who express feminine gender identities. The Samoan word fa'afafine literally translates as 'like' or 'in the manner' of—fa'a—'a woman'—fafine, but there is no easy translation for the word as a whole" (Schmidt 2003, 417). Some dress as women, some do not. Many have sex with men yet they do not easily fit the category of homosexual; some modify their embodiment to look more like women. Overall, it is difficult to apply the notion of transsexual to fa'afafine (Schmidt 2003).

Popular discourses suggest that fa'afafine are an accepted part of Samoan life. The *Lonely Planet* tourist guide for Samoa notes fa'afafine are "very much an integral part of the fabric of Samoan society" (Talbot and Swaney 1998, 29). It seems that fa'afafine are both accepted and marginalized in Samoa. Their identities hang in the balance between tradition and modernization, between cultural discourses of family, respect, and social status and Western ideas about sexual liberation, individual freedom, and the right to emotionally sustaining relationships (Schmidt 2003). These discourses have impacted on the way in which fa'afafine understand themselves, as well as other Samoans understand fa'afafine. Traditionally, fa'afafine are identified at a young age by the virtue of their propensity for feminine tasks, as one fa'afafine remembers: "When I was young, I know I was like this. I do all the girl's work when I was young. I do the washing, and my sister's just mucking around, cleaning the house, but my job at home is cooking, washing, ironing—everything" (quoted in Schmidt 2003, 419). Traditions, however, are complex and at times contradictory. Fa'afafine sometimes operate as go betweens for young women and men who wish to socialize. It is suggested that they have been, and still are, a significant point of contact with a feminine person outside their families, and young boys may learn about sex with a woman from fa'afafine (Schmidt 2003). In contemporary Samoa, fa'afafine may play a role that was once played by pre-Christian girls in nighttime exchanges of entertainment (Mageo 1992). Their "current role represents a novel cultural stratagem for assisting real girls to play idealized roles and for defusing an increased pressure toward violence in public gatherings" (Mageo 1992, 444).

Changes in Samoan cultures, due to processes of globalization and capitalism, have increased individuation of what has been traditionally a group-oriented indigenous society. Labor is becoming less significant in relation to gendered identities and there is more emphasis on gendered appearance and bodily expression. The expression of sexuality is more obvious, particularly in spaces such as nightclubs, which offer opportunities for sexually explicit dancing (Schmidt 2003). For fa'afafine these social and cultural changes mean that their feminine labor in the home is no longer a predominant marker of gender. Westernization has also had an impact on the sexuality of fa'afafine. Urban fa'afafine may now express a specific form of sexualized femininity, which in the past, in accordance with Samoan traditions, was unacceptable.

Beauty pageants, similar to Tonga's Miss Galaxy pageant, are frequently held in bars in Apia, the capital of Samoa. These pageants are entwined with traditional and Western ideas of fa'afafine femininity. At the pageants fa'afafine may display their feminine abilities yet also redeem their reputations within Samoan society. They entertain and provide a public forum which is an integral part of Samoan life, and proceeds from the pageant are donated to places such as the local rest home. The redistribution of wealth, and show of generosity, is believed to be one way in which Samoans can gain "social credit" (Schmidt 2003, 426). The pageants also represent social movement in a way that might echo Western queer politics to counter social marginalization and exclusion. Schmidt (2003,

426) explains: "More than one informant suggested that the formation of subcultures such as those they saw in the exclusive gay clubs of New Zealand created an artificial, exclusionary environment, suggesting that for fa'afafine, social isolation, even of a voluntary nature, is not desirable." It is important to highlight that what transgendered citizenship means depends on place. We have given some examples of transsexual and transgendered (even the terms are problematic because they do not easily cross cultures) embodiment, practices, and social acceptability in different places and cultures. In the section that follows we extend this discussion about the subjectivities and rights of trans citizens by relaying the story of a transsexual who became a mayor and then a Member of Parliament (MP) in the New Zealand Government. We ask why the bodies of MPs matter when it comes to considering sexual citizenship and nation-states? We also ask what are the implications when a politician's body does not fit the dominant norm, that is, white, male, middle class, and heterosexual? The story of Georgina Beyer—the world's first transsexual mayor and MP—is instructive.

THE STORY OF GEORGINA BEYER

Georgina Beyer began her political career when she was elected to the Carterton District Council in 1993. She became the first transsexual mayor in the world in 1995 when she was elected Mayor of Carterton (Georgina Beyer.com 2008). Perhaps somewhat surprisingly, a conservative, mostly Pākehā (white, European) rural community voted Beyer into power with the knowledge that she is transsexual, Māori, and a former sex worker. As she puts it:

> I'd become the first woman to be mayor not only in Carterton but also in Wairarapa. I'd also become the first Māori in Carterton and Wairarapa to be elected as mayor, and one of only four Māori mayors elected nationally. There were lots of people celebrating my win with me on election night. I was told later that election-night parties by gay communities around the country went absolutely wild when news of my election got out. (Beyer and Casey 1999, 155)

The celebrations were "wild," we suggest, because with Beyer as mayor members of marginalized communities felt they might have more sway in New Zealand's legal and policymaking institutions. Beyer realized that she was carrying with her the hopes and dreams of many oppressed groups into office and from a human rights perspective her election as mayor was a major victory (Beyer and Casey 1999).

In 1999 Beyer went on to national politics and was elected as a Member of Parliament representing the Wairarapa district. This begs the question of whether the election of a Māori transsexual into New Zealand's parliament indicates that New Zealand is a nation that is accepting of sexual minorities. The answer is both yes and no. At the time of election Beyer claimed that her transsexuality was "not an issue."

> Only the media now focus on it [transsexuality], not the people who elected me into office. . . . It is an example of overcoming the odds and I am proud of that, and I am proud if it motivates people like myself in all minorities who struggle to achieve their dreams. . . . Against the adversity of society's disapproval and discrimination people from all minorities can achieve and do something positive. (*Press* 1999, 3)

The election of Beyer into national politics provides an opportunity to reflect on the relationship between gender, sexed embodiment, sexuality, and citizenship.

> When the elected member departs from the archetype in their class position, gendered difference, ethnicized difference, or other forms of embodied difference, their partiality is immediately apparent, and we need to turn to a consideration of how any individual can claim to represent a group made up of diverse citizens. (Mackie 2001, 190)

Discussions about citizenship and difference shed some light on this issue of representation. Democracy is supposed to enable people to "transcend their localized and partial concerns, getting beyond the narrow materialism of special interest to address the needs of the community instead" (Philips 1993, 92). However, the recognition of social hierarchies such as class, gender, and ethnic difference inevitably impacts on those who differ from an abstracted universalized ideal. In most Western democracies, the abstracted universalized ideal is embodied in white, heterosexual, and middle-class men.

Politicians whose embodiment differs from this construction tend to be disadvantaged. Nirmal Puwar (2004) has studied black women members of the British Parliament. Historically these spaces of governance have excluded women and nonwhites. Within these spaces there is an undeclared white masculine body underlying the modernist universal construction of the "individual." Yet clearly the individual is embodied and it is the white male figure who is actually taken as the central point of reference. "It is against this template, one that is defined in opposition to women and non-whites—after all, these are the relational terms in which masculinity and whiteness are constituted—that women and 'black' people who enter these spaces are measured" (Puwar 2004, 141). Yet, it seems obvious to say that voices from different groups need to be heard when formulating legislation and policy. Moira Gatens (1998, 5–6; italics in original) explains the importance of embodiment in relation to theories of democracy and the politics of difference:

> Gender norms construct specific forms of human embodiment as socially meaningful. Hence, it is possible to "impartially" apply norms which nevertheless impact differentially on embodied men and women (for example, laws prohibiting *any person* to procure an abortion; the normative expectation that child care is a private, rather than a corporate matter; the laws of provocation and self-defence). When social inequality is associated with embodied differences—for example, sexual and racial differences—norms may be "universally" applied without "universality" affecting all classes, or types of person. These particular cases of norms of partiality are precisely the kind . . . that offer the "ideal" means of domination and coercion.

In Puwar's (2004) study of black women in parliament she asks a series of questions including "what happens when bodies not expected to occupy certain spaces, do so?" and "what happens when women and racial minorities take up privileged positions not 'reserved' for them for which, they are not, in short, the somatic norm?" (Puwar 2004, 1). Significantly, as noted above, Beyer claimed that her transsexuality was "not an issue." Based on strong support from her constituents and electors due to years of dedicated service to community organizations and her advocacy for a number of groups such as youth, homeless, and unemployed, Beyer effectively told the media that she was able to transcend the particularities of her embodiment. In media reports Beyer understandably attempts to downplay her embodied difference to other politicians. Her book *Change for the Better* (Beyer and Casey 1999), however, provides a space for personal reflection that complicates her stated position in media.

As a minority herself, Beyer was determined to represent the needs of all citizens and went to extraordinary efforts to do so. She remarks: "I felt I mixed well with the citizens of Carterton from top to bottom, and was able to empathise and offer understanding to them all" (Beyer and Casey 1999, 136). Beyer spent a lot of time talking with and listening to her constituents. "Consequently I was in touch with the issues that concerned them. I appealed to and treated with respect low-income people who had been neglected by successive conservative councils" (Beyer and Casey 1999, 136). Perhaps it *is* her embodied difference that helped make Beyer such an effective politician.

Soon after Beyer was elected as a councillor at Carterton she was invited to a conference for local authority politicians. In this arena, she came up against some resistance. One conservative MP—Warren Cooper—joked in his conference speech that "he had just had an operation on his foot and made some sexual remark about cutting off a toe rather than a little further up" (Beyer and Casey 1999, 139). When it was Beyer's turn to face the audience she recalls: "I managed to get a dig back at Warren Cooper. I said something like, 'Maybe if they had cut it off, he'd be a better person,' or words to that effect. Warren was in the audience and my remark was met with stony silence, until a lone brave person tittered and then the whole place just laughed" (Beyer and Casey 1999, 139).

Not long after Beyer became mayor she received an invitation from the Queen of England to attend a royal garden party at Government House in New Zealand. She was introduced to the queen and they had a short conversation. Beyer was also introduced to the prime minister's wife, Joan Bolger, who remarked that she had noticed Beyer talking with the queen. Beyer comments: "Without thinking about what I was saying, I said, 'Oh yes, I'm terribly proud of that. She's the first real queen I've ever met!' Joan Bolger laughed and I suddenly realised what I'd said. We both had a bit of a chuckle" (Beyer and Casey 1999, 160). On the one hand, this informal and humorous interaction may be understood as arising from the peculiarities of a small country whose democratic leaders, and their partners, do not always follow political protocols based on colonial legacies. On the other hand, this interaction may be understood as politically subversive. A bold transsexual mayor jokes about queens with the wife of the prime minister and gets away with it. While this may seem an insignificant encounter, it does provide an example of the way in which a transsexual politician may contest accepted norms. At this meeting with the queen, Joan Bolger was relaxed with Beyer; her husband, however, the Prime Minister Jim Bolger, was not, as Beyer recounts:

> While I was talking to Tipene O'Regan [Sir Tepene O'Regan is a well-respected Māori elder and leader] and other Māori leaders, I backed into Jim Bolger. Our bodies were very close together and I said, "Oh Prime Minister!" He looked at me quite startled and he said, "Oh, Your Worship, congratulations." He obviously knew who I was and proceeded to shake my hand. However, his body language was absolutely negative and he stood as far away from me as he could. (Beyer and Casey 1999, 159)

The discomfort that the prime minister felt, Beyer suggests, was due to being physically close to a transsexual. Bolger's body fitted the norm for politicians; Beyer's did not.

The next time the prime minister and Beyer met was on Waitangi Day when they were formally introduced for the first time. Waitangi Day marks the anniversary of the signing of the Treaty of Waitangi in 1840, which was an agreement between Māori chiefs and the British Crown. Beyer took advantage of the occasion: "Well, being Waitangi Day I had to hongi [the traditional Māori greeting of nose pressing/sharing of breath]. So I shook his hand and grabbed him, and we hongied and we hongied and we hongied! I hung on to him for dear life, and I have the photo to prove it. He'd tried to keep as far away from me as he could the first time we met: this time I held him close!" (Beyer and Casey 1999, 160; see figure 7.1). In this exchange Beyer insists on physical closeness with the prime minister in order to test his levels of acceptance of difference. Using the occasion of Waitangi Day, she followed Māori protocol, which enabled her to cross boundaries—boundaries of physical proximity but also racialized, gendered, and sexual boundaries.

Approximately a decade on from when Beyer was elected into New Zealand's parliament, Clive Aspin (Aspin 2007), an editor of *Sexualities and the Stories of Indigenous People*, interviewed her about being an MP.

Figure 7.1.   Mayor Georgina Beyer and Prime Minister Jim Bolger "hongi" on Waitangi Day in New Zealand. Photograph appears courtesy of Photography by Woolf and with the permission of Georgina Beyer.

Beyer explained that her pathway to politics can be traced to her child-hood and whakapapa (genealogy which is tied closely to cultural iden-tity). Members of her extended family were activists and high achievers.

> Hana Te Hemara, a Māori activist in the preservation of the Māori language, on the one hand, and Sir Paul Reeves, an activist at the other end of the po-litical spectrum. I guess that's where I look for qualities that will sustain me. I had no advantages over anyone else. If anything, I had greater disadvan-tages because I was Māori, takatāpui, and I wanted to be a woman. (Beyer quoted in Aspin 2007, 71)

Beyer speaks of her challenges and struggles but says that being Māori has also given her strength. "I've been on the street and I've been on the [unemployment] benefit, and I've had my arse kicked a few times for no good reason other than I was a poofter, trash, and my spirit rejected that. It came from a sense of pride, of mana [influence and power]" (Beyer quoted in Aspin 2007, 71).

It is perhaps the *intersection* of identities—being Māori, takatāpui, and transsexual—which has had the greatest impact on Beyer's life experi-ences and her public service to many communities in New Zealand. Beyer reflects on what she thinks needs to happen for equality for all New Zea-land citizens:

> Kiwi [an informal term used to refer to New Zealanders] citizens, brought up as we were, we turn out not bad people who punch above their weight. The challenge for the queer community is to not be complacent about how far we have come and to continue to get those things that still matter very much to us. (Beyer quoted in Aspin 2007, 77–78)

Beyer is referring to rights-based legislation, mainly the Homosexual Law Reform Bill that was passed in New Zealand in 1986 after a sus-tained period of protest by conservative and church-based groups. The Homosexual Law Reform Act decriminalized sexual relations between men aged sixteen and over. Prior to 1986 men having consensual sex with each other were liable to prosecution and a prison sentence. Lesbi-ans did not exist in legislation, hence sex between women was legal, yet many lesbians suffered the same social discrimination as gay men. As legal citizens lesbians were able to be public and staunch supporters of the reform movement, participating in protests and lobbying politicians. Other groups, such as Heterosexuals Unafraid of Gays (HUG), formed to show solidarity and support for the reform. The campaign to reform the law moved beyond queer communities and into wider issues of human rights and discrimination. Four MPs started antigay petitions such as the

Coalition for Concerned Citizens, while others such as MP Marilyn Waring came out.

Beyer was not an MP at the time of the Homosexual Law Reform and when asked if she has been affected by homophobia in Parliament, she replied:

> Not at all. Chris Carter [an openly gay MP] went through the ignominy of that when he was elected. Tim Barnett [another openly gay MP] may have suffered a little too, but, by and large, when John Banks [a right-wing conservative MP] left parliament so did much of that venal stuff. I haven't experienced overt discrimination, and they would have been foolish if they did so. They just need to look at my electoral record and note my standing. To attack me on that would be fatal. (Beyer quoted in Aspin 2007, 79)

During her time in Parliament Beyer supported the passing of the Civil Union Bill that allows couples of any gender to register their relationship, and the Prostitution Law Reform Bill which passed in June 2003. The Prostitution Law Reform Act decriminalized prostitution in New Zealand and put in place provisions to protect the health and safety of sex workers and their clients. The act prohibits anyone under eighteen years old working as a prostitute. Anyone who would like to operate a prostitution business must hold a certificate (Ministry of Justice 2008).

Beyer retired from Parliament in 2007 after serving more than seven years as an MP. In her Parliamentary Valedictory Speech she says:

> In my maiden speech I made a flippant comment that became synonymous with Georgina Beyer. I will repeat it. I stated at that time that this was the stallion that became a gelding and then a Mayor, and now, as it was at the time, I have found myself to be a member. Can I say to you at this point that while I have relished the opportunity of being a member in this House, I am glad I do not possess one. (Georgina Beyer.com 2008)

Thirteen years after Beyer was first elected Mayor of Carterton, across the Pacific Ocean, the United States is swearing into power its first transgendered mayor, Stu Rasmussen. Rasmussen told reporters: "I identify mostly as a heterosexual male. But I just like to look like a female. . . . Some guys' mid-life crisis is motorcycles or sports cars or climbing mountains or trophy wives or whatever. I always wanted cleavage, so I went out and acquired some" (GayNZ.com News Staff 2008a). Rasmussen will be representing the citizens of Silverton, Oregon.

In this chapter we have examined sexual citizenship as a form of social identification, which some writers claim is replacing more traditional forms of national identity. Nations often assume their citizens are heterosexual men or women who engage in natural or normal sex. Natural sex is acceptable while Other kinds of sex such as sodomy and oral sex are not. We also discussed transsexuality (in particular the story of Georgina Beyer) and the role of the state, churches, and pressure groups in relation to both straight and queer marriage. Gay and lesbian struggles over the civil recognition of domestic partnership and the right to marry have for a number of years been at the forefront of debates within lesbian and gay groups. At the heart of these struggles may be a desire to be seen as normal and ordinary gay citizens.

This has led to critics' concerns about a "new homonormativity" (Duggan 2002), which foregrounds the dangers of pitching rights claims based on the right of access to heteronormative privilege. On the one hand, it is important that sexual citizenry is not overdetermined by a politics of assimilation so that critical questions about the kinds and desires of sexual citizenry can still be posed. On the other hand, the mainstreaming of previously marginalized and/or demonized sexual identities and practices "opens out the sphere of sexual citizenship in new trajectories away from a narrowly prescribed normativity" (Bell and Binnie 2006, 870). Multiple strategies may be useful, and politically necessary, if new ideas of sexual citizenship are to be inclusive.

8

Global Intimacies

How do desire, romance, and sex transcend national boundaries and travel across the globe? As discussed in the previous chapter, the rise of information technologies and the rapid pace of a globalized economy and culture mean that citizens no longer necessarily remain bounded within their own nation-states. People are now far more likely to be mobile. We can now travel between places far more rapidly than in the past. Time and space have converged. In the past, places tended to remain relatively isolated. Today, if we have the resources of time and money, we can get on a train or plane and be somewhere else in a short space of time.

This chapter focuses on flows of intimacy, romance, and sex in relation to globalization. The topics explored are tourist (or destination) weddings in New Zealand, mail-order and cyberbrides from Latin America and Asia (including female sex trafficking), and sex and romance in the beach tourism destinations of the Caribbean. We also ask if there is a new globalized sexual citizen. Global travel companies are increasingly courting gay customers. The growth of queer tourism has led to greater visibility of lesbians and gay men as consumers (Johnston 2005a). We explore whether a global "pink economy" is based on uniformity and conformity to normative aspects of sexuality, or if the pink economy produces difference. In doing so we bring together the following areas of scholarship—embodied geographies of sexualities, sex and romance tourism, and formations of transnational citizenship—to highlight global contemporary sexual politics, identities, and practices.

WEDDING TOURISM

"An exotic South Pacific wedding and honeymoon in New Zealand is 100% pure romance" (Cashmere Heights Weddings 2004). The construction of "100% pure romance" in New Zealand relies on images of white glaciers, rugged mountains, lush green subtropical forests, blue water coastlines, and golden beaches. Weddings as rituals in nature present a type of natural heterosexuality that may conceal historical and material changes. Weddings may be powerful markers of a couple's normality, morality, productivity, and gendered subjectivities. Hubbard (2000, 194; italics in original) explains:

> Particular expressions of heterosexuality are constructed as moral or immoral in particular spatial and temporal contexts, with the boundary between what is considered "normal" and what is regarded as "perverted" being struggled over in a variety of sites (which, importantly, also exist as visual *sights*).

Examining the moral geographies of heterosexual performances at tourist weddings enables a critical examination of how heterosexuality is naturalized in and through the spaces of nature. Hubbard (2000, 206) comments: "There appears to be little overt consideration of how moral heterosexual performances are naturalized in a variety of 'everyday' social settings, either public or private." This is why we consider the stories of tourists who come to New Zealand to get married surrounded by beautiful and natural landscapes. It is one way of considering how moral heterosexual performances are naturalized in a particular setting.

A great deal of business is generated by the New Zealand wedding tourism industry, which has increased by 300 percent over the last ten years. In 2003, one thousand couples came to New Zealand to marry. In 2004, it increased to twelve hundred couples. This business is estimated to contribute approximately $30 million each year to the New Zealand economy (TVNZ 2004). The Television New Zealand documentary *I Do Down-Under* (TVNZ 2004) examines the phenomenon of tourist weddings in New Zealand. It follows a successful wedding tourism operator—Vanessa Leeming—who ran one of New Zealand's largest wedding planner companies, Cashmere Heights Weddings (which appears to have been recently renamed Romantic New Zealand). The weddings portrayed in this documentary show couples getting married in iconic landscapes such as Mount Cook, the beaches on the West Coast, Lake Tekapo, and Queenstown.

We draw on this material to illustrate how particular powerful performances of sexuality and nature encourage the global movement of couples to travel "down under." The nature spaces of New Zealand are constituted as "romantic and 100% natural" and important components of the couples' wedding ceremonies. Gillian Rose (1993, 89) states: "Whether written or painted, grown or built, a landscape's meanings draw on the cultural codes of the society for which it was made."

New Zealand has become synonymous with nature tourism. The country's tourism board sells the country as "100% Pure" and promotes the nation's reputation as one of the world's premier natural destinations (New Zealand Tourism Board 2002; Cloke and Perkins 1998). As seen in chapter 7, spaces of nature and wilderness are often places for the expression of very conventional forms of heterosexuality (Little 2007; Woodward 1998, 2000) and wedding tourism plays a key role in helping to solidify New Zealand's nature spaces as 100% pure, natural, and heterosexual (Johnston 2006).

Couples in the *I Do Down-Under* documentary learned of New Zealand's natural landscapes through media such as film, television, websites, and literature. They chose New Zealand for their wedding ceremony because of its dramatic landscapes. A couple from Germany explain:

> Klaus: I first learnt about New Zealand, I think when I was a boy, on this television channel there was a documentation [sic] about New Zealand's fern trees and they were special to New Zealand. You can't see them anywhere in the world. So I saw this and I wanted to go to New Zealand. It's like a dream.
>
> Petra: I too also wanted to go to New Zealand because of the beautiful surroundings. Nature untouched and unspoilt and that's something you don't get in Europe, in Germany (TVNZ 2004).

New Zealand is regularly constructed as unspoiled, natural, and exotic, and this is most often found in tourism marketing. In 2008 the official Pure New Zealand tourism website ran a video showing "100% Pure" landscapes such as awe, wonder, exhilaration, welcome, indulgence, and escape (New Zealand Tourism Board 2008). The website shows remote and beautiful nature spaces where couples (supposedly "in love" with each other and the landscape) ride horses along beaches, sail yachts close to waterfalls in Fiordland, walk through native tree forests and stroke the trees, ski down snowy mountains, and stay in isolated bush huts on the edge of rivers. Couples appear happy and excited with both each other and their holiday choice. Their various expressions of sexuality are constructed to appear highly desirable and New Zealand's wild and exotic nature becomes a loving and romantic space. The more natural the landscape, the more enticing it is for tourists who, by many accounts, seek Other experiences (MacCannell 1999; Shields 1991; Urry 1990).

One wedding tourism operator, Aaron, who had been in the business since 1987, said the following about the 100% Pure New Zealand tourism marketing campaign.

> A pure place is pure in thoughts, it's going to be a welcoming place um. . . . The word "pure" is a magnificent word because it translates uniquely into, um, special cleanliness. The Japanese translation, I've forgotten it now, but the Japanese translation of pure is like six words but it actually means "open to you," un, un-dirtied, or un-muddied. But also in our [Pākehā European New Zealander] attitudes we sort of see the other side of dirt as pure. Pure is always good. (personal interview, February 15, 2006, Johnston 2006, 198)

Aaron offers what he considers to be a Japanese interpretation of "pure" to make connections between nature and heterosexual relationships. Along with other tourism wedding operators he made comments about selling New Zealand's "clean and green" image to wedding tourism clients. His Japanese interpretation of pure is used to make links to a European (Western) interpretation of pure—that which is *not* dirty. Dirt, or the impure, may provoke anxiety and disgust by those who seek a moral geography such as New Zealand's romantic love spaces (Johnston 2006).

These landscapes (both real and imagined) are crucial for defining normative forms of heterosexuality, wedding tourism, and nature. Sexual practices and performances are imbued with moral values which encourage and normalize the creation of idealized pure heterosexual couples and place. These expressions of heterosexuality are "in place" in New Zealand's natural landscapes. The notion of 100% Pure has particular resonance in relation to constructions of heterosexual love.

Feminists have discussed meanings of romantic love, focusing on the relationship between romance, emotion, women's agency, and power in the context of heterosexual love (Jackson 1999; Langford 1999). Stevi Jackson (1999, 103) notes romantic love serves to "validate sexual activity morally, aesthetically and emotionally" and helps alleviate fears about sexual and emotional exploitation. The transformative power of love is comparable to the transformative power of being a tourist; put simply, it has the power to overcome mundane and everyday routines.

> Hence the transformative power of (romantic) love, its ability to turn frogs into princes. One of the most obvious appeals of romantic fiction is that it enables readers to relive the excitement of romantic passion without having to confront its fading and routinization. In real life we too often discover that our prince was only a frog after all. (Jackson 1999, 116)

What is operating here is a discursive system that produces and regulates the sexual identities of bodies and places. When the bride and groom are gathered together down under in a natural locale, heterosexuality is enfolded into nature, and vice versa. The wedding, usually followed by a honeymoon in the same country, extends the emotion, erotic and exotic, between man and woman to New Zealand landscapes (Johnston 2006).

Isolation is an important feature of these tourist weddings. The shift from people visiting the couple's wedding party, to the couple visiting wedding places suggests that the consumption of an unfamiliar environment becomes increasingly central to the production of nuptial privacy. Couples—alone together in nature—are able to distinguish their marriage from, and elevate it above, other affectionate bonds with their family and friends. The function and meaning of weddings has changed according to different times and spaces. Elizabeth Freeman (2002) sketches a history of weddings and notes that marriage was once a means of subordinating a couple's relationship to a larger social framework. It is now "more and more a means of separating a couple from broader ties and obligations" (Freeman 2002, 11).

In the documentary *I Do Down-Under* the couple from the Netherlands, Arianne and Sebastiaan, request a wedding in "a secluded West Coast beach [Punakaiki]" with a "real New Zealand feel to the whole, whole wedding . . . a really New Zealand wedding" (TVNZ 2004). For their wedding Arianne wears a flowing white dress and Sebastiaan wears a suit. They walk with bare feet on the sandy beach. The nature space of their wedding—a deserted beach—is wholly embraced by the couple in that their bodies are regulated by conventions of both wedding *and* beach attire. The secluded beach looks like an advertisement from the 100% Pure New Zealand advertising campaign, reinforcing for viewers New Zealand as remote, exotic, pure, and isolated (Johnston 2006). The couple has chosen nature to witness their wedding, rather than family and friends. Sebastiaan and Arianne explain:

> Sebastiaan: Our marriage here is a big, big secret. The idea was to go off somewhere and marry and then come back and tell our family. This New Zealand wedding is practical because we both have *mothers that want something to do with it.*
>
> Arianne: My mother thinks we are in Greece.
>
> Sebastiaan: My mother thinks we are in Italy. (TVNZ 2004, cited in Johnston 2006, 200; italics in original)

It is useful to remember that a couple's agency over their wedding changes over space and time due to the institutionalization of a variety of social practices, rituals, and laws. What seems normal for heterosexual weddings is a recent construction. Marriage and weddings have been regulated by various institutions. The history of the white wedding ritual predates Western countries' control of marriage.

> Before the Christianisation of Europe, fathers, families, and community customs regulated marriage, to be followed by priests and the church, then by magistrates and the civil law, now inflected by a commercial industry, with the couple's authority over their own marriage waxing and waning alongside these institutions. (Freeman 2002, 11)

Today's wedding ritual contains residual elements of different historical periods. The betrothal process was a prominent feature of pre-Christian weddings and this took precedent over the wedding ceremony. It was generally families that created a couple's social status, rather than religious or legal institutions. Early Christian wedding rituals became standard around the beginning of the first millennium and the church incorporated some pre-Christian elements such as the "giving of the ring, the handclasp, and the exchange of kisses" (Freeman 2002, 14). When the Catholic Church focused on the wedding ritual itself, it diminished the power of bodily acts to "make" a marriage and focused on spiritual aspects instead. Corporeal tokens and fertility rituals were frowned upon. It was the church that established the verbal consent "I do," which also acted to take precedence over parental and community involvement of the nuptials. The "I do" consensus exchange was accompanied by a strict doctrine which meant marriage was indissoluble except by church dispensation (Freeman 2002).

The white wedding became standard in the United States during the mid to late nineteenth century. During the first half of the twentieth century, federal taxation and the distribution of resources such as welfare and social security became locked into marital status. Puritan regulations remain in the modern US civil marriage, for example, "the subsumption of women's entitlements into the household structure, maintenance of opposite and incommensurate racial categories, differential access to citizenship and/or social services, privileging of physically healthy people, and heterosexual supremacy" (Freeman 2002, 24).

The standard white wedding is undoubtedly a product of capitalism peppered with residual sacramental enthusiasms. "Hen parties" (bridal showers) and "stag dos" (bachelor parties) are the prewedding dramas before the veiled bride in a white satin dress, the groom, attendants in matching dresses, rings, flower bouquets, and special music are gathered together in a specific place.

Back in New Zealand, the couple from the Netherlands (Sebastiaan and Arianne), a marriage celebrant, and a photographer perform their various wedding roles on a secluded West Coast beach under a perfect blue sky. Vows are made, rings are exchanged, and the champagne cork is popped. The viewers of the documentary are treated to a shot of the newlyweds walking barefoot, arms linked, along the beach as the afternoon sun dips below the sparkling watery horizon. Arianne confirms: "This is exactly what we wanted to do, without family, just two of us, just cosy" (TVNZ 2004, cited in Johnston 2006, 201). Ironically, the couple must of course also have had several other people at the ceremony—those who were involved in filming the documentary. Their wedding was also viewed by thousands watching the documentary.

Being close to, and in, nature is seen to enhance social well-being, reduce the stress of a traditional wedding, and allow a couple time to fully commit to each other (but not necessarily to each other's family and friends). To be married in what has become one of the world's premier nature spaces—New Zealand—implies a total commitment to the relationship which is contrasted to the unnatural stress and fuss of weddings at home with family. Ideas of nature are used to support heteronormativity and provide a defense of existing power relations in the construction and performance of sexual relationships (Little 2003).

Wedding tourism separates the couple from their social networks and elevates their relationship with one another over their ties to parents, extended family, friends, and other lovers, past and present. In their place, nature steps in. Escaping to a tourist wedding in New Zealand romanticizes both nature and heterosexuality as the couple, like the landscapes, are deemed to be pure, natural, exciting, and romantically "meant to be." Tourist weddings in New Zealand nature spaces make heterosexuality seem natural, inevitable, and sacred (Johnston 2006).

This in-depth look at wedding tourism demonstrates the value of thinking about love, romance, sex, and sexuality transnationally. Over the past few years with the increasing compression of time and space, new sites of opportunity have opened up for intimate encounters. New Zealand's nature spaces are not innocent backdrops; rather, they are produced and marketed as nature par excellence. Building on suggestions that heterosexuality can take different forms in different spaces (Hubbard 2000; Little 2003) New Zealand tourist weddings (and their various representations) can be understood as pure, romantic, exotic, and natural. Wedding tourism, therefore, is a useful lens through which to highlight the production and global flow of heterosexual bodies.

It is also important to recognize that the nature spaces of wedding tourism described above are not the only landscape option available for wedding tourists. Within the United States, Las Vegas, Nevada, is a popular destination for weddings. Its wedding tourism industry differs remarkably from New Zealand's nature destinations. Couples may choose a quiet chapel in a casino, then engage in some gambling after the ceremony (see figure 8.1 of a bride at a Las Vegas casino).

Couples may even decide to marry beside the famous Welcome to Fabulous Las Vegas sign (see Weddings Las Vegas 2009). The sign is at the north end of Las Vegas Boulevard—the Strip—where there are also a dozen or so wedding chapels. Couples say "I do" to each other in chapels with names such as Viva Las Vegas Wedding Chapel (also known as Elvis Wedding Chapel), Wedding Drive Thru, The Candlelight Chapel, and the famous Little White Wedding Chapel. Ken Van Vechten's (2005) book *Neon Nuptials: The Complete Guide to Las Vegas Weddings* compares and rates fifty "Sin City" venues for kitsch, outdoor ceremonies, stand-alone chapels, casino options, churchlike chapels, and resort settings.

Another global flow of love, romance, sex, and sexuality is mail-order brides.

Figure 8.1. A bride gambles in a Las Vegas casino. Photograph by Lynda Johnston.

MAIL-ORDER BRIDES

Transnational marriages are more alluring to some than others. Over the past decade some men from Western countries have begun to seek out and marry women from non-Western countries. Henry Makow comments: "I am an explorer in the undiscovered continent of love, a scientist in the laboratory of masculine longing. Can a middle-aged man, scarred by sex wars at home, find a new beginning on a tropical island where women are still feminine?" (Makow 2000, back cover). There are a set of complicated politics, economics, and realities that speak to "sex wars" at home and the desire for mail-order brides, but broadly speaking, as more First World women all over the world move outside of the home to work, more Third World women are sought to uphold ideologies of patriarchal and nuclear families. Women moving from poorer countries to spouses in richer countries tend to arouse negative responses from the media, the general public, and scholars. The recent shift from letter writing between prospective partners to using the Internet to broker introductions has added to the anxieties and moral panic surrounding marriage migration (Robinson 2007).

The desire for mail-order brides is provocatively encapsulated by Americus Mitchell, aged sixty-seven and husband to Maria Victoria Malevo. Maria Victoria Malevo is twenty-one and from Quezon City, Philippines. The couple currently live in the town of Kilmarnock in Virginia. Mitchell explains: "American women put themselves on a pedestal and are neglecting US men. . . . It's the same thing as when Ford and General Motors keep turning out bad products. You turn to the Japanese" (So 2006, 395). This analogy reveals a great deal about the status of US and Asian women in the global capitalist era. Mitchell draws on the 1980s and 1990s backlash against US women who work outside the home and the economic threat that Asia represents. He confirms a "globalist capitalist vision of Asian women as automatons" (So 2006, 395). Global capitalist discourses—entwined with raced and gendered ideas—contribute to the notion that Asian wives might be as easily exchanged or acquired as any other Asian "products." Asian women are imagined to be more firmly located within patriarchal familial structures and, paradoxically, are represented as being more suited than First World (usually white) women to maintain "traditional" family values. It is clear from Mitchell's statement above that the incorporation of Asian mail-order brides into US families reveals a type of growing anxiety surrounding the globalization of the US family (So 2006).

It is difficult to estimate the number of marriages that occur each year through international matchmaking services. Surveys of matchmaking companies estimate the number of marriages to be between four thousand

and six thousand in 1998, and mail-order marriages make up between 2.7 and 4.1 percent of female spouse immigration (Scholes 1997). Matchmaking agencies continue to grow in number. Christine So (2006, 415) explores "America's nostalgia for the nuclear family, the continuing backlash against the feminist movement, the anxiety over disintegrating national borders, and a fragmented culture" and suggests that the desire for immigrant Asian wives is about, ironically, rescuing and reconsolidating the US family and nation.

There are concerns for women that enter into mail-order marriages and these center, primarily, on fears that they will be socially and economically dependent on their husbands and that they may become victims of domestic abuse without knowledge of support systems available to effect escape (So 2006). Women's organizations and activist groups such as GABRIELA Network USA (2008) work on behalf of Filipinas in the United States. They agitate governments to halt the traffic of women and push for the regulation of international matchmaking organizations. In *Romance on a Global Stage: Pen Pals, Virtual Ethnography, and "Mail-Order" Marriages* Nicole Constable (2003) discusses Filipino and Chinese mail-order brides. Rather than focusing solely on the exploitation of these women, she offers another means to understand their experiences:

> If this study succeeds in its humanistic project of depicting women as something other than mail-order brides, desperate victims, or hyper-agents, motivated solely by economic hardship and desperation and willing to marry any western man who approaches them, and if the men (many of them, anyway) can be seen as something other than simply consumers of women as commodities, then this work will have succeeded, at least in part. (Constable 2003, 9)

Importantly, these marriage arrangements need to be understood as gendered and raced practices rather than as representing simple economic dualistic power relations between haves (men) and have-nots (women). To understand mail-order marriages in this way is to assume a unified exercise of power (male/capitalist domination) and obscure women's agency, rendering them as commodified bodies and as dupes of the brokers who run the websites and the men who seek to marry them (Robinson 2007). Kathryn Robinson (2007) makes a convincing argument for the need to understand these transnational marriages as an aspect of the new ways in which personal relationships are being renegotiated on a global level and facilitated by the global reach of capitalism. Globalization involves a "spatial reorganisation of social relations" in the context of international flows and movements and a "power geometry of time-space compression" (Massey 1994, 12 and 14), which allows individuals multiple and different ways to access power in relation to those flows and movements.

Felicity Schaeffer-Grabiel (2005) focuses on the impact of the Internet on transnational marriages. In "Planet-Love.com: Cyberbrides in the Americas and the Transnational Routes of US Masculinity" Schaeffer-Grabiel (2005, 332) argues: "The emergence of agencies on the internet with services in Latin America has resulted in attracting women from a mostly middle-class and/or professional clientele, although male participants come from various regional, economic, and class backgrounds." Schaeffer-Grabiel's study echoes the findings of Robinson's (2007), So's (2006), and Constable's (2003) research, that is, that the matchmaking industry does not merely commodify relationships into binaries of white male buyer and ethnic female seller, but it involves a more complex global space of social, racial, national, and gendered subjectivities. Schaeffer-Grabiel points out that in most feminist writing on mail-order brides women's and men's voices remain silent. She discusses the ways in which middle-class Mexican women interpret their desire to marry US men (Schaeffer-Grabiel 2004), and turning to men, she demonstrates a contemporary way that national identity and globalization resurface through men's loves, practices, and forms of intimacy (Schaeffer-Grabiel 2005).

It is through the Internet—Planet Love's chat room—that men's quest for a bride takes on new and interesting dimensions. The website Planet Love states:

> Welcome to Planet Love! Planet Love (PL)—The Foreign Bride Guide is the premier and most progressive resource available for being successful with a Foreign Bride. At Planet Love you will uncover the truth through highly relevant factual robust discussions about International Relationships and understand the immense benefits as well as the risks that you may face regarding women from Latin American and Asian countries. (Planet Love 2008)

The website claims to inform potential clients of the truth about foreign brides. Many websites idealize Latin American women as having better genes or, as one of Schaeffer-Grabiel's (2005, 333) participants put it, "raw materials." Latin American women are imagined as untainted by modern capitalist relations while also in need of being "saved" from their own anachronistic nation. Some men in the United States imagine themselves saving globally disadvantaged women abroad as well as saving the US nation from the "so-called disintegration of the family brought about by feminism, women's entrance into the labor force, and US women of color, who are stereotyped as welfare recipients (viewed as unruly and lazy laborers)" (Schaeffer-Grabiel 2005, 335). Latin American women, in imagined contrast, embody the "last frontier" and in chat room discussions men from various ethnicities, classes, and professions enact fantasies of colonialism and nationalism while at the same time appearing to be cosmopolitan citizens of the globe. Schaeffer-Grabiel (2005) found that the Internet plays a vital role in these constructions of gendered subjectivities. She found that it altered patterns of intimacy and subjectivity, as well as essentializing Latin American women's bodies as reproducers of the new nation.

After spending time in chat rooms, interviewing more than forty men on Vacation Romance tours (held in five-star hotels—men pay as much as US$1,200 and travel expenses to attend, while women are invited for free), and analyzing guidebooks Schaeffer-Grabiel (2005) found that US men seeking foreign brides tend to display forms of "disempowered masculinity"; that is, they tend to feel alienated from US culture and society. One participant, Jason, said, "My whole life is abstract . . . so on some level, going outside my country is an attempt to, you know, get past that cynical, detached experience that I have here" (Schaeffer-Grabiel 2005, 338). Jason's exodus to Latin America is a way to "break out of the mold" and leave behind relationships overdetermined by capitalist exchange. Jason was tired of working in the highly competitive market of the Silicon Valley where he experienced an influx of highly skilled and lower paid technicians from South Asia. Divorced from his previous wife, he had to work long hours to maintain a high quality of life in California. His situation prevented him from realizing the American dream of owning a house and having a family (Schaeffer-Grabiel 2005).

Some men, harboring resentful feelings, are prompted to take action against "ungrateful women" and take charge of their lives by finding a foreign, supposedly less demanding, and more docile wife (Schaeffer-Grabiel 2005). Below is a testimony from a man who felt ready for such a change.

My final decision to pursue a foreign bride resulted from an argument I heard between my mother and her new husband. Mother was bitching moaning and carrying on about how her new life was drudgery and how she felt unappreciated. Her new husband got tired of her whining and shouted, "Fran YOU have a brand new $250,000 dream home in the suburbs with every furnishing and knick knack you wanted, a new Isuzu Trooper, a healthy bank account, a very comfortable living, a husband who has bent over backwards to make you happy . . . WHAT THE HELL MORE DO YOU WANT!" . . . This is when I realized that the odds are stacked against me finding happiness with an American wife, which has led me to say, "IT IS TIME FOR NEW GENES." (Clark, February 23, 2001, www.planet-love.com/gclark/gclark/gclark02/, uppercase in original; cited in Schaeffer-Grabiel 2005, 340)

Clark's cybernarrative envisions a better future by infusing "new genes" in a transracial family. He represents his mother as a "spoiled" suburban white woman who does not appreciate what she has and implies that most American women "do not reciprocate with docile bodies in exchange for a capitalist and patriarchal order in the workplace and home" (Schaeffer-Grabiel 2005, 340). Earlier in Clark's story he describes his mother as having feminist views which resulted in him being raised in an "unhealthy male-bashing environment." Male participants, like Clark, in Schaeffer-Grabiel's (2005) study wanted less liberated women who were less "spoiled" and materialistic than US women. The focus on genes reemerges in various forms in chat room discussions, during interviews, and on websites.

Through these discourses Latin American and other "foreign women" become naturalized as having the right biological makeup and cultural grooming, constructing them as more feminine, traditional, and better mothers. "Unlike nineteenth-century constructions of racial mixing as degenerative, in this instance foreign genes are constructed as regenerative. This shift in racial construction connects with individualistic ideals of multiculturalism in the global marketplace (Schaeffer-Grabiel 2005, 341). Some men in chat rooms tended to describe themselves as active participants in assimilating women into the American dream.

Schaeffer-Grabiel (2005) concludes her study by noting that the role of the Internet in facilitating visual and interactive fantasies and marriage illustrates another way US individualism and capitalism are powerful means for men to experience themselves as decentered subjects, rather than the hegemonic center. Many men are turning to Latin American and other foreign women and cultures in the hope of living outside of the tyranny of capitalism, materialism, and rugged individualism. However, "many simply seek a fantasy-ridden image of women as the object of change they seek to import back home without having to change anything about themselves" (Schaeffer-Grabiel 2005, 353).

There are other darker sides of global issues related to sex, sexuality, and bodies, in particular sex trafficking and prostitution. In an in-depth analysis of female sex trafficking involving young girls from Nepal, Cambodia, and Philippines, Vidyamali Samarasinghe (2008) argues that the sexual exploitation of women and children is an expression of patriarchy—that is—female subordination and male dominance. While not all female sex trafficking is about minor girls from poor backgrounds, "to be young and female are essential prerequisites of recruitment into the sex industry. They meet the demand for a particular 'taste' in a service activity, which prefer youthful bodies. Power dynamics based on age and gender ensure that young females from poor countries are easily controlled both by older people and by males" (Samarasinghe 2008, 2). None of the girls that Samarasinghe (2008) spoke with had been abducted or kidnapped; rather, they had been misled. Girls from Nepali homes, for example, are taken to Mumbai by people known to them. Usually the recruiters are relatives or familial or even young men posing as prospective husbands. Others may masquerade as "employment agents, 'concerned' older women, and truck drivers who make regular runs across the border to India" (Samarasinghe 2008, 77). Alongside this trickery, girls may be willing to leave their difficult rural working conditions in Nepal, particularly when they are promised jobs as housemaids for affluent Indian families or factory workers.

The trafficked sex worker may be sold several times and the younger she is the higher the "resale" value. In the case of the sex industry in Mumbai, Samarasinghe (2008) notes, clients are local Indian men as well as expatriate Nepali men, plus some men from the Gulf States. There is an increasing demand for young female virgins in the Indian sex industry. This demand relates to the myth that "male virility is enhanced and sexually transmitted disease may be cured by sexual intercourse with virgins. . . . Males who frequent brothels in search of commercial sex will pay a premium price for a young female virgin in order to eliminate the risk of HIV/AIDS infection" (Samarasinghe 2008, 79). Girls are either not paid at all, or they are given a small allowance to buy food, water, and toiletry items. If Nepali women or children are rescued or escape from the brothel, the stigma of being a sex worker means they are not welcomed back in their family homes and villages.

The horrors of this kind of sexual exploitation are not replicated by women seeking men or boys and this is not surprising given the resilience of patriarchy operating to exploit women and girls. Sometimes, however, women seek "exotic men." One example is Western, mainly US, women tourists who visit the Caribbean for sex, romance, and sometimes longer term partnerships with "local" men. This is known in the academic literature as "ethnosexual" tourism and is the topic of the next section.

SEX, ROMANCE, AND BEACHES

While it is now common for academics in tourism studies to respond to the sexual and erotic component of tourism, very few accounts make explicit reference to embodied sexuality (but see Johnston 2005a, 2005b, 2007; Frohlick 2007; Veijola and Jokinen 1994). This is surprising given that the connection between bodies, sexuality, romance, and love are at the forefront of tourism marketers' minds (Ingraham 1999). Susan

Frohlick (2007, 2008) notes in her ethnographic study that over the past few years new erotic subjectivities have emerged in Puerto Viejo, Costa Rica. Intimacy plays a vital role between women tourists and local men. Frohlick untangles the complicated intimacies, cultures, social and economic flows between Western white foreign women and—as the Costa Rica *Rough Guide* says—"resident dreadlocked hustlers" (McNeill 2001, 173). Costa Rica is an important site for tourism, which has been growing since the late 1980s, and during the late 1990s ethnosexual tourism has become much more prominent. Many foreign tourists, including European and North American women tourists, head to this area in "search of Caribbean culture and a Caribbean aesthetic (beauty and other sensory pleasures associated with the Caribbean)" (Frohlick 2007, 140). The interactions between Western women and local men unfold in a myriad of ways. Some foreign women become involved in "situational" forms of sexual tourism (Phillips 1999); others may conduct long-term romantic relationships which result in women staying longer than they had planned or returning repeatedly to spend time with their local lover.

Costa Rica is a global tourist destination divided spatially by gender and race where "white North American and European men travel to the Pacific Coast for sex with local women (*Ticas*), and white female tourists tend to prefer the Caribbean coast known for sexually appealing Caribbean men" (Frohlick 2007, 140). Guidebook descriptions contribute to popular imaginings of Puerto Viejo as a "female sex tourism" destination. Within the literature female sexual tourism is usually understood as "sex tourists" or "romance tourists" with both concepts underscoring the economic exchanges between tourist and local. Hence privileged First World women are seen as consumers of sex and romance, and underprivileged dark-skinned men are commoditized.

The relationship is not so clear-cut, however, as Sheila Jeffreys (2003, 207) argues, "by virtue of male privilege and the construction of male dominant sexuality" female tourists are just as likely to "service" their local lovers, rather than the other way around. It seems that some women engaging in ethnosexual tourism appear more interested in being "swept away" by their local male lovers rather than asserting control over them. Taking a global view, women from First World countries do exert their relative economic control over local lovers and others in Third World countries but the power associated with masculinity complicates the encounters.

Frohlick (2007) is not the only one to examine Western white women travelers in the Caribbean. Other scholars have also written about women tourists in the Caribbean (Jeffreys 2003; Kempadoo 2004; Mullings 2000), specifically Jamaica (Pruitt and LaFont 1995; Sánchez Taylor 2001), the

Dominican Republic (O'Connell Davidson and Sánchez Taylor 2005), and
Barbados (Phillips 1999 and 2002). What Frohlick adds to this literature
is the idea that sexual relations between tourists and locals depend upon
gendered and racialized boundaries being both maintained and broken.
Gender matters when it comes to ethnosexual tourism. Puerto Viejo is like
many other ethnosexual tourist destinations where men avail themselves
sexually for foreign women yet these local men do not see themselves as
prostitutes, gigolos, or sex workers; rather, they consider themselves to be
"players" and "boyfriends" (Frohlick 2007; Phillips 2002). The ambiguity
of economic exchange is bound up with women's fantasies for romance
and emotional gratification rather than just sex with a local partner.
Monetary exchange does, however, take place. "Some men hustle women
upfront for cash or stuff. Other men want only sex (but nevertheless hope
to gain some material benefits), while some want to impregnate foreign
women" (Frohlick 2007, 142). As one male resident of Puerto Viejo says:
"We all say that girls from Europe are hot, really wild, they like sex"
(Frohlick 2007, 145). Other men may hope for land for a house or an air-
plane ticket to take them out of the country. Intimacy holds a significant
exchange value—it is what foreign women want from local lovers. Local
men use intimacy to both lure women into paying them and to regulate
foreign women's mobility.

In these sexual encounters with tourist women, men learn early on
that sexuality is bound up with race and ethnicity. Boys learn about sex
from older boys' and men's anecdotes. Luis, a Caribbean man who grew
up in Puerto Viejo, recalls: "You listen to men's stories and how they
used to have sex on the beach. The old men. Then you start to think of
that. Maybe I can take a walk on the beach with this girl. Then you see
this girl, and you try it" (Frohlick 2007, 149). Foreign women bring ideas
about black Caribbean men to Puerto Viejo and describe local black
men's beauty and well-toned physiques in terms of culture, history,
and genetics "effectively colonizing individual men into a stereotype of
pre-modern black male sexuality" (Frohlick 2007, 150). In the Caribbean,
black masculinity is sexualized through naturalizing global discourses
about erotic Others as attractive, virile, and masterful (Frohlick 2007;
Kempadoo 2004; Phillips 2002). A Canadian woman in her twenties told
Frohlick (2007, 151): "The men here are naturally buff. They fish. They
surf. They play soccer on the beach. They don't sit at desks all day, not
ever. They have inherited these genes from their Jamaican ancestors who
were slaves." Other women told Frohlick (2007) that men offer them access to material, corporeal, and proximate kinds of intimacy that they
cannot obtain at home:

There's an instant intimacy you get from the men here that you don't find at home. . . . They want you close to them. They cook for you. They wash your clothes for you. One boyfriend took care of me when I was sick, bringing me medicinal plants. They want to live with you as soon as they meet you. (Frohlick 2007, 154)

Feelings of intimacy are inscribed not only on to bodies, but also on to landscapes. Women reported to Frohlick (2008, 129) that they felt "more sexy here" in the Caribbean than in their Western homes. Through contemporary touristic mobilities these women are able to assert a sexual identity and agency.

One of Frohlick's participants, Zoe—a blonde, slim, attractive, white woman from the United States—engaged in ethnosexual tourism within the Caribbean "paradise" explaining it was not long after her arrival that she "found herself" sexually involved with a local man, who she described as "beautiful" and "like no man" she had ever met, a mixture of "a macho guy" (with scars from a brawl over a woman to prove it) and a "sweet-natured" domesticated "jungle man" who cooked for her (Frohlick 2008). Being in Puerto Viejo made Zoe, and other women in her situation, feel physically and sexually free. Zoe had not expected to become involved with anyone but was attracted to this particular man because he was "different" (from other local men and from US men). Zoe's perception of him as a naturalized feature of the Caribbean landscape (in the jungle cooking soup from wild native plants) draws upon discourses of the liberation of white femininity through travel mobility and "primitive," natural black male sexuality.

Her whiteness and his blackness meshed in the context of a Caribbean vacation and sensual landscape such that their mutual desire seemed "natural," yet played out through particular gendered, racialised, and sexualised mobilities, as well as a much wider and complicated history of contestations over white women with black men. (Frohlick 2008, 131)

Women's dreams, therefore, are firmly enmeshed in the fecund and ecologically lush environment; yet some women struggled bitterly when they found out about men's infidelity. Women felt they were in competition with each other for local lovers. One participant told Frohlick (2007, 159):

Women just don't talk to one another in this town. It's all kind of secret really. Women seem to compete with one another when they first arrive to attract a black Costa Rican man and nobody says anything because word spreads like fire. The men are very possessive, and intolerant of women who cheat. Yeah, double standards for sure. You never really know what they're doing during the day but they sure know what you're up to!

Female tourists arrive with money and dreams and a desire to play and relax in the Caribbean. Fantasies of Caribbean paradise have often been formed from childhood days. When they arrive they desire the closeness of a Caribbean man to help them fulfill their fantasies about a simple, pure and natural lifestyle. "Their ideas are often romantic, hopeful, and naïve about the harsher realities of being seen as a *gringa* from which to make money or to manipulate through sex and intimacies" (Frohlick 2007, 162). When these women choose to stay in the area to seek out relationships with local men their mobility is compromised. There are other costs for these women, such as a loss of their self-esteem, a feeling of "giving too much," and a loss of identity. Also, some women experience domestic abuse and poverty during their stay.

Before leaving the Caribbean tourist beach scene it is useful to also reflect on nonheterosexual intimate tourist encounters. Jasbir Puar (2001) recounts a series of events that occurred in the Caribbean starting with a gay cruise liner originating in the United States being refused docking privileges in the Cayman Islands. When other Caribbean governments heard about the cruise ship they too expressed an intention to refuse entry to that ship and any other gay cruise ship that might follow. Press releases reported that in the Bahamas a cruise ship with nine hundred gay and lesbian passengers had become "a test for tourist-dependent Caribbean Islands after the Cayman Islands refused the ship landing rights" (*Trinidad Express* 1998, 29; cited in Puar 2001, 1041). Island residents were not happy, even offended, when previous gay tours had landed. Gay male tourists were seen openly showing affection, such as kissing and holding hands, in public. While this controversy had played out in the Bahamas and Cayman Islands, gay and lesbian activists from Trinidad—the Caribbean Forum of Lesbians, All-Sexuals and Gays (C-FLAG), the Gay Enhancement Advocates of Trinidad and Tobago (GE-ATT), and the Artists Against AIDS—were outraged that the gay and lesbian cruise ships could be denied docking privileges. Furthermore, a US-based gay rights organization called on then British Prime Minister Tony Blair to intervene, which he did, saying that codes outlawing gays and lesbians breached the International Covenant of Human Rights (Puar 2001).

This example brings to our attention the irony of the United Kingdom and United States advocating protection for gay and lesbian cruise ships in the Caribbean while refusing to grant such "absolute rights" for the same passengers upon their return home. Furthermore, the official actions and statements of the two nations may well allow European-American cruise goers to leave the Caribbean with only a surface understanding of the complex homophobia of local governments, of local cultural assumptions about modes of sexual repression and liberations. (Puar 2001, 1045)

Since this incident, the number of gay and lesbian tourists interested in Trinidad as a tourist site has (somewhat ironically perhaps) increased. This is attributed to Trinidad's Carnival, which is known to be a gay-friendly event. The editors of *Out and About* (1996) note that "Trinidad's Carnival is the biggest gay event in the region" and claim "the gay community here is relatively closeted. . . . Gays play an important role in the social fabric of the country, especially the arts and in Carnival." The Carnival is held in the capital, Port-of-Spain, which is described as being

> diverse and sports a sizeable gay and lesbian population but, like many former British colonies, it is a bit conservative and the community is not readily visible to visitors, although it may surprise some visitors that gay men and lesbians regularly patronize a number of primarily straight bars. Visiting one of these . . . is recommended to visitors who want to make contact with local gay men and lesbians. From there, it's easy to take a taxi to a gay and lesbian nightspot. (Gay.com 2008)

The information about Trinidad at Gay.com nods to the complexity of what it means to be gay in Trinidad. Gay tourism is prompting a flow of Western queers, which prompts the question, what are the implications of this to sexual politics in the Caribbean? In the context of theorizing global intimacies queer identities are often difficult to translate across social and material spaces. In other words, people experience being queer differently in different spaces.

To continue the theme of queers moving across the globe to attend special events such as Trinidad's Carnival in the next section we focus on the Sydney Gay and Lesbian Mardi Gras. This is an annual gay pride parade or festival. It is the largest of its type in the world and attracts both local and international visitors. In 2008 Air New Zealand offered a special "gay flight" to take passengers from the United States, via New Zealand to Sydney for the festival. In the section that follows we focus on this flight to understand more about the various ways in which lesbians and gay men are constructed as global citizens and consumers.

FEATHER BOAS AND BOEING JETS

There is a growing literature on international queer tourism that acknowledges and analyzes gender and sexuality as key cultural constructs in the social construction of place, space, and global landscapes (see Aitchison 1999, 2001, 2003; Binnie 2004a; Puar 2002a, 2002b, 2002c; Del Casino and Hanna 2000; Richardson 2005). What we focus on here is a trend among some travel companies to target their marketing on the basis of sexual identity. Air New Zealand, for example, has attempted to reach gay, lesbian, bisexual, and transgendered customers by becoming a major sponsor of the Sydney Gay and Lesbian Mardi Gras festival. Early in 2008 Air New Zealand launched its Pink Flight, a Boeing 777 that took passengers from San Francisco to Sydney for the annual event (see Air New Zealand 2008b). This first ever North American gay-themed flight was decked out with pink décor (pink is a color often used to reflect gay identity). The outside of the Boeing was also given a makeover. The Boeing donned a 70-foot pink boa and 13-inch pink feathers were strategically placed to look like eyelashes (see figure 8.2).

Air New Zealand's flight crew also wore pink boas, pink hats, and gave a cabaret performance at the preparty held at the terminal's departure gate. Passengers received pink canapés and pink cocktails. Air New Zealand enlisted the entertainment services of comedian and Emmy-award winner diva Kathy Griffin, as well as drag queens. In a press release, Air New Zealand's vice president (US) said: "We knew that this party needed a hostess befitting of the eclectic and diverse group we are inviting on board for this celebration and who better than Kathy Griffin?" (Reuters 2008).

In addition to Griffin's performance, the Pink Flight offered onboard shows including drag shows, music, contests, screenings of gay-themed films, and scheduled beauty sleep periods. Onboard food was "pinked-up" and passengers made selections from pink cocktails, goodies bags, and had a "party wake up" before landing (Reuters 2008). According to Air New Zealand's US director of marketing, Jodi Williams: "Air New Zealand isn't an ordinary airline. . . . With us, our passengers' vacation starts as soon as they come on board. We make travel fun and relaxing for our guests, ensuring that their vacation experience begins long before they arrive to their final destination" (Reuters 2008).

In-flight attendents or "hostesses" including Miss Ribena, Buckwheat, Tess Tickle, Dallas Vixon, and Venus Mantrapp entertained and served guests (see figure 8.3). Passengers seemed appreciative of the effort that went toward the Pink Flight. One from Palm Springs in California commented: "As soon as we heard about this flight, we knew we had to signup. In fact, we were the first ones to purchase our tickets!" Another said: "The crew was fantastic. I've never seen an airline do something like this before!" (Reuters 2008). The pink celebrations took on a South Pacific feel during the last leg of the journey from Auckland to Sydney. Not only

Figure 8.2.   Air New Zealand's Pink Flight, nonstop from San Francisco to Sydney, on its way to Mardi Gras. Photograph appears courtesy of Air New Zealand Limited.

did customers receive pink feather boas, they also received leis (Hawaiian garlands), which were draped on them by Air New Zealand staff.

The 2008 Pink Flight followed Air New Zealand's inaugural Flight of the Fairies, which flew between Auckland and Sydney in 2007. Akersten (2008) interviewed "young people who were going to Mardi Gras for the first time, cool people, hot people. Merry talking heads giving us good

Figure 8.3. **Venus Mantrapp serving refreshments on Air New Zealand's Pink Flight to Sydney. Photograph by Matt Akersten, used with permission.**

Vox Pops about how 'fabulous,' 'exciting' and 'awesome' it all was." Air New Zealand provided retro-style zip-up travel cases and passengers were delighted to find one on each seat, "bright pink of course, with 'Pink Flight of Fabulousity' printed on the back, and containing a few 'goodies' like pink travel socks and VIP vouchers for Sydney nightspots. . . . And *Priscilla Queen of the Desert* was a very appropriate in-flight movie" (Akersten 2008). Recognizing that many gay, lesbian, bisexual, and transgendered people face discrimination and oppression when traveling, Air New Zealand constructed a queer-friendly in-flight space—high above the globe—to make their queer customers feel comfortable.

What this story about the Pink Fight and the Flight of the Fairies makes apparent is that gay identities are increasingly forged through consumption practices and this is especially the case in relation to international tourism. Over the years the development of queer global tourist destinations such as San Francisco, Sydney, Amsterdam, London, New York, and Paris has been very important to those wishing to attract the pink dollar or pink pound. Therefore, while we do not wish to diminish the fun and "fabulousity" of Air New Zealand's flights, it is important to place this example within the context of the global pink economy, an economy that Bob Cant suggests is potentially based upon uniformity and conformity. Cant (1997, 11) warns:

> The spread of McDonald's has been noted as one of the main results of the globalization of the economy. What could emerge for the lesbian and gay communities is the spread of McPink—a global pink economy which promotes a series of ever-changing lifestyle options. The pink economy could be the unaccountable motor of a new conformity that packages the desirable and rejects those who do not fit in as vigorously as did any traditional community.

This point has also been made by other scholars who argue that lesbians and gay men as global consumer citizens may mean support for, and adherence to, dominant cultural norms and values as key mechanisms of social inclusion (Bell and Binnie 2000; Cooper 2004; Evans 1993; Richardson 2005). One can see this in the arguments developed by neoconservative gay writers such as Bruce Bawer (1993) who asserts that the lifestyle of most mainstream gays is identical to that of most heterosexual couples in similar professional and economic circumstances. Another gay writer, Andrew Sullivan (1995), advances a similar argument claiming that the majority of lesbian and gay individuals have the same aspirations, goals, and lifestyles as most heterosexuals and desire nothing more than to be fully integrated into society as consuming global citizens. If queers are to be mainstreamed then sameness is asserted over difference. Marginalized from this global mainstream McPink economy are those who are "trapped in poverty, unable to buy into the 'global gay lifestyle'" (Bell and Binnie 2000, 116).

As a major sponsor of the Sydney Gay and Lesbian Mardi Gras, Air New Zealand is following US trends. Gay pride groups used to be independent and community-funded but are now reliant upon sponsorship deals with mainstream transnational corporations such as Absolut Vodka and American Airlines (Woods 1995). Alexandra Chasin (2000) argues that as gay pride events in the United States have become more commercialized they have had to transform themselves into professional organizations, with paid positions for parade organizers whose job is to obtain corporate sponsorship. The shift to larger, national organizations with scaled up budgets supported by transnational corporate funding can benefit lesbian and gay movements through increased visibility and "authority" (Bawer 1993) yet there are tensions, in particular, the ways in which such changes may constrain political activity (Richardson 2005). For example:

> among gay-related causes, the smaller, more local, more grassroots organisa- tions, and those working for radical social change, are surely those the least favoured by funders. As a result, market related funding mechanisms— while providing increased visibility for the larger national service-oriented organizations—can contribute to the invisibility and/or the de-resourcing of less mainstream organisations. (Chasin 2000, 202)

There is a new level of accountability evident in lesbian and gay politics. Political organizations are increasingly accountable not only to their political constituency but also to the corporate interests who fund them. "Where these relationships of accountability are in conflict with one an- other, then organisations may feel constrained to act in ways that satisfy funders and further mainstreaming can occur" (Richardson 2005, 528).

If there are funding tensions for the Sydney Gay and Lesbian Mardi Gras organizers, they are not obvious. Air New Zealand continues to build on the success of the Pink Flight and more are planned. A dedicated "Gay and Lesbian Travel Air New Zealand" webpage greets potential customers with the following message:

> Whichever way you go, Air New Zealand takes you there. We have flights to great gay and lesbian friendly destinations in New Zealand and Australia and the UK. The famous Sydney Mardi Gras (The Gay Pride Parade and par- ties) in March, London Gay Pride in July and New Zealand Gay Ski Week at the end of August are just a few exciting events we can take you to. We celebrate diversity—it's the Kiwi [New Zealand] way! (Air New Zealand 2008a)

Potential passengers are directed to a series of links that offer advice on travel for gays and lesbians including tours. There is also a link to a sec- tion titled "Interesting Facts about New Zealand's Civil Rights." We are not suggesting, therefore, that globalization *always* produces sameness, yet to some extent it may deny local specificity and exclude those whose identities, for whatever reason, are not founded on consumption prac- tices. The danger associated with a globalized notion of sexual citizenship is that *being gay* may become synonymous with a homogenous identity based on the ability to *buy* particular lifestyles. Assumed homogeneity, however, may mask a multitude of local differences.

In this chapter we have presented just four examples of global intima- cies. These examples speak to the diversity of desire, romance, sex, and love that cross national, social, cultural, and racial borders. While these examples are global they are also local in a sense (individuals who are part of a community who cross the globe to meet other individuals and in the process form new communities). To reiterate a point made at the outset, the production of scale is itself a political process. Different scales overlap, are fluid and contingent. We think it is useful, therefore, to examine sexual subjectivities and practices from a range of different scales, each one representing an intersection between a range of different people and places.

9

Conclusion

It is never easy summing up what one has written in a book—arriving at the end and needing to formulate something profound and coherent about what it all might mean and where one might go to from this point. In concluding *Geographies of Sexualities* (2007, 215) Lim, Brown, and Browne wanted to offer something that was *not* coherent and that

> didn't offer a single conclusion, or even a number of conclusions. Rather, I [Kath] wanted to finish messy—to have something that highlighted not just the variety of views we the editors have on queer theory, queer geographies and geographies of sexualities, but also something that showed how co-writing both enriches texts and has an excess where individualities are necessarily co-opted into a broader frame.

This helped us think about how we have written this book from some shared places and spaces but also from some different ones. We both work in the Geography Department at the University of Waikato but one of us is offered on a daily basis all the privileges of leading a life that is considered to be normal (married with two sons) while the other faces challenges of being lesbian/queer in the academy and more generally. While some previously marginalized sexualities have now become more socially and politically accepted (even fashionable and cosmopolitan as we have argued in this book), this can certainly not be relied upon and many social situations can end in an awkward silence or worse. This is not to say that one of us is completely positioned as normal and the other as dissident. There are contradictions here (even at the level that not all heterosexual practices can be considered "normal"). Both of us are white and aged in our midforties. However, one of us has long struggled with being large or fat and all the prejudice that engenders; the other is petite. One of us is from an urban background; the other grew up in a rural setting. Co- and multiauthored texts, however, tend to offer a unified voice that makes these embodied differences—sexual and other—invisible. We could have chosen to write this conclusion by each contributing a section in our own voice (like Lim, Brown, and Browne 2007) but decided given that there is at least as much, if not more, that has united us rather than divided us in this project we would write the chapter, like the rest of the book, jointly.

While *Space, Place, and Sex* is certainly not specific to Aotearoa New Zealand in that we draw on information from a variety of sources and countries, we are aware in looking back over the text that it does contain a number of examples that draw on our experiences of living "down under." Perhaps this is somewhat inevitable given that as we noted in the preface, all knowledge is "positioned"; that is, it comes from somewhere. As geographers we are especially aware of this and in New Zealand we tend to occupy something of a paradoxical position in relation to geographical scholarship (Berg and Kearns 1998; Binnie, Longhurst, and Peace 2001). We think this makes our experiences interesting. On the one hand, we are very much part of and contribute to Anglo-American geographies. Most of us think and write in English and publish mainly in Anglo-American journals and books. On the other hand, geographers in New Zealand tend to respond to "down under" issues (see the collection "Geographies of Sexuality and Gender 'Down Under'" in *Australian Geographer* 2008, vol. 39, no. 3) such as colonization, rural subjectivities and spaces, and Māori geographies.

We hope this paradoxical positioning has resulted in a book that readers from elsewhere (close to and well beyond the shores of New Zealand) will be able to appreciate as both connecting to their own experiences as well as offering new insights from another place. As we have researched and written the book we have talked with and listened to people at home and overseas while at the same time trying to understand ourselves, including our academic practices. During the years of writing we have been prompted to think about the production and politics of academic knowledge. Sibley (1995, 121) argues that the "issue of what, within the academy, counts as legitimate knowledge is a complex one." Sibley notes that it matters *who* produces the knowledge (for example, white and female academics). It also matters where knowledge is produced.

THE ARGUMENT

The aim of this book was to illustrate that in order to understand the production and expression of sexual identities and practices whether they be lesbian, gay, bisexual, transsexual, intersex, queer, heterosexual, or something else we can enrich our understanding by considering space and place at a variety of spatial scales. The research draws on feminist poststructuralist theory to argue that the body is discursively produced but is also more than text. It has an undeniable materiality.

Over the past decade there has emerged a substantial corpus of research on sex and sexuality within geography. However, Lim, Brown, and Browne (2007, 219) suggest that there are "some strands of work that are, as yet, underdeveloped within the geographies of sexualities literature" [Gavin]. One strand of work is that which uses the notion of geographical scale for thinking about specific kinds of sexual-social activities. Issues of space, place, territories, borders, and boundaries in relation to sex and sexuality need to be explored in greater depth and at a range of scales. Bodies, homes, communities, cities, rural spaces, nations, and the globe are mutually constituted in uneven ways that are rarely reiterated uniformly. It is important to think about space, place, and sex at a variety of spatial scales, from the micro level to the macro level. The sexed body is as political as the nation-state. As a generalization, geographers have been effective at looking at the broader picture but this has sometimes been at the expense of finer detail—the sexually embodied geographies. In order to understand the relationships between people and places it is necessary to address a variety of scales. The purpose of this book was to make a contribution in this area. We wanted to unravel some of the diversity and complexity that surrounds and inhabits the embodied experiences of sex and sexuality and illustrate that sexed bodies are constructed through different social and cultural entanglements and through different spaces and places at a range of spatial scales.

Space, Place, and Sex illustrates that sexed bodies and spaces are neither autonomous nor coherent. It is important to recognize complex practices surrounding the subjectivities and spaces of sexuality at a variety of different spatial scales. Throughout the book we filtered sexed bodies through a geographical lens. At no point was the plan to offer a comprehensive account of sex and sexuality but rather a series of snapshots using different lenses—from micro to macro scale—to prompt new ways of thinking about what it means to "perform" different sexual subjectivities in particular spaces and places.

We have drawn from our own experiences and research over the past decade and on the work of others, especially but not solely gay, lesbian, queer, feminist, social, and cultural geographers. We have read, cut out, and reported on articles that caught our attention in newspapers and other popular media. We have also sought information online. While some of this information may not be considered to be particularly scholarly, we maintain that the Internet is a rich source of material on sex and sexuality that reflects and reinforces social trends, community groupings, and conversations that are also happening in "real" space.

THE IMPLICATIONS

In 1997 Jon Binnie made an important intervention into geographical knowledge by calling for a queering of the discipline. He argued that it was imperative not simply to add knowledge about sex and sexuality to an unchanged geographical canon but to shake up the dispassionate rationalism of the academy by exposing its silences and institutionalized homophobia (also see Keith 1992 on "angry writing"). Binnie and Valentine (1999) argue that although there has been rapid growth in work on geographies of sexualities over the past decade there is still a great deal of homophobia within the discipline as a whole. Of course this homophobia exists not just in the discipline of geography but also in other disciplines, and well beyond the academy.

This book is about sex and sexuality but arguably it is also about more than this. It is about queering knowledge and opening up a small space in which it is possible to talk about the sexed, sexy, sensual, and sexual body. As one of us has argued elsewhere, although geographers began in the 1990s to examine more explicitly the politics of embodiment and spatiality, often the body under examination was a kind of "disembodied body." It was a body that did not seem to have specific genitalia or that broke its boundaries (Longhurst 2001). It seemed to be a fleshless kind of "tidy" body that really did little to disrupt the rationalism of the discipline of geography. The fleshiness of the sexed, sexy, sensual, and sexual body—of skin, desire, love, fluid, stains, leakage, friction, orgasm—was missing, and is still missing for the most part from most geography texts on sexual theory and practices. We think it is fair to say that geography has been queered by a focus on sexed bodies but perhaps just "a little bit . . . the institutional and institutionalized homophobia and erotophobia at the heart of geography is still there, arguably as strong as ever" (Bell 2007, 86).

This book, then, is just one more small step along the way to being able to talk about bodies, power, sex, sexuality, the erotic, love, desire, pain, pleasure, and geography in the same breath. Discussing topics such as asexuality, polyamory, homeless people having sex, a small town that became known as the sex change capital of the world, and bestiality pushes the boundaries of what geographers perceive to be important and relevant as sites of investigation. More, however, remains to be done if the task of creating new knowledge about the diversity of sexualities and spaces is to be realized. A continued interrogation of "space, place, and sex" is required in order to further understand the myriad of ways in which power and knowledge filter through sexed, sexy, sensual, and sexual bodies.

References

Adam, Barry D. 1995. *The Rise of the Gay and Lesbian Movement.* Boston: Twayne.

———. 2003. "The Defense of Marriage Act and American Exceptionalism: The 'Gay Marriage' Panic in the United States." *Journal of the History of Sexuality* 12, no. 2: 259–76.

Agathangelou, Anna M. 2004. *The Global Political Economy of Sex: Desire, Violence and Insecurity in Mediterranean Nation-States.* New York: Palgrave.

Air New Zealand. 2008a. "Gay and Lesbian Travel." www.airnewzealand.com/bookings/gayandlesbiantravel/default.htm (accessed November 29, 2008).

———. 2008b. "Pink Flight." www.airnewzealand.com/pinkflight (accessed November 26, 2008).

Aitchison, Cara. 1999. "New Cultural Geographies: The Spatiality of Leisure, Gender and Sexuality." *Leisure Studies* 18: 19–39.

———. 2001. "Theorizing Other Discourses of Tourism, Gender and Culture: Can the Subaltern Speak (in Tourism)?" *Tourist Studies* 1, no. 2: 133–47.

———. 2003. *Gender and Leisure: Social and Cultural Perspectives.* London: Routledge.

Aizura, Aren. 2006. "Of Borders and Homes: The Imaginary Community of (Trans)sexual Citizenship." *Inter-Asian Cultural Studies* 7, no. 2: 289–309.

Akersten, Matt. 2008. "Mission to Mardi Gras: Gays on a Plane." GayNZ.com, March 7, www.gaynz.com/articles/publish/21/article_5671.php (accessed March 8, 2008).

Alexeyeff, Kalissa. 2000. "Dragging Drag: The Performance of Gender and Sexuality in the Cook Islands—Dancing." *Australian Journal of Anthropology* 11, no. 3: 297–308.

Anderson, Benedict. 1983. *Imagined Communities: Reflections on the Origin and Spread of Nationalism.* London: Verso.

Anderson, Kay. 1995. "Culture and Nature at the Adelaide Zoo: At the Frontiers of 'Human Geography.'" *Transactions, Institute of British Geographers* 2, no. 3: 275–94.

Angeles, Leonora, and Sirijit Sunanta. 2007. "'Exotic Love at Your Fingertips': Intermarriage Websites, Gendered Representation and the Transnational Migration of Filipino and Thai Women." *Kasarinlan: Philippine Journal of Third World Studies* 22, no. 1: 3–31.

Asexuality Aotearoa New Zealand. 2008. "News." August. www.asexuality.org.nz/news.htm (accessed August 23, 2008).

Asis, Maruja, B. Milagros, Shirlena Huang, and Brenda S. A. Yeoh. 2004. "When the Light of the Home Is Abroad: Unskilled Female Migration and the Filipino Family." *Singapore Journal of Tropical Geography* 25, no. 2: 198–215.

Aspin, Clive. 2007. "Of Two Spirits: An Interview with Georgina Beyer, Member of Parliament." In *Sexuality and the Stories of Indigenous People*, ed. Jessica Hutchings and Clive Aspin, 70–81. Wellington, NZ: Huia Press.

Atkinson, David, Peter Jackson, David Sibley, and Neil Washbourne. 2005. "Introduction: Borders and Boundaries." In *Cultural Geography: A Critical Dictionary of Key Concepts*, ed. David Atkinson, Peter Jackson, David Sibley, and Neil Washbourne, 153–54. New York: I. B. Tauris.

Australian Geographer. 2008. "Geographies of Sexuality and Gender 'Down Under.'" Special issue, 39, no. 3.

AVEN, the Asexuality Visibility and Education Network. 2008. www.asexuality.org/home/ (accessed November 14, 2008).

Bain, Alison L., and Catherine J. Nash. 2006. "Undressing the Researcher: Feminism, Embodiment and Sexuality at a Queer Bathhouse Event." *Area* 38, no. 1: 99–106.

Baker, Andrea. 2000. "Two by Two in Cyberspace: Getting Together and Connecting Online." *CyberPsychology & Behaviour* 3, no 2: 237–42.

Banim, Maura, Eileen Green, and Ali Guy. 2001. "Introduction." In *Through the Wardrobe: Women's Relationships with Their Clothes*, ed. Ali Guy, Eileen Green, and Maura Banim, 1–17. Oxford: Berg.

Barraket, Jo, and Millsom Henry-Waring. 2004. "'Everybody's Doing It': Examining the Impacts of Online Dating." The Australian Sociological Association Conference, La Trobe University, Beechworth Campus, December 8–11, 2004.

Bawer, Bruce. 1993. *A Place at the Table: The Gay Individual in American Society*. New York: Poseidon Press.

BBC News. 2007. "Australian Pub Bars Heterosexuals." May 28, news.bbc.co.uk/2/hi/asia-pacific/6697469.stm (accessed August 30, 2007).

Beck, Ulrich. 2002. "The Cosmopolitan Society and Its Enemies." *Theory, Culture and Society* 19, 17–44.

Beere, Paul. 2007. "The Fast and the Spurious: Geographies of Youth Car Culture in Hamilton, New Zealand." Master's thesis, University of Waikato, Hamilton, New Zealand.

Bell, David. 1992. "What We Talk About When We Talk About Love: A Comment on Hay (1991)." *Area* 24: 409–10.

———. 1994a. "Erotic Topographies: On the Sexuality and Space Network." *Antipode* 2, no. 1: 96–100.

———. 1994b. "In Bed with M E Robinson." *Area* 26: 86–89.

———. 2000a. "Eroticising the Rural." In *De-Centring Sexualities: Politics and Representations Beyond the Metropolis,* ed. Richard Philip, David Watt, and Diane Shuttleton, 83–101. London: Routledge.

———. 2000b. "Farm Boys and Wild Men: Rurality, Masculinity, and Homosexuality." *Rural Sociology* 65, 547–61.

———. 2003. "Homosexuals in the Heartland: Male Same-Sex Desire in the Rural United States." In *Country Visions,* ed. Paul Cloke, 178–94. London: Prentice Hall.

———. 2006. "Bodies, Technologies, Spaces: On 'Dogging.'" *Sexualities* 9, no. 4: 387–407.

———. 2007. "Fucking Geography, Again." In *Geographies of Sexualities: Theories, Practices and Politics,* ed. Kath Browne, Jason Lim, and Gavin Brown, 81–86. Aldershot: Ashgate.

Bell, David, and Jon Binnie. 2000. *The Sexual Citizen: Queer Politics and Beyond.* Cambridge: Polity Press.

———. 2002. "Sexual Citizenship: Marriage, the Market and the Military." In *Handbook of Lesbian and Gay Studies,* ed. Diane Richardson and Steven Seidman, 443–57. London: Sage.

———. 2006. "Editorial: Geographies of Sexual Citizenship." *Political Geography* 25, no. 8: 869–73.

Bell, David, Jon Binnie, Julia Cream, and Gill Valentine. 1994. "All Hyped Up and No Place to Go." *Gender, Place and Culture: A Journal of Feminist Geography* 1, no. 1: 31–47.

Bell, David, and Ruth Holliday. 2000. "Naked as Nature Intended." *Body and Society* 6, no. 3–4, 127–40.

Bell, David, and Gill Valentine, eds. 1995a. *Mapping Desire: Geographies of Sexualities,* London: Routledge.

———. 1995b. "Queer Country: Rural Lesbian and Gay Lives." *Journal of Rural Studies* 11, 113–22.

Berg, Lawrence, and Robin Kearns. 1998. "American Unlimited." *Environment and Planning D: Society and Space* 16, 128–32.

Berlant, Lauren. 1998. "Intimacy: A Special Issue." *Critical Inquiry* 24, no. 2: 281–88.

Berlant, Lauren, and Michael Warner. 1998. "Sex in Public." *Critical Inquiry* 24, no. 2: 547–66.

Besio, Kathryn, Lynda Johnston, and Robyn Longhurst. 2008. "Sexy Beasts and Devoted Mums: Narrating Nature through Dolphin Tourism." *Environment and Planning A* 40, no. 5: 1219–34.

Besnier, Niko. 2002. "Transgenderism, Locality, and the Miss Galaxy Beauty Pageant in Tonga." *American Ethnologist* 29, no. 3: 534–66.

———. 2004. "The Social Production of Abjection: Desire and Silencing among Transgender Tongans." *Social Anthropology* 12, no. 3: 301–23.

Beyer, Georgina, and Cathy Casey. 1999. *Change for the Better: The Story of Georgina Beyer as told to Cathy Casey*. Auckland: Random House.

Bhatti, Mark, and Andrew Church. 2000. "'I Never Promised You a Rose Garden': Gender, Leisure and Home-Making." *Leisure Studies*, 19, no. 3: 183–97.

Binnie, Jon. 1995. "Trading Places: Consumption, Sexuality and the Production of Queer Space." In *Mapping Desire*, ed. David Bell and Gill Valentine, 182–99. London: Routledge.

———. 1997. "Coming Out of Geography: Towards a Queer Epistemology." *Environment and Planning D: Society and Space* 15, no. 2: 223–37.

———. 2000. "Cosmopolitanism and the Sexed City." In *City Visions*, ed. David Bell and Azzedine Haddour, 166–78. Harlow: Prentice Hall.

———. 2004a. *The Globalization of Sexuality*. London: Sage.

———. 2004b. "Quartering Sexualities: Gay Villages and Sexual Citizenship." In *City of Quarters: Urban Villages in the Contemporary City*, ed. David Bell and Mark Jayne, 163–72. Aldershot: Ashgate.

———. 2007. "Sexuality, the Erotic and Geography." In *Geographies of Sexualities*, ed. Kath Browne, Gavin Brown, and Jason Lim, 29–38. London: Ashgate.

Binnie, Jon, Robyn Longhurst, and Robin Peace. 2001. "Upstairs/Downstairs— Place Matters, Bodies Matter." In *Pleasure Zones: Bodies, Cities, Spaces*, ed. David Bell, Jon Binnie, Robyn Longhurst, and Robin Peace, vii–xiv. Syracuse, NY: Syracuse University Press.

Binnie, Jon, and Gill Valentine. 1999. "Geographies of Sexuality—A Review of Progress." *Progress in Human Geography* 23, no. 2: 175–87.

Bird, Susan. 2002. "Case Note: *Re Kevin (Validity of Marriage of Transsexual) [2001] FamCA 1074*," *Southern Cross Law Review*, 6: 364–71.

Blundell, Kay. 2008. "Kapiti Coast Beaches Going Nude?" *The Dominion Post*, September 15, Stuff.co.nz www.stuff.co.nz/4692491a11.html (accessed September 18, 2008).

Blunt, Alison. 2002. "'Land of Our Mothers': Home, Identity, and Nationality for Anglo-Indians in British India 1919–1947." *History Workshop Journal* 5, no. 1: 49–72.

———. 2005. "Cultural Geography: Cultural Geographies of Home." *Progress in Human Geography* 29, no. 4: 505–15.

Blunt, Alison, and Robyn Dowling. 2006. *Home*. Oxon: Routledge.

Blunt, Alison, and Ann Varley. 2004. "Geographies of Home." *Cultural Geographies* 11, no. 1: 3–6.

Boswell, J. 1950. *Boswell's London Journal*. London: Heinmann.

Brown, Michael. 2000. *Closet Space: Geographies of Metaphor from the Body to the Globe*. London: Routledge.

Brown, Michael, and Claire Rasmussen. 2009. "Bestiality and the Queering of the Human Animal." *Environment and Planning D: Society and Space*, online advanced publication.

Browne, Kath. 2004. "Genderism and the Bathroom Problem: (Re)Materialising Sexed Sites, (Re)Creating Sexed Bodies." *Gender, Place and Culture: A Journal of Feminist Geography* 11, no. 3: 331–46.

———. 2006a. "'A Right Geezer-Bird (Man-Woman)': The Sites and Sights of 'Female' Embodiment." *ACME: An International E-Journal for Critical Geographies* 5, no. 2: 121–43.

———. 2006b. Review of "Queer Migrations: Sexuality, US Citizenship and Border Crossings." *Gender, Place and Culture: A Journal of Feminist Geography* 13, no. 4: 461–63.

———. 2007. "Drag Queens and Drab Dykes: Deploring and Deploying Femininities." In *Geographies of Sexualities: Theory, Practice and Politics*, ed. Kath Browne, Jason Lim, and Gavin Brown, 113–24. London: Ashgate.

Browne, Kath, Jason Lim, and Gavin Brown, eds. 2007. *Geographies of Sexualities: Theories, Practices and Politics*. Aldershot: Ashgate.

Bryld, Mette, and Nina Lykke. 2000. *Cosmodolphins: Feminist Cultural Studies of Technology, Animals and the Sacred*. London: Zed Books.

Bryson, Mary. 2004. "When Jill Jacks In: Queer Women and the Net." *Feminist Media Studies* 4, no. 3: 239–54.

Butler, Judith. 1990. *Gender Trouble: Feminism and the Subversion of Identity*. London: Routledge.

———. 1993. *Bodies That Matter: On the Discursive Limits Of Sex*. London: Routledge.

Califia, Pat. 1994. *Public Sex: The Culture of Radical Sex*. Pittsburgh: Cleis.

Campbell, Hugh. 2000. "The Glass Phallus: Pub(lic) Masculinity and Drinking in Rural New Zealand: Rural Masculinities." *Rural Sociology* 65, no. 4: 562–81.

Campbell, Hugh, Robin Law, and James Honeyfield. 1999. "What It Means to Be a Man: Hegemonic Masculinity and the Reinvention of Beer." In *Masculinities in Aotearoa/New Zealand*, ed. Robin Law, Hugh Campbell and John Dolan, 166–86. Palmerston North, NZ: Dunmore Press.

Cant, Bob. 1997. "Introduction." In *Invented Identities: Lesbians and Gays Talk About Migration*, ed. Bob Cant, 1–18. London: Cassell.

Cashmere Heights Weddings. 2004. www.chc-weddings.co.nz/ (accessed July 3, 2004).

Cater, John, and Trevor Jones. 1989. *Social Geography: An Introduction to Contemporary Issues*. London: Edward Arnold.

Chasin, Alexandra. 2000. *Selling Out: The Gay and Lesbian Movement Goes to Market*. New York: St Martin's Press.

Chauncey, George. 1994. *Gay New York: Gender, Urban Culture, and the Making of the Gay Male World, 1890–1940*. New York: Basic Books.

Cherlin, Andrew. 2004. "The Deinstitutionalization of American Marriage." *Journal of Marriage and Family* 66, 848–61.

Chow-White, Peter A. 2006. "Race, Gender and Sex on the Net: Semantic Networks of Selling and Storytelling Sex Tourism." *Media Culture Society* 28, no. 6: 883–905.

Cloke, Paul, and Jo Little, eds. 1997. *Contested Countryside: Otherness, Marginality and Rurality*. London: Routledge.

Cloke, Paul, and Harvey Perkins. 1998. "'Cracking the Canyon of the Awesome Foursome': Representations of Adventure Tourism in New Zealand." *Environment and Planning D: Society and Space* 16, no. 2: 185–218.

———. 2005. "Cetacean Performance and Tourism in Kaikoura, New Zealand." *Environment and Planning D: Society and Space* 23, no. 6: 903–24.

Cody, Paul, and Peter Welch. 1997. "Rural Gay Men in Northern New England: Life Experiences and Coping Styles." *Journal of Homosexuality* 33, no. 1: 51–67.

Cohen, Roger. 2000. "Night Moves of All Kinds: Berlin." *New York Times*, September 17, Travel section, 11.

Constable, Nicole. 2003. *Romance on a Global Stage: Pen Pals, Virtual Ethnography, and "Mail-Order" Marriages*. Berkeley: University of California Press.

Cooper, Davina. 2004. *Challenging Diversity: Rethinking Equality and the Value of Difference*. Cambridge: Cambridge University Press.

Country Living. 1999. "The Farmer Wants a Wife." November, 50, 53–61.

Country Living. 2004. "Reviving Rural Romance." February, 44–66.

Cream, Julia. 1995. "Re-Solving Riddles: The Sexed Body." In *Mapping Desire: Geographies of Sexualities*, ed. David Bell and Gill Valentine, 31–40. London: Routledge.

Creed, Gerald, and Barbara Ching. 1997. "Recognizing Rusticity: Identity and the Power of Place." In *Knowing Your Place: Rural Identity and Cultural Hierarchy*, ed. Gerald Creed and Barbara Ching, 1–38. New York: Routledge.

Cresswell, Tim. 1999. "Embodiment, Power and the Politics of Mobility: The Case of Female Tramps and Hobos." *Transactions of the Institute of British Geographers* 24, no. 2: 175–92.

———. 2005. "Moral Geographies." In *Cultural Geography: A Critical Dictionary of Key Concepts*, ed. David Atkinson, Peter Jackson, David Sibley, and Neil Washbourne, 231–48. London: I. B. Tauris.

Currah, Paisley, and Shannon Minter. 2000. "Unprincipled Exclusions: The Struggle to Achieve Judical and Legislative Equality for Transgendered People." *William and Mary Journal of Women and Law* 7, no. 1: 37–64.

d.vice. 2008. "Vibrators." www.dvice.co.nz/sex-toys/vibrators/pearl+%26+tickler/5756-pearl-dolphin-deluxe (accessed November 17, 2008).

Daily Mail Online. 2008. "Amazing Pictures of Pregnant Man as He Tells Oprah 'People May Try to Kill My Baby.'" April 4, www.dailymail.co.uk/news/article-555473/Amazing-pictures-pregnant-man-tells-Oprah-people-try-kill-baby.html (accessed June 19, 2008).

Daley, Christine. 2005. "From Bush to Beach: Nudism in Australasia." *Journal of Historical Geography* 31: 149–67.

Davidson, Joyce, and Christine Milligan. 2004. "Editorial. Embodying Emotion Sensing Space: Introducing Emotion Geographies." *Social & Cultural Geography* 5, no. 4: 523–32.

Davies, Gail. 2000. "Virtual Animals in Electronic Zoos: The Changing Geographies of Animal Capture and Display." In *Animal Places, Beastly Places: New Geographies of Human-Animal Relation*, ed. Chris Philo and Chris Wilbert, 243–67. London: Routledge.

Defoe, Daniel. 1978. *The Fortunes and Misfortunes of the Famous Moll Flanders*. Harmondsworth: Penguin.

Dekkers, Midas. 2000. *Dearest Pet: On Bestiality*. London: Verso.

Delaney, David, and Helga Leitner. 1997. "The Political Construction of Scale." *Political Geography* 16, no. 2: 93–97.

Del Casino, Vincent J., Jr., and Stephen P. Hanna. 2000. "Representations and Identities in Tourism Map Spaces." *Progress in Human Geography* 24, no. 1: 23–46.

Doan, Petra L. 2007. "Queers in the American City: Transgendered Perceptions of Urban Space." *Gender, Place and Culture: A Journal of Feminist Geography* 14, no. 1: 57–74.

Doane, Seth. 2008. "The Sex Change Capital of the U.S." CBS News, September 7, www.cbsnews.com/stories/2008/09/07/sunday/main4423154.shtml (accessed November 7, 2008).

Dobash, R. Emerson, and Russell P. Dobash. 1998. "Cross-Border Encounters: Challenges and Opportunities." In *Rethinking Violence against Women*, ed. R. Emerson Dobash and Russell P. Dobash, 1–21. London: Sage.

Dominion Post. 2007. "Cleavage Complaint Likely to Fail." September 26, www.stuff.co.nz/stuff/dominionpost/4215209a6479.html (accessed September 26, 2007).

Domosh, Mona. 1998. "Geography and Gender: Home, Again?" *Progress in Human Geography* 22: 276–82.

Doran, Matt. 2007. "Gay Pub Can Ban Heterosexual Drinkers." News.com.au, May 28, www.news.com.au/story/0,23599,21804872-2,00.html (accessed May 28, 2007).

Douglas, Mary. 1966. *Purity and Danger: An Analysis of Concepts of Pollution and Taboo*. London: Routledge and Kegan Paul.

——. 1975. *Implicit Meanings: Essay in Anthropology*. London: Routledge.

Downey, Robyn. 2008. "Bachelor Likes 'a Real Woman.'" June 18, www.stuff.co.nz/northland/4586846a1927.html (accessed November 12, 2008).

Duggan, Lisa. 2002. "The New Homonormativity: The Sexual Politics of Neoliberalism." In *Materializing Democracy: Towards a Revitalized Cultural Politics*, ed. Russ Castronova and Dana Nelson, 175–94. Durham NC: Duke University Press.

Duncan, Nancy. 1996. *Body Space: Destabilizing Geographies of Gender and Sexuality*. London: Routledge.

Dwyer, Claire. 1999. "Veiled Meanings: Young British Muslim Women and the Negotiation of Differences." *Gender, Place and Culture: A Journal of Feminist Geography* 6, no. 1: 5–26.

Elder, Glen, Jennifer Wolch, and Jody Emel. 1998. "*Le Pratique Sauvage*: Race, Place, and the Human-Animal Divide." In *Animal Geographies*, ed. Jennifer Wolch and Jody Emel, 72–90. London: Verso.

Elwood, Sarah A. 2000. "Lesbian Living Spaces: Multiple Meanings of Home." *Journal of Lesbian Studies* 4, no. 1: 11–27.

Embarrassing Problems.com. 2003. "Breasts in Men." www.embarrassingproblems.co.uk/breasts_g.htm (accessed September 12, 2003).

Emerton, Robyn. 2006. "Finding a Voice, Fighting for Rights: The Emergence of the Transgender Movement in Hong Kong." *Inter-Asia Cultural Studies* 7, no. 2: 243–69.

Enting, Carolyn. 2008. "Yummy Mummy or Hot Momma?" *Dominion Post*, July 25, at www.stuff.co.nz/print/4631530a11215.html (accessed September 2, 2008).

Evans, David. 1993. *Sexual Citizenship: The Material Construction of Sexualities*. London: Routledge.

Faderman, Lillian. 1991. *Odd Girls and Twilight Lovers: History of Lesbian Life in Twentieth-Century America*. New York: Columbia University Press.

Featherstone, Mike. 1998. The *Flâneur*, the City and Virtual Public Life, *Urban Studies* 35: 909–25.

Federation of Gay Games (FGG). 2008. "The Gay Games Can and Are Changing the World!" www.gaygames.com.en/federation/index.htm (accessed September 20, 2008).

Fellows, William D. 1996. *Farm Boys: Lives of Gay Men from the Rural Midwest*. Madison: University of Wisconsin Press.

Fieldays. 2008. "The Largest Agricultural Event in the Southern Hemisphere." www.fieldays.co.nz/ (accessed October 8, 2008).

Fifth Season. 2008. www.fifthseason.co.nz/ (accessed September 25, 2008).

Floyd, Janet. 2004. "Coming Out of the Kitchen: Texts, Contexts and Debates." *Cultural Geographies* 11, no. 1: 61–73.

Foucault, Michel. 1977. *Discipline and Punish: The Birth of the Prison*. Alan Sheridan, trans. London: Penguin.

———. 1978. *The History of Sexuality, vol. 1: An Introduction*. Robert Hurley, trans. London: Penguin.

Forsyth, Ann. 1997a. "'Out' in the Valley." *International Journal of Urban and Regional Research* 21: 38–62.

———. 1997b. "NoHo: Upscaling Main Street on the Metropolitan Edge." *Urban Geography* 18: 622–52.

Fox, Margalit. 2006. "Stanley H. Biber, 82, Surgeon Among First to do Sex Changes, Dies." *New York Times*, January 21, www.nytimes.com/2006/01/21/national/21biber.html?_r=1&oref=slogin (accessed November 12, 2008).

Freeman, Elizabeth. 2002. *The Wedding Complex: Forms of Belonging in Modern American Culture*. Durham and London: Duke University Press.

Frohlick, Susan. 2007. "The Negotiation of Intimacy between Tourist Women and Local Men in a Transnational Town in Caribbean Costa Rica." *City and Society* 19, no. 1: 139–68.

———. 2008. "'I'm More Sexy Here': Erotic Subjectivities of Female Tourists in the 'Sexual Paradise' of Caribbean Costa Rica." In *Gendered Mobilities*, ed. Tanu Priya Uteng and Tim Cresswell, 129–42. Aldershot: Ashgate.

Fuss, Diana. 1989. *Essentially Speaking: Feminism, Nature and Difference*. London: Routledge.

Fyfe, Nick. 2004. "Zero Tolerances, Maximum Surveillance: Deviance, Difference and Crime Control in the Late Modern City." In *The Emancipatory City? Paradoxes and Possibilities*, ed. Loretta Lees, 40–56. London: Sage.

Gabb, Jaqui. 2004. "'I Could Eat My Baby to Bits': Passion and Desire in Lesbian Mother-Children Love." *Gender, Place and Culture: A Journal of Feminist Geography* 11, no. 3: 399–415.

———. 2005. "Locating Lesbian Parent Families: Everyday Negotiations of Lesbian Motherhood in Britain." *Gender, Place and Culture: A Journal of Feminist Geography* 12, no. 4: 419–32.

GABRIELA Network USA. 2008. www.gabnet.org/ (accessed November 23, 2008).

Gatens, Moira. 1991a: "A Critique of the Sex/Gender Distinction." In *A Reader in Feminist Knowledges*, ed. Sneja Gunew, 139–57. New York: Routledge.

———. 1991b. *Feminism and Philosophy: Perspectives on Difference and Equality.* Cambridge: Polity Press.

———. 1998. "Institutions, Embodiment and Sexual Difference." In *Gender and Institutions: Welfare, Work and Citizenship*, ed. Moira Gatens and Alison McKinnon, 1–15. Cambridge: Cambridge University Press.

Gauthier, Deann, and Nancy Chaudoir. 2004. "Tranny Boyz: Cyber Community Support in Negotiating Sex and Gender Mobility among Female to Male Transsexuals." *Deviant Behavior* 2, no. 4: 375–98.

"Gay Aussie Hotel Wins Right to Ban Heterosexuals, Lesbians." 2007. www.breitbart.com/article.php?id=070528090003.xafs5doi&show_article=1 (accessed May 28, 2007).

Gay.com. 2008. "Trinidad—It's a Carnival Kind of Town." www.gay.com/travel/article.do?sernum=6761&page=1 (accessed November 22, 2008).

GayNZ.com News Staff. 2008a. "America's First Transgendered Mayor." November 16, www.gaynz.com/articles/publish/3/article_6755.php (accessed November 17, 2008).

GayNZ.com News Staff. 2008b. "Ellen and Portia Marry in White." www.gaynz.com/articles/publish/3/printer_6364.php (accessed August 18, 2008).

Geddes, Andrew, and Jill Brewis. 1986. *Home Landscape Design for New Zealanders.* Auckland: Reed Methuen.

Georgina Beyer.com. 2008. www.georginabeyer.com/ (accessed October 6, 2008).

Gerhard, Jane. 2005. "Sex and the City." *Feminist Media Studies* 5, no. 1: 37–49.

Gissing, G. 1980. *The Odd Women.* London: Virgo.

Goldsmith, Raquel Rubio. 1994. "Seasons, Seeds, and Souls: Mexican Women Gardening in the American Mesilla, 1900–1940." In *Women of the Mexican Countryside, 1850–1900: Creating Spaces, Shaping Transitions*, ed. Heather Fowler-Salamini and Mary Kay Vaughan, 140–56. Tucson: University of Arizona Press.

Gorman-Murray, Andrew. 2006a. "Gay and Lesbian Couples at Home: Identity Work in Domestic Space." *Home Cultures* 3, no. 2: 145–68.

———. 2006b. "Homeboys: Uses of Home by Gay Australian Men." *Social & Cultural Geography* 7, no. 1: 53–69.

———. 2006c. "Queering Home or Domesticating Deviance? Interrogating Gay Domesticity through Lifestyle Television." *International Journal of Cultural Studies* 9, no. 2: 227–47.

———. 2007. "Rethinking Queer Migration through the Body." *Social & Cultural Geography* 8: 105–21.

———. 2008. "Masculinity and the Home: A Critical Review and Conceptual Framework." *Australian Geographer* 39, no. 3: 367–79.

Gorman-Murray, Andrew, Gordon Waitt, and Chris Gibson. 2008. "A Queer Country? A Case Study of the Politics of Gay/Lesbian Belonging in an Australian Country." *Australian Geographer* 39, no. 2: 171–91.

Groothuis, Doug. 2003. "Technology's Subtle Assault on the Personal." May 7, Doug Groothius.com, www.ivpress.com/groothuis/doug/archives/000129.php (accessed February 14, 2008).

Grosz, Elizabeth. 1994. *Volatile Bodies: Toward a Corporeal Feminism.* St Leonards: Allen and Unwin.

Gurney, Craig. 2000. "Transgressing Public/Private Boundaries in the Home: A Sociological Analysis of the Coital Noise Taboo." *Venereology* 13, no. 1: 39–46.

Hamilton Pride. 2007a. "Hamilton Pride 2007," www.hamiltonpride.co.nz (accessed November 20, 2008).

Hamilton Pride. 2007b. "Hamilton Pride 07, 1st to 9th December." Leaflet. www.hamiltonpride.co.nz (accessed October 10, 2008).

Hanly, Gil. (photographs). 2000. *Heroic Gardens.* Auckland: Reed Books.

Hannah, J. V. 2008. "Contracts Required for Same-Sex Ball Partners." *express: New Zealand's Gay Magazine*, September 10–23, 3.

Hannerz, Ulf. 1996. *Transnational Connections. Culture, People, Places.* London: Routledge.

Harris, Jordon. 2005. *Ko Ia: He or She.* Booklet produced and distributed in New Zealand, unpublished (available from authors).

Hartley, John. 1999. *Uses of Television.* New York: Routledge.

Hay, Iain, ed. 2005. *Qualitative Research Methods in Human Geography*, 2nd ed. South Melbourne: Oxford University Press.

Hay, Robert. 1991. "Parallels between Love Relations and Our Relations with Place." *Area* 23: 256–59.

Hemmings, Clare. 2002. *Bisexual Spaces: A Geography of Gender and Sexuality.* New York: Routledge.

Heroic Gardens. 2006. Heroic Gardens Festival, www.heroicgardens.org.nz/ (accessed March 17, 2006).

Hester, Jo Bob, and Rhonda Gibson. 2007. "The Agenda-Setting Function of National versus Local Media: A Time-Series Analysis for the Issue of Same-Sex Marriage." *Mass Communication and Society* 10, no. 3: 299–317.

Hockey, Jenny, Angela Meah, and Victoria Robinson. 2004. *Mundane Heterosexualities: From Theory to Practices.* Basingstoke: Palgrave Macmillan

Holt, Martin, and Christine Griffin. 2003. "Being Gay, Being Straight and Being Yourself: Local and Global Reflections on Identity, Authenticity and the Lesbian and Gay Scene." *European Journal of Cultural Studies* 6, no. 3: 404–25.

Hoyt, Erich. 2000. *Whale Watching 2000: Worldwide Tourism Numbers, Expenditures and Expanding Socioeconomic Benefits.* Washington, DC: International Fund for Animal Welfare.

Hubbard, Phil. 2000. "Desire/Disgust: Moral Geographies of Heterosexuality." *Progress in Human Geography* 24, no. 2: 191–217.

———. 2001. "Sex Zones: Intimacy, Citizenship and Public Space." *Sexualities* 4: 51–71.

———. 2004. "Cleansing the Metropolis: Sex Work and the Politics of Zero Tolerance." *Urban Studies* 41, no. 9: 1687–702.

———. 2005. "Space/Place." In *Cultural Geography: A Critical Dictionary of Key Concepts*, ed. David Atkinson, Peter Jackson, David Sibley, and Neil Washbourne, 41–48. London: Taurus.

Hughes, Anne. 1997. "Rurality and Cultures of Womanhood: Domestic Identities and Moral Order in Rural Life." In *Contested Countryside Cultures: Otherness, Marginalisation and Rurality*, ed. Paul Cloke and Jo Little, 123–37. London: Routledge.

Hutchings, Jessica, and Clive Aspin, eds. 2007. *Sexuality and the Stories of Indigenous People*. Wellington, NZ: Huia Press.

Ihaka, James. 2008. "She'll Be Sweet Says Bachelor Hopeful." *New Zealand Herald*, www.nzherald.co.nz/nz/news/article.cfm?c_id=1&objectid=10515632 (accessed November 9, 2008).

Ingraham, Chrys. 1999. *White Weddings: Romancing Heterosexuality in Popular Culture*. New York: Routledge.

Isin, Engin, and Patricia Wood. 1999. *Citizenship and Identity*. London: Sage.

Jackson, Stevi. 1995a. "Even Sociologists Fall in Love: An Exploration of the Sociology of Emotions." *Sociology* 27, no. 2: 201–20.

———. 1995b. "Women and Heterosexual Love: Complicity, Resistance and Change." In *Romance Re-Visited*, ed. Lynne Pearce and Jackie Stacey, 49–61. London: Lawrence and Wishart.

———. 1999. *Heterosexuality in Question*. London: Sage.

Jamieson, Lynn. 1998. *Intimacy: Personal Relations in Modern Society*. Oxford: Polity Press.

Jeffreys, Shelia. 2003. "Sex Tourism: Do Women Do It Too?" *Leisure Studies* 22 (July): 223–38.

Johnson, Louise C. 2006a. "Browsing the Modern Kitchen—a Feast of Gender, Place and Culture" (part 1). *Gender, Place and Culture: A Journal of Feminist Geography* 1, no. 2: 123–32.

———. 2006b. "Hybrid and Global Kitchens—First and Third World Intersections" (part 2). *Gender, Place and Culture: A Journal of Feminist Geography* 13, no. 6: 647-52.

Johnson, Louise, with Jackie Huggins, and Jane Jacobs. 2000. *Placebound. Australian Feminist Geographies*. Melbourne: Oxford University Press.

Johnston, Lynda. 2001. "(Other) Bodies and Tourism Studies." *Annals of Tourism Research: A Social Science Journal* 28, no. 1: 180–201.

———. 2005a. *Queering Tourism: Paradoxical Performances at Gay Pride Parades*. New York: Routledge.

———. 2005b. "Transformative Tans: Gendered and Raced Bodies on Beaches." *New Zealand Geographer* 61: 110–16.

———. 2006. "'I Do Down-Under': Wedding Tourism in Aotearoa, New Zealand." *Acme: An International E-Journal for Critical Geographies* 5, no. 2: 191–208.

———. 2007. "Mobilizing Pride/Shame: Lesbians, Tourism and Parades." *Social & Cultural Geography* 8, no. 1: 29–45.

Johnston, Lynda, and Gill Valentine. 1995. "Wherever I Lay My Girlfriend, That's My Home: The Performance and Surveillance of Lesbian Identities in Domestic Environments." In *Mapping Desire: Geographies of Sexualities*, ed. David Bell and Gill Valentine, 99–113. London: Routledge.

Johnston, Ron, Derek Gregory, Geraldine Pratt, and Michael Watts, eds. 2000. *The Dictionary of Human Geography*, 4th ed. Malden, MA: Blackwell.

Jones, Owain. 1999. "Tomboy Tales: The Rural, Nature and the Gender of Childhood." *Gender, Place and Culture: A Journal of Feminist Geography* 6, no. 2: 117–36.

Jones, Steve. 1999. *Doing Internet Research: Critical Issues and Methods for Examining the Net*. Thousand Oaks, CA: Sage.

Keith, Michael. 1992. "Angry Writing: Representing the Unethical World of the Ethnographer." *Environment and Planning D. Society and Space* 10: 551–68.

Kellner, Douglas. 1994. "Madonna, Fashion, and Identity." In *On Fashion*, ed. Shari Benstock and Suzzane Ferriss, 159–82. New Brunswick, NJ: Rutgers University Press.

Kempadoo, Kamala. 2004. *Sexing the Caribbean: Gender, Race and Sexual Labor*. New York: Routledge.

Kentlyn, Sue. 2008. "The Radically Subversive Space of the Queer Home: 'Safety House' and 'Neighbourhood Watch,'" *Australian Geographer* 39, no. 3: 327–37.

Kirkey, Kenneth, and Ann Forsyth. 2001. "Men in the Valley: Gay Male Life on the Suburban-Rural Fringe." *Journal of Rural Studies* 17: 421–41.

Kirkland, Anna. 2006. "What's at Stake in Transgender Discrimination as Sex Discrimination?" *Signs: Journal of Women in Culture and Society* 32, no. 1: 83–111.

Knopp, Lawrence. 1995. "Sexuality and Urban Space: A Framework for Analysis." In *Mapping Desire: Geographies of Sexualities*, ed. David Bell and Gill Valentine, 149–61. London: Routledge.

———. 1998. "Sexuality and Urban Space: Gay Male Identity Politics in the United States, the United Kingdom, and Australia." In *Cities of Difference*, ed. Ruth Fincher and Jane Jacobs, 149–76. New York: The Guilford Press.

———. 1999. "Out in Academia: The Queer Politics of One Geographer's Sexualisation." *Journal of Geography in Higher Education* 23, no. 1: 116–23.

Kristeva, Julia. 1982. "Motherhood According to Giovanni Bellini." In *Desire in Language: A Semiotic Approach to Literature and Art*, ed. Julia Kristeva, Leon S. Roudiez, Alice Jardine, and Thomas Gora, 237–69. Oxford: Basil Blackwell.

Kurtz, Stanley. 2006. "*Big Love*, From the Set." National Review online, March 13, 2007, www.nationalreview.com/kurtz200603130805.asp (accessed February 13, 2007).

Langford, Wendy. 1999. *Revolutions of the Heart: Gender, Power and the Delusions of Love*. London: Routledge.

Lesbian and Gay Archives of New Zealand [laganz]. 2008. www.laganz.org.nz/ (accessed October 5, 2008).

Lim, Jason, Gavin Brown, and Kath Browne. 2007. "Conclusions and Future Directions, or Our Hopes for Geographies of Sexualities (and Queer Geographies)." In *Geographies of Sexualities: Theories, Practices and Politics*, ed. Kath Browne, Jason Lim, and Gavin Brown, 215–24. Aldershot: Ashgate.

Lima, Ieti. 2001. "Some Changes and Continuities in the Gardening Practices of Samoans in Aotearoa/New Zealand." In *Flowers, Fale, Fanau and fa'a Polynesia,* ed. Richard Bedford, Robyn Longhurst, and Yvonne Underhill-Sem, 215–24. Asia Pacific Migration Research Network, Working Paper No. 8, Centre of Asia Pacific Social Transformation Studies, University of Wollongong, Australia.

Little, Jo. 2003. "'Riding the Rural Love Train': Heterosexuality and the Rural Community." *Sociolgia Ruralis* 43, no. 4: 401–17.

———. 2007. "Constructing Nature in the Performance of Rural Heterosexualities." *Environment and Planning D: Society and Space* 25: 851–66.

Little, Jo, and Michael Leyson. 2003. "Embodied Rural Geographies: Developing Research Agendas." *Progress in Human Geography* 27, no. 3: 257–72.

Llewellyn, Mark. 2004. "Designed by Women and Designing Women: Gender, Planning and the Geographies of the Kitchen in Britain 1917–1946." *Cultural Geographies* 11, no. 1: 42–60.

Lloyd, Genevieve. 1993. *The Man of Reason: "Male" and "Female" in Western Philosophy.* London: Routledge.

Longhurst, Robyn. 1997. "(Dis)embodied Geographies." *Progress in Human Geography* 21, no. 4: 486–501.

———. 1999: "Gendering Place." In *Explorations in Human Geography: Encountering Place,* ed. Richard Le Heron, Laurence Murphy, Pip Forer, and Margaret Goldstone, 151–72. Auckland: Oxford University Press.

———. 2000. "Corporeographies of Pregnancy: 'Bikini Babes.'" *Environment and Planning D: Society and Space* 18, no. 4: 453–72.

———. 2001. *Bodies: Exploring Fluid Boundaries.* London: Routledge.

———. 2005. "(Ad)dressing Pregnant Bodies in New Zealand: Clothing, Fashion, Subjectivities and Spatialities." *Gender, Place and Culture: A Journal of Feminist Geography* 12, no. 4: 433–46.

———. 2006a. "A Pornography of Birth: Crossing Moral Boundaries." *ACME: An International E-Journal for Critical Geographies* 5, no. 2: 209–29.

———. 2006b. "Plots, Plants and Paradoxes." *Social & Cultural Geography* 7, no. 4: 581–93.

———. 2008. "Afterword—Geographies of Sexuality and Gender 'Down Under.'" *Australian Geographer* 39, no. 3: 381–87.

Lukenbill, W. Bernard. 1998. "Observations on the Corporate Culture of a Gay and Lesbian Congregation." *Journal for the Scientific Study of Religion* 37, no. 3: 440–52.

Lupton, Deborah. 1998. *The Emotional Self.* London: Sage.

Lynn, William. 1998. "Animals, Ethics, and Geography." In *Animal Geographies: Place, Politics, and Identities in the Nature-Culture Borderlands,* ed. Jennifer Wolch and Jody Emel, 280–97. London: Verso.

MacCannell, Dean. 1999. *The Tourist: A New Theory of the Leisure Class.* Berkeley: UC Press.

Mackie, Vera. 2001. "The Trans-sexual Citizen: Queering Sameness and Difference." *Australian Feminist Studies* 16, no. 35: 185–92.

Mageo, Jeanette-Marie. 1992. "Male Transvestism and Cultural Change in Samoa." *American Ethnologist* 19, no. 3: 443–59.

Makow, Henry. 2000. *A Long Way to Go For a Date.* Winnipeg: Silas Green.

Mansvelt, Juliana, and Lawrence D. Berg. 2005. "Writing Qualitative Geographies, Constructing Geographical Knowledges." In *Qualitative Research Methods in Human Geography*, ed. Iain Hay (2nd ed.), 248–65. South Melbourne: Oxford University Press.

Marie Claire. 2004. "Rumpy in the Country?" May, 153–56.

Marks, Kathy. 2007. "Australian Pub Bars Heterosexuals." *The Independent*, May 29, findarticles.com/p/articles/mi_qn4158/is_20070529/ai_n19179705 (accessed August 30, 2007).

Markwell, Kevin. 2002. "Mardi Gras Tourism and the Construction of Sydney as an International Gay and Lesbian City." *GLQ* 8: 81–99.

Marston, Sallie. 2000. "The Social Construction of Scale." *Progress in Human Geography* 24: 219–42.

Martin, Sue. 2001. "On Our Selection: Class, Gender and the Domestic Garden in Nineteenth-Century Australia." *History of Gardens and Designed Landscapes: An International Quarterly* (formerly the *Journal of Garden History*) 21: 27–32.

Massey, Doreen. 1994. *Space, Place and Gender.* Cambridge: Polity Press.

Matejskova, Tatiana. 2007. "Straights in a Gay Bar: Negotiating Boundaries through Time-Spaces." In *Geographies of Sexualities: Theory, Practices and Politics*, ed. Kath Browne, Jason Lim, and Gavin Brown, 137–49. Aldershot: Ashgate.

McCormack, Derek. 1999. "Body Shopping: Reconfiguring Geographies of Fitness." *Gender, Place and Culture: A Journal of Feminist Geography* 6, no. 2: 155–77.

McCowan, Judy A., Diane Fischer, Ryan Page, and Michael Homant. 2001. "Internet Relationships: People Who Meet People." *CyberPsychology and Behaviour* 4, no. 5: 593–96.

McDowell, Linda. 1999. *Gender, Identity and Place: Understanding Feminist Geographies.* Minneapolis: University of Minnesota Press.

McDowell, Linda, and Joanne P. Sharp, eds. 1999. *A Feminist Glossary of Human Geography.* London: Arnold.

McLelland, Mark. 2002. "The Newhalf Net: Japan's 'Intermediate Sex' On-Line." *International Journal of Sexuality and Gender Studies* 7, no. 2: 163–75.

McNeil, Jean. 2001. *The Rough Guide to Costa Rica.* London: Rough Guides.

Meyerowitz, Joanne. 2002. *How Sex Changed: A History of Transsexuality in the United States.* Cambridge, MA: Harvard University Press.

Middlemarch. 2008. "Welcome to Middlemarch." www.middlemarch.co.nz/ (accessed November 8, 2008).

Ministry of Justice (New Zealand). 2008. "Prostitution Law Reform." www.justice.govt.nz/plr/ (accessed October 6, 2008).

Mitchell, Don. 2001. "Post-Modern Geographical Praxis? Post-Modern Impulse and the War against Homeless People in the Post-Justice City." In *Postmodern Geography: Theory and Praxis*, ed. Claudio Minca, 57–92. Oxford: Blackwell.

Mohammad, Robina. 2005. "British Pakistani Muslim Women: Marking the Body, Marking the Nation." In *A Companion to Feminist Geography*, ed. Lise Nelson and Joni Seager, 379–97. Malden, MA: Blackwell.

Monahan, Kate. 2008. "Solving the Man Drought." Duck Soup, June 13, www.ducksoup.co.nz/dating-tips/solving-the-man-drought/ June 13, 2008 (accessed November 9, 2008).

Monk, Felicity. 2008. "Glad to be A." *Sunday Star-Times Magazine*, June 8, 16–19.

Monsarrat, Ann. 1973. *And the Bride Wore . . . The Story of the White Wedding*. New York: Dodd, Mead and Company.

Moon, Dawne. 1995. "Insult and Inclusion: The Term Fag Hag and Gay Male 'Community.'" *Social Forces* 74, no. 2: 487–510.

Moore, Adam. 2008. "Rethinking Scale as a Geographical Category: From Analysis to Practice." *Progress in Human Geography* 32, no. 2: 203–25.

Moss, Pamela, ed. 2002. *Feminist Geography in Practice: Research and Methods*. Oxford: Blackwell.

Moss, Pamela, and Isabel Dyck. 2002. *Women, Body, Illness: Space and Identity in the Everyday Lives of Women with Chronic Illness*. Lanham, MD: Rowman & Littlefield.

Mullings, Beverley. 2000. "Fantasy Tours: Exploring the Global Consumption of Caribbean Sex Tourism." In *New Forms of Consumption: Consumers, Culture, and Commodification*, ed. Mark Gottdiener, 227–50. Lanham, MD: Rowman & Littlefield.

Munro, Surya, and Lorna Warren. 2004. "Transgendering Citizenship." *Sexualities* 7, no. 3: 345–62.

Munt, Sally R. 2001. "The Butch Body." In *Contested Bodies*, ed. Ruth Holliday and John Hassard, 95–106. London: Routledge.

Murphy, Dean, Patrick Rawstorne, Martin Holt, and Ryan Dermot. 2004. "Cruising and Connecting Online: The Use of Internet Chat Sites by Gay Men in Sydney and Melbourne." National Centre in HIV Social Research, Faculty of Arts and Social Sciences, The University of New South Wales (NCHSR), Monograph 2/2004.

Namaste, Ki. 1996. "Genderbashing: Sexuality, Gender, and the Regulation of Public Space." *Environment and Planning D: Society and Space* 14, no. 2: 221–40.

Nast, Heidi. 2002. "Queer Patriarchies, Queer Racisms, International." *Antipode* 35: 874–909.

———. 2006. "Critical Pet Studies?" *Antipode* 38, no. 5: 894–906.

Nast, Heidi, and Steve Pile, eds. 1998. *Places through the Body*. London: Routledge.

Natalier, Kristin. 2004. *Gender and Domestic Life: Changing Practices in Families and Households*. Basingstoke: Palgrave Macmillan.

Nelson, Lise. 1999. "Bodies (and Spaces) Do Matter: The Limits of Performativity." *Gender, Place and Culture: A Journal of Feminist Geography* 6, no. 4: 331–53.

Newton, Esther. 1993. *Cherry Grove, Fire Island: Sixty Years in America's First Gay and Lesbian Town*. Boston: Beacon Press.

New Zealand Herald. 2003. "Rural Bachelor of the Year." May 7, www.nzherald.co.nz/nz/news/article.cfm?c_id=1&objectid=3500532 (accessed November 9, 2008).

New Zealand Herald. 2007. "Breasts Complaint Casino Reviewing Dress Code." September 25, www.nzherald.co.nz/section/1/story.cfm?c_id=1&objectid= 10465828 (accessed September 26, 2007).

New Zealand Polyamory Group. 2008. www.nzpoly.org.nz/ (accessed June 16, 2008).

New Zealand Tourism Board. 2002. "Pure New Zealand." www.purenz.com/ (accessed August 30, 2002).

New Zealand Tourism Board. 2008. "100% Pure New Zealand." Television commercial, www.newzealand.com/travel/souvenirs/video-library/super-tvc/ super-tvc_home.cfm (accessed November 26, 2008).

Nip, Joyce Yee-man. 2004. "The Relationship Between Online and Offline Communities: The Case of the Queer Sisters." *Media, Culture and Society* 26, no. 3: 409–28.

Nzgirl. 2008. "Internet Dating Protocol." www.nzgirl.co.nz/articles/8019 (accessed February 4, 2008).

NZPA Images. 2006. "Hamilton Lobby Groups Protest Against Home Based Brothels Outside High Court." May 15, www.nzpaimages.co.nz/events. php?event_id=1332 (accessed September 2, 2008).

O'Connell Davidson, Julia, and Jacqueline Sánchez Taylor. 2005. "Travel and Taboo: Heterosexual Sex Tourism in the Caribbean." In *Regulating Sex: The Politics of Intimacy and Identity*, ed. Elizabeth Bernstein and Laurie Schaffner, 83–99. New York: Routledge.

Oswin, Natalie. 2008: "Critical Geographies and the Uses of Sexuality: Deconstructing Queer Space." *Progress in Human Geography* 32, no. 1: 89–103.

Otago Daily Times. 2008. "Thousands Flock to Fieldays." Online edition, June 12, www.odt.co.nz/news/farming/9287/thousands-flock-fieldays (accessed September 29, 2008).

Out and About. 1996. "Carnival around the World." December, 145–52.

———. 1998. "Cayman Islands: Boycott Update." March, 27–28.

Pain, Rachel. 1997. "Social Geographies of Women's Fear of Crime." *Transactions of the Institute of British Geographers* 22: 231–44.

Phelan, Shane. 2001. *Sexual Strangers. Gays, Lesbians and Dilemmas of Citizenship.* Philadelphia: Temple University Press.

Philips, Anne. 1993. *Democracy and Difference.* Cambridge: Polity Press.

Phillips, Joan. 1999. "Tourist-Oriented Prostitution in Barbados: The Case of the Beach Boy and the White Female Tourist." In *Sun, Sex and Gold: Tourism and Sex Work in the Caribbean*, ed. Kamala Kempadoo, 183–200. Lanham, MD: Rowman & Littlefield.

———. 2002. "The Beach Boys of Barbados: Postcolonial Entrepreneurs." In *Transnational Prostitution: Changing Global Patterns*, ed. Susanne Thorbek and Bandana Pattanaik, 42–55. New York: Zed Books.

Phillips, Richard, Diane Watt, and David Shuttleton eds. 2000. *De-Centring Sexualities: Politics and Representations beyond the Metropolis.* London: Routledge.

Philo, Chris, and Chris Wilbert. 2000. "Animal Places, Beastly Places: An Introduction." In *Animal Places, Beastly Places: New Geographies of Human-Animal Relations*, ed. Chris Philo and Chris Wilbert, 1–34. London: Routledge.

Planet Love. 2008. "Welcome to Planet Love!" www.planet-love.com/ (accessed November 23, 2008).

Press (Christchurch). 1999. "World's First Transsexual MP Hides from Spotlight." Monday, November 29, 3.

Pritchard, Annette, and Nigel Morgan. 2005. "'On Location': Re(Viewing) Bodies of Fashion and Places of Desire." *Tourist Studies* 5, no. 3: 283–302.

Proulx, Annie. 1999. "Brokeback Mountain." In *Close Range: Wyoming Stories,* 252–83. New York: Scribner.

Pruitt, Deborah, and Suzanne LaFont. 1995. "For Love and Money: Romance Tourism in Jamaica." *Annals of Tourism Research: A Social Science Journal* 22: 422–40.

Puar, Jasbir. 2001. "Global Circuits: Transnational Sexualities and Trinidad." *Signs: Journal of Women in Culture and Society* 26, no. 4: 1039–65.

———. ed. 2002a. "Introduction." *GLQ: A Journal of Lesbian and Gay Studies* 8 no. 1–2: 1–6.

———. 2002b. "Circuits of Queer Mobility: Tourism, Travel and Globalisation." *GLQ: A Journal of Lesbian and Gay Studies* 8, no. 1–2: 101–38.

———. 2002c. "A Transnational Feminist Critique of Queer Tourism." *Antipode: A Radical Journal of Geography* 34, no. 5: 935–46.

———. 2006. "Mapping US Homonormativities." *Gender, Place and Culture: A Journal of Feminist Geography* 13, no. 1: 67–88.

Puwar, Nirmal. 2004. *Space Invaders: Race, Gender and Bodies Out of Place.* Oxford: Berg.

Radley, Alan, Darrin Hodgetts, and Andrea Cullen. 2006. "Fear, Romance and Transience in the Lives of Homeless Women." *Social & Cultural Geography* 7, no. 3: 437–61.

Reed, Jennifer. 2005. "Ellen Degeneres: Public Lesbian Number One." *Feminist Media Studies* 5, no.1: 23–36.

Reimer, Suzanne, and Deborah Leslie. 2004. "Identity, Consumption and the Home." *Home Cultures* 1, no. 2: 187–208.

Reuters. 2008. "Air New Zealand's Pink Flight Takes Passengers to New Heights." February 29, www.reuters.com/article/pressRelease/idUS280812+29-Feb-2008+BW20080229 (accessed February 29, 2008).

Rich, Adrienne. 1986. "Notes Towards a Politics of Location." In *Blood, Bread and Poetry: Selected Prose 1979-1985,* 210–31. New York: W. W. Norton.

Richardson, Diane. 2000. *Rethinking Sexuality.* London: Sage.

———. 2005. "Desiring Sameness? The Rise of a Neoliberal Politics of Normalisation." *Antipode* 37, no. 3: 515–35.

Riff Raff Statue. 2008. "The Embassy: Home." www.riffraffstatue.org/ (accessed December 3, 2008).

Robinson, Kathryn. 1996. "Of Mail-Order Brides and 'Boys' Own' Tales: Representations of Asian-Australian Marriages." *Feminist Review*, no. 52, The World Upside Down: Feminisms in the Antipodes. (Spring): 53–68.

———. 2007. "Marriage Migration, Gender Transformations, and Family Values in the 'Global Ecumene.'" *Gender, Place and Culture: A Journal of Feminist Geography* 14, no. 4: 483–97.

Robinson, M. E. 1994. "Ask Not For Whom: A Comment on Bell (1992)." *Area* 26: 84–86.

Robinson, Victoria, Jenny Hockey, and Angela Meah. 2004. "'What I Did . . . on My Mother's Settee': Spatialising Heterosexuality." *Gender, Place and Culture: A Journal of Feminist Geography* 11, no. 3: 417–35.

Rocky Horror Picture Show. 2009. "The Rocky Horror Picture Show: The Official Fan Site!" www.rockyhorror.com/ (accessed June 12, 2009).

Rodriguez, Eric M., and Suzanne C. Ouellette. 2000. "Gay and Lesbian Christians: Homosexual and Religious Identity Integration in the Members and Participants of a Gay-Positive Church." *Journal for the Scientific Study of Religion* 39, no. 3: 333–47.

Romantic New Zealand. 2009. "New Zealand Weddings & Wedding Services." www.chc-weddings.co.nz/ (accessed June 16, 2009).

Rose, Gillian. 1993. *Feminism and Geography: The Limits of Geographical Knowledge.* Cambridge: Polity Press.

Ross, Michael W. 2005. "Typing, Doing, and Being: Sexuality and the Internet." *Journal of Sex Research* 42, no. 4: 342–52.

Rubin, Gayle. 1993. "Thinking Sex: Notes for a Radical Theory on the Politics of Sexuality." In *The Lesbian and Gay Studies Reader*, ed. Henry Abelove, Michele A. Barale, and David M. Halperin, 3–44. London: Routledge.

Rushbrook, Dereka. 2002. "Cities, Queer Space and the Cosmopolitan Tourist." *GLQ: A Journal of Lesbian and Gay Studies* 8, no. 1–2: 183–206.

Rust, Paula C. 2001. "Make Me a Map: Bisexual Men's Images of Bisexual Community." *Journal of Bisexuality* 1, no. 2/3: 49–108.

Samarasinghe, Vidyamali. 2008. *Female Sex Trafficking in Asia: The Resilience of Patriarchy in a Changing World.* New York and London: Routledge.

Sánchez Taylor, J. 2001. "Dollars Are a Girl's Best Friend? Female Tourists' Sexual Behaviour in the Caribbean." *Sociology* 35, no. 3: 749–64.

Saussure, Ferdinand de. 1974. *A Course in General Linguistics.* London: Fontana.

Schaeffer-Grabiel, Felicity. 2004. "Cyberbrides and Global Imaginaries: Mexican Women's Turn from the National to the Foreign." *Space and Culture: International Journal of Social Science* 7, no. 1: 33–48.

———. 2005. "Planet-Love.com: Cyberbrides in the Americas and the Transnational Routes of US Masculinity." *Signs: Journal of Women in Culture and Society* 31, no. 2: 331–56.

Schalet, Amy. 2000. "Raging Hormones, Regulated Love: Adolescent Sexuality and the Constitution of the Modern Individual in the United States and the Netherlands." *Body and Society* 6, no. 1: 75–105.

Schmidt, Johanna. 2001. "Redefining Fa'afafine: Western Discourses and the Construction of Transgenderism in Samoa." *Intersections: Gender, History and Culture* 6: 1–16, intersections.anu.edu.au/issue6/schmidt.html.

———. 2003. "Paradise Lost? Social Change and Fa'afafine in Samoa." *Current Sociology* 51, no. 3–4: 417–32.

Scholes, Robert. 1997. "The Mail-Order Bride Industry and Its Impact on US Immigration." In *International Matchmaking Organizations: A Report to Con-*

gress, www.uscis.gov/files/article/Mobrept_full.pdf (accessed November 22, 2008).

Schorb, Jodi R., and Tania N. Hammidi. 2000. "Sho-Lo Showdown: The Do's and Don'ts of Lesbian Chic." *Tulsa Studies in Women's Literature* 19, no. 2: 255–68.

Sedgwick, Eve D. 1990. *Epistemology of the Closet.* New York: Harvester Wheatsheaf.

Sengupta, Joydeep. 2002. "Gay Rights and European Citizenship." *Gay and Lesbian Review Worldwide,* Nov–Dec, findarticles.com/p/articles/mi_hb3491/is_/ai_n28954031 (accessed November 17, 2008).

Serlin, David. 1996. "The Twilight (Zone) of Commercial Sex." In *Policing Public Sex: Queer Politics and the Future of AIDS Activism,* ed. Dangerous Bedfellows, 45–52. Boston: South End Press.

Sex Workers Pride. 2002. "May Day 2002." www.sexworkerspride.org.uk/interview.html (accessed November 7, 2008).

Shields, Rob. 1991. *Places on the Margin.* London: Routledge.

Shilling, Chris. 1993. *The Body and Social Theory.* London: Sage.

Sibley, David. 1995. *Geographies of Exclusion: Society and Difference in the West.* London: Routledge.

Silk, John. 1999. "The Dynamics of Community, Place and Identity." *Environment and Planning A* 31: 5–17.

Silverman, Steven. 2008. "Ellen DeGeneres Reacts to Gay Marriage Ban." *People,* Thursday, November 6, www.people.com/people/article/0,,20238579,00.html?xid=rss-fullcontentcnn (accessed November 18, 2008).

Simonsen, Kirsten. 2000. "Editorial: The Body as Battlefield." *Transactions of the Institute of British Geographers* 25, no. 1: 7–9.

Skeggs, Beverley. 1999. "Matter Out of Place: Visibility and Sexualities in Leisure Spaces." *Leisure Studies* 18, no. 3: 213–32.

Smith, Darren, and Holt, Louise. 2005. "'Lesbian Migrants in the Gentrified Valley' and 'Other' Geographies of Rural Gentrification." *Journal of Rural Studies* 21, no. 3: 313–22.

Smith, Neil. 1992. "Geography, Difference and the Politics of Scale." In *Postmodernism and the Social Sciences,* ed. Jo Doherty, Elspeth Graham, and Mo Malek, 57–59. London: Macmillan.

———. 1993. "Homeless/Global: Scaling Places." In *Mapping the Futures,* ed. Jon Bird, 87–119. London: Routledge.

Smith, Wesley. 2005. "Horse Sense." *Weekly Standard,* Monday, August 29.

So, Christine. 2006. "Asian Mail-Order Brides, the Threat of Global Capitalism, and the Rescue of the U.S. Nation-State." *Feminist Studies* 32, no. 2: 395–419.

Somerville, Peter 1992. "Homelessness and the Meaning of Home: Rooflessness or Rootlessness." *International Journal of Urban and Regional Research* 16, no. 4: 529–39.

Sothern, Matthew. 2004. "(Un)queer Patriarchies: or, 'What We Think When We Fuck.'" *Antipode* 36: 183–90.

Statistics New Zealand. 2006. "Census, 2006." www.stats.govt.nz/census/default.htm (accessed June 13, 2008).

Steiner, Emil. 2007. "Aussie Pub Bars Heterosexuals." *Washingtonpost.com.* May 30, blog.washingtonpost.com/offbeat/2007/05/aussie_gay_pub_bans_ heterosexu.html (accessed August 30, 2007).

Stoller, Robert. 1968. *Sex and Gender.* London: Hogarth.

Sullivan, Andrew. 1995. *Virtually Normal: An Argument about Homosexuality.* New York: Alfred A. Knopf.

Sunday Star-Times. 2008. "Mother's Day, Father's Day—or April Fool's Day?" March 30, A17.

Synott, Anthony. 1993. *The Body Social: Symbolism, Self and Society.* London: Routledge.

Talbot, Dorinda, and Deanna Swaney. 1998. *Lonely Planet: Samoa.* Hawthorn: Lonely Planet Publications.

Taylor, Affrica. 1998. "Lesbian Space: More Than One Imagined Territory." In *New Frontiers of Space, Bodies and Gender,* ed. Rose Ainley, 129–41. London: Routledge.

Television New Zealand [TVNZ]. 2001. *Love Train Sparks Easter Romance.* One News, April 15, tvnz.co.nz/view/page/423466/36496 (accessed November 9, 2008).

———. 2004. *I Do Down-Under: Document New Zealand.* Documentary aired April 5.

———. 2006. *Sex Change Capital of the World.* Documentary aired March 31.

Thien, Deborah. 2004. "Love's Travels and Traces: The Impossible Politics of Luce Irigaray." In *Women and Geography Study Group: Gender and Geography Reconsidered,* ed. Jo Sharp, Kath Browne, and Deborah Thien, 43–48. CD-ROM. Women and Geography Study Group.

Toepfer, Karl Eric. 1997. *Empire of Ecstasy: Nudity and Movement in German Body Culture, 1910–1935.* Berkeley: University of California Press.

Trinidad Express. 1998. "Gay Cruise Leaves Bahamas." February 10, 29.

Tuan, Yi-Fu. 1974. "Topophilia: A Study of Environmental Perception, Attitudes, and Values." Englewood Cliffs, NJ: Prentice-Hall.

Tyler, Imogen. 2001 "Celebrity, Pregnancy and Subjectivity." In *Thinking through the Skin,* Sara Ahmed and Jacquie Stacey, 69–83. London: Routledge.

Urry, John. 1990. *The Tourist Gaze.* London: Sage.

Valentine, Gill. 1992. "Images of Danger: Women's Sources of Information about the Spatial Distribution of Male Violence." *Area* 24: 22–29.

———. 1993. "Negotiating and Managing Multiple Sexual Identities: Lesbian Time-Space Strategies." *Transactions of the Institute of British Geographers* 18, no. 2: 237–48.

———. 1994. "Toward a Geography of the Lesbian Community." *Women and Environments* 14, no. 1: 8–10.

———. 1995a. "Creating Transgressive Space: The Music of KD Lang." *Transactions of the Institute of British Geographers* 20, no. 4: 474–85.

———. 1995b. "Out and About: Geographies of Lesbian Landscapes." *International Journal of Urban and Regional Research* 19, no. 1: 96–111.

———. 1996. "(Re) Negotiating the 'Heterosexual Street': Lesbian Productions of Space." In *Bodyspace: Destabilizing Geographies of Gender and Sexuality,* ed. Nancy Duncan, 146–55. London: Routledge.

———. 1997. "Making Space: Separatism and Difference." In *Thresholds in Feminist Geography: Difference, Methodology and Representation,* ed. John Paul Jones III, Heidi Nast, and Susan Roberts, 65–75. Lanham, MD: Rowman & Littlefield.

———. 2000. "Introduction: From Nowhere to Everywhere: Lesbian Geographies." *Journal of Lesbian Studies* 4, no. 1: 1–9.

———. 2001. *Social Geographies: Space and Society.* Harlow, UK: Pearson Education.

Valentine, Gill, and Sarah L. Holloway. 2002. "Cyberkids? Exploring Children's Identities and Social Networks in On-line and Off-line Worlds." *Annals of the Association of American Geographers* 92, no. 2: 302–19.

Valentine, Gill, Tracey Skelton, and Ruth Butler. 2003. "Coming Out and Outcomes: Negotiating Lesbian and Gay Identities With, and In, the Family." *Environment and Planning D: Society and Space* 21, no. 4: 479–99.

Van Vechten, Ken. 2005. *Neon Nuptials: The Complete Guide to Las Vegas Weddings.* Las Vegas: Huntington Press.

Veijola, Soile, and Eeva Jokinen. 1994. "The Body in Tourism." *Theory, Culture and Society* 11: 125–51.

Waitt, Gordon. 2003. "Gay Games: Performing 'Community' Out From the Closet of the Locker Room." *Social & Cultural Geography* 4, no. 2: 167–83.

———. 2004. "Gay Games, Queer Community Space." *Inter-Cultural Studies: A Forum on Social Change and Cultural Diversity* 4, no. 1: 42–51.

Waitt, Gordon, and Andrew Gorman-Murray. 2007. "Homemaking and Mature Age Gay Men 'Down-Under': Paradox, Intimacy, Subjectivities, Spatialities, and Scale." *Gender, Place and Culture: A Journal of Feminist Geography* 14, no. 5: 569–84.

Waikato Times. 2008. "Ball Contracts Under Fire." August 30, A7.

Walkowitz, Judith R. 1992. *City of Dreadful Delight: Narratives of Sexual Danger in Late-Victorian London.* Chicago: University of Chicago Press.

Wan, Gok. 2007. *How to Look Good Naked: Shop For Your Shape and Look Amazing.* London: Harper Collins.

Warf, Barney, and Mort Winsberg. 2008. "The Geography of Religious Diversity in the United States." *Professional Geographer* 60, no. 3: 413–24.

Warner, Michael. 1991. "Introduction: Fear of a Queer Planet." *Social Text* 29, no. 4: 3–17.

Warrington, Molly. 2001. "'I Must Get Out': The Geographies of Domestic Violence." *Transactions of the Institute of British Geographers* 26, no. 3: 365–82.

Waters, Sarah. 1999. *Tipping the Velvet.* New York: Riverhead Books.

Watt, Emily. 2008. "Two's Company, Three's Better." *Waikato Times,* March 22, E5.

Webber, Melvin M. 1963. "Order in Diversity: Community without Propinquity." In *Cities and Space,* ed. L. Wirigo, 25–54. Baltimore: Johns Hopkins University Press.

Weddings Las Vegas. 2009. "Vegas Attitude." www.weddingslasvegas.com/las_vegas_sign (accessed April 7, 2009).

Weeks, Jeffery. 1998. "The Sexual Citizen." *Theory, Culture and Society* 15: 35–52.

Wekerle, Gerda R. 2001. "Creating Cultural Landscapes: Immigrants and Their Garden." Paper presented at the Association of American Geographers' 97th Annual Meeting of the AAG, February 27–March 3, New York.

Wells, Peter. 2000. "Creating a Sovereign Space: Geoffrey Marshal, John Hayward." In *Heroic Gardens*, Gil Hanly (photographs), 109–15. Auckland: Reed Books.

Westneat, Danny. 2005. "Horse Sex Story Was Online Hit." *Seattle Times*, Friday, December 30, B1.

Whittle, Steven, ed. 1994. "Consuming Differences: The Collaboration of the Gay Body and the Cultural State." In *The Margins of the City: Gay Men's Urban Lives*, 27–41. Aldershot: Arena.

Whitty, Monica T. 2005. "The Realness of Cybercheating: Men's and Women's Representations of Unfaithful Internet Relationships." *Social Science Computer Review 23*, no. 1: 57–67.

Wikipedia. 2008. s.vv. "gay games." en.wikipedia.org/wiki/Gay_Games (accessed September 10, 2008).

Williams Paris, Jenell, and Rory E. Anderson. 2001. "Faith-Based Queer Space in Washington, DC: The Metropolitan Community Church-DC and Mount Vernon Square." *Gender, Place and Culture: A Journal of Feminist Geography* 8, no. 2: 149–68.

Wilson, Angelia R. 2000. "Getting Your Kicks on Route 66! Stories of Gay and Lesbian Life in Rural America *c.*1950_1970s." In *De-Centring Sexualities: Politics and Representations Beyond the Metropolis*, ed. Richard Phillips, Diane Watt, and David Shuttleton, 199–216. London: Routledge.

Wilson, Elizabeth. 1991. *The Sphinx in the City*. London: Virago.

Wolch, Jennifer. 2002. "Anima Urbis." *Progress in Human Geography* 26, no. 6: 721–42.

Wolfson, Evan. 1996. "Why Should We Fight for the Freedom to Marry: The Challenges and Opportunities That Will Follow a Win in Hawaii." *Journal of Gay, Lesbian, and Bisexual Identity* 1: 79–89.

Woods, Chris. 1995. *State of the Queer Nation: A Critique of Gay and Lesbian Politics in 1990s Britain*. London: Cassell.

Woods, Michael. 2000. "Fantastic Mr. Fox? Representing Animals in the Hunting Debate." In *Animal Places, Beastly Places: New Geographies of Human-Animal Relations*, ed. Chris Philo and Chris Wilbert, 182–202. London: Routledge.

Woodward, Curt. 2006. "State Senator Offers Bill to Ban Bestiality." Associated Press State and Local Wire, Friday, January 13.

Woodward, Rachel. 1998. "'It's a Man's Life!': Soldiers, Masculinity and the Countryside. *Gender, Place and Culture: A Journal of Feminist Geography* 5: 277–300.

Woodward, Rachel. 2000. "Warrior Heroes and Little Green Men: Soldiers, Military Training, and the Construction of Rural Masculinities." *Rural Sociology* 65: 640–57.

Woolf, Virginia. 1919. *Night and Day*. London: Hogarth.

———. 1924. *A Room of One's Own*. London: Virago.

———. 1984. "Street Haunting." In *The Virginia Woolf Reader*, ed. Mitchell Leaska, 246–59. San Diego: Harcourt Brace Jovanovich.

Wotherspoon, Garry. 1986. *Being Different: Nine Gay Men Remember*. Alexandria, Australia: Hale & Iremonger.

Young, Iris Marion. 1990a. *Justice and the Politics of Difference*, Princeton, NJ: Princeton University Press.

———. 1990b. *Throwing Like a Girl and Other Essays in Feminist Thought*. Bloomington and Indianapolis: Indiana University Press.

———. 1990c. "The Ideal of Community and the Politics of Difference." In *Feminism/Postmodernism*, ed. Linda J. Nicholson, 300–23. London: Routledge.

Index

187

About the Authors

Lynda Johnston is associate professor in the Department of Geography, Tourism and Environmental Planning, University of Waikato, New Zealand. She has published on topics such as wedding tourism, gay pride parades, suntanning, bodybuilding, and feminist and queer methodologies. Her publications include *Queering Tourism: Paradoxical Performances of Gay Pride Parades* (2005) and *Subjectivities, Knowledges and Feminist Geographies: The Subjects and Ethics of Social Research* (2002), which she coauthored.

Robyn Longhurst is professor of geography at University of Waikato and an editor of *Gender, Place and Culture: A Journal of Feminist Geography*. She is author of *Bodies: Exploring Fluid Boundaries* (2001) and *Maternities: Gender, Bodies and Spaces* (2008) and coauthor of *Pleasure Zones: Bodies, Cities, Spaces* (2001). She has published on issues relating to pregnancy, mothering, "fat" bodies, visceral geographies, masculinities, and the politics of knowledge.